2nd Edition

Social Work

Documentation

A Guide to Strengthening Your Case Recording

Nancy L. Sidell

NASW PRESS

National Association of Social Workers
Washington, DC

Darrell P. Wheeler, PhD, MPH, ACSW, President
Angelo McClain, PhD, LICSW, Chief Executive Officer

Cheryl Y. Bradley, *Publisher*
Stella Donovan, *Acquisitions Editor*
Sharon Fletcher, *Marketing Manager*
Julie Gutin, *Project Manager*
Stefanie Lazer, *Copyeditor*
Julie Palmer-Hoffman, *Proofreader*
Lori Holtzinger, Zinger Indexing, *Indexer*

Cover by Diane Guy, Blue Azure
Interior design and composition by Xcel Graphic Services
Printed and bound by Sheridan Books

Library of Congress Cataloging-in-Publication Data

Sidell, Nancy.
  Social work documentation: a guide to strengthening your case recording / Nancy L. Sidell.—2nd edition.
      pages cm
  Revised edition of the author's Social work documentation, 2011.
  Includes bibliographical references and index.
  ISBN 978-0-87101-486-3 (pbk.)—ISBN 978-0-87101-487-0 (e-book) 1.   Social case work reporting. 2.   Social service—Records and correspondence. 3.   Communi-cation in social work. I.   Title.
  HV43.S52 2015
  651.5'042—dc23
                                                                                          2015018571

Printed in the United States of America

To Michael J. Sidell, for his unwavering love and support.

To Gayle M. Kreitzer and Alyssa L. Hoffman, without whom this work would not have been completed.

Table of Contents

About the Author

Nancy L. Sidell, PhD, is professor of social work at Mansfield University, Mansfield, Pennsylvania. She has served as BSW program director and department chair during her tenure at Mansfield University. Sidell has over 18 years of practice experience as a social worker in health, mental health, and nursing home settings. She is an item development consultant with the Association of Social Work Boards and a coauthor (with Denise K. Smiley) of *Professional Communication Skills in Social Work*. She has also authored numerous journal articles. She lives in Wellsboro, Pennsylvania, and enjoys quilting, road biking, and hiking.

Acknowledgments

Appreciation is extended to the following people for their assistance and their support of this project: Mary Daly, Tiffany Welch, Joshua Battin, J. P. Burke, Francis Hendricks, Shirley Teckman, and Andrea Scibana. For providing helpful research assistance, thanks go to Matthew Syrett, Damolla Hayward, Elizabeth Paisley, Alana Jamieson, and Haley Fitzwater. Additional recognition is offered to Lavina Harless, Monica Roth-Day, Karen Tamminga, and Vicki Coy. I am also extremely grateful for the care and attention this project has received from the staff of NASW Press.

A special thank-you to the BSW students at Mansfield University who have tested these concepts and exercises over the years. It has been a pleasure to know each of you. Last, I am grateful to the memory of Fawn M. Stager for the lessons she taught me and the bonds we shared.

About This Book

The purpose of this book is to provide practical, hands-on experience to social workers wishing to improve their documentation skills. It stems from concerns about the wearing away of basic writing skills, hastened by a reduced emphasis on grammar and spelling at all levels of education and a devaluation of the written word. One example of this erosion is the appearance in formal kinds of writing of shorthand abbreviations, previously acceptable only in informal electronic communications.

Social workers must document the services they provide, regardless of their educational level or the setting in which they are employed. Many are unprepared for this responsibility. Social work programs teach skills necessary for effective social work practice but often leave instruction about professional documentation to agency field instructors. Social workers should arrive at the workplace well prepared to document, but often they do not, and most agencies hiring new social workers must train them on the job.

Undergraduate and graduate students, as well as seasoned social workers, can benefit from instruction in the basics of social work documentation. This book is written with the goal of improving social workers' writing skills and better preparing them for the written demands of their work. It can be useful as a reference tool in agency settings where employees need assistance with documentation concepts.

This book reviews common formats and examples. It cannot, however, cover all of the documentation requirements that social workers may find during their careers or all of the settings in which social workers practice. The term "agency" is most commonly used to refer to the workplace throughout this book for efficiency purposes and in no way conveys the richness of the numerous settings in which social workers are employed. Neither does this book replace specific agency guidelines or jurisdictional rulings. Not all examples will be useful in every setting, given the wide variation in documentation requirements. But although this book cannot replace agency policy documents or supervisory guidance, it can serve as a learning tool.

The book is divided into three sections. The first four chapters give a general overview of documentation—its history, considerations that need to be addressed before documentation begins, and special issues. The second portion of the book reviews in turn the different components of a typical case file. The last section focuses on ways in which documentation can be evaluated and improved. Continuous skill improvement and supervisory issues are covered here, along with a look at future trends and directions. Over 120 exercises are found throughout the book, designed to build confidence about and knowledge of important aspects of documentation.

The exercises are designed to elicit written answers, which can be kept in a separate notebook or folder. Many of them are best completed with one or more peers who work through the exercises at the same time. Although the term "peer" is used throughout the exercises, a supervisor, fellow student, or colleague can fill this role. For example, a social worker may find that a supervisor's feedback about the exercises is helpful to his or her professional growth. Alternatively, working with a peer who is also interested in improving documenting skills may be beneficial. Both social workers can work through the exercises and provide one another with helpful feedback. Specific and constructive feedback from a supervisor or peer can promote more polished and professional recording abilities. These skills will greatly enhance a social worker's professionalism and ultimately result in better service to clients.

PART I

Understanding Documentation

This section provides an introductory basis for understanding the importance of documentation. The history of documentation and efforts to teach it are covered in the first chapter. The second chapter is devoted to issues surrounding social work documentation today, including ethical and technological impacts on recording. The third chapter lays a foundation for understanding the major components of a case record. The fourth chapter discusses special issues in grammar and word usage that often confound social workers. It also includes information about risk management guidelines that are important to keep in mind when choosing the words used in case recording. A social worker can minimize the chance of a lawsuit, for example, by following the noted guidelines.

CHAPTER 1

Introduction to Social Work Documentation

Social work documentation, like any good writing, is a skill that is built. "You might believe that good writing comes naturally for some people, but even for the experienced writer, it is hard work" (Szuchman & Thomlison, 2008, p. xi).

The Oxford English Dictionary Online defines *documentation* as "the accumulation, classification, and dissemination of information" ("Documentation," 2013). In social work, its meaning is even more specific. The term is well known to students and practitioners alike, despite the fact that it does not appear in the sixth edition of the *Social Work Dictionary* (Barker, 2014). It is a communication tool with which social workers record their work; the means by which cases are managed; and the manner in which services are evaluated, assessed, and often reimbursed. It is a required professional social work function, a permanent record of client service provision.

Social workers often have a negative response to documentation—it is the bane of many professionals' existence. To many social workers, it means spending time away from their true passion of working with clients, responding to unnecessary bureaucratic demands, and tending to tedious and boring details. Overworked social workers do not appreciate the requirement for case recording and often delay the task. The phrase "if it's not documented, it's not done" is commonly used to encourage better documentation habits, but the particulars of how to do so are less well noted.

HISTORY OF DOCUMENTATION

The lack of appreciation for case recording is nothing new. Colcord and Mann (1930) wrote that "the charity organization group learned early to keep records, and some of their number, as time went on, became very much dissatisfied with the clumsy way of doing things revealed by these records" (p. 585).

From the beginning of organized social work, efforts were made to record information about cases. Often, these notes were kept in public files in local offices and had minimal content (Strode, 1940). Timms (1972, p. 9) noted that early recording of service delivery took the form of a registry in which poor-relief workers entered the name of the client; the amount of cash assistance provided; the client's residence; and a few remarks such as "destitute," "very aged," or "large family." These cursory notes were often the only record of service delivery.

The next phase of documentation, beginning in the last half of the 19th century, was characterized by more detail and verification of key facts (Timms, 1972). Guidelines presented at the first national Conference of Boards of Public Charities in 1874 illustrate this type of documentation. They advised including the following items in the record:

- Kinds of mental and moral perversion;
- Descriptions of morbid and debasing conditions of the mind;
- Points at which neglect of social and moral duties began;
- Information regarding the totally idiotic or weak-minded in three generations, living and dead;
- Total inebriates in three generations, living and dead; and
- Capacity for self-support without the direction and control of a superior authority or constant advice and supervision. (Conference of Boards of Public Charities, 1874, pp. 88–89)

Documentation content has changed since 1874, but it is still a work in progress for the profession. In 1922, Mary Richmond wrote that "the habit of full recording is not yet well established" (p. 30). Depending on the location in which services were provided, the habit seemed to vary widely. In the same year that Richmond wrote these words, Josephine Brown, a pioneer in rural social work, advised against keeping notes on services delivered: "The taking of notes is even less advisable in the country than in the city. . . . Unless some obvious reason for using paper and pencil exists—such as securing information for the court—notes are out of the question" (Brown, 1922, p. 188).

Disagreeing with Brown five years later was Harold J. Mathews:

One of the greatest sins of the rural case worker, which she is more guilty of than the city worker, is that she does not keep as good records. Too many times we find them with only copies of letters and a few ragged notes, if anything at all. This is not fair to the profession and the development of the work in rural sections, to say nothing of being unfair to the client and the next case worker who comes along. It is bad business to say the least. (Mathews, 1927/1980, p. 172)

In 1932, Brown wrote this of rural case records: "If any information about a family receiving relief is on record anywhere, it may be in the pocket notebook of a county supervisor" (p. 17). Clearly, inconsistency and loose practices seemed to be prevalent and accepted.

Case notes were a challenge for more than just rural social workers. When the Federal Emergency Relief Administration was established in 1933, there was an immediate need to obtain information about relief given to the unemployed and their families across the United States. A research division tasked with developing a standardized means of reporting relief statistics was created for the first time in the country's history:

> There were in existence few satisfactory state systems for reporting the numbers of relief recipients and the amounts of expenditures. As a result, a vague uncertainty prevailed concerning the size of the relief problem. . . . Little was known about the characteristics or composition of the relief population. (Brown, 1940, p. 194)

In 1934, poor-relief workers still kept little or no permanent record of their services:

> Check book stubs, loose sheets of paper, duplicate order blanks, and pocket note books are frequently the only evidence of such uses to which public funds have been put. In several instances even such informal memoranda are lacking. Some poor directors have destroyed their records upon going out of office. (Pennsylvania Department of Public Welfare, 1934, p. 87)

Records were often inadequate and inaccurate. Prior to 1937 and the passage of the Public Assistance Law, 967 people were responsible for the administration of poor relief in Pennsylvania's 425 established districts. The organization of relief in Pennsylvania was likely not unique. Administrators there maintained very few records, which were described as

> usually fragmentary and unsatisfactory. . . . They supplied but little information regarding relief expenditures or the circumstances of the recipients which justified helping them with public funds. The records often consisted of no more than the lists of names of relief recipients which were printed in annual reports of the county government or in the newspapers, supplemented by the financial reports of the county treasurers which gave unitemized amounts of grocers' bills and the accounts of other tradesmen who furnished goods to the poor. (Brown, 1940, pp. 15–16)

In the late 1930s, the trend in social work documentation turned from scant notes to process recordings (Timms, 1972). Although never practiced on a day-to-day basis, process recordings signified an attempt to document everything. From there, the pendulum swung back to a compromise between keeping a simple register and detailing everything: differential recording, which involved selectively choosing what was considered the most important content to record. A narrative summary account of services provided, based on the unique nature of the case, gradually emerged.

By the mid-1950s, the selective and analytic diagnostic record was widely used (Kagle, 1984b). This type of record existed primarily to show the worker's supervisor how the case was being approached. Changes in the 1960s and 1970s included an increased demand for accountability, early computer technology, and new complexities in service funding, all of which had an impact on the record-keeping practices of social workers. A survey conducted in 1979 and 1980 revealed that educational supervision was no longer the primary function of social work records. They were being used increasingly for purposes such as ensuring continuity of services, evaluating effectiveness of service delivery, and enabling professionals involved in the same case to communicate with one another (Kagle, 1984b). Audiences included other service providers, clients, and funding sources. During this period, the conviction emerged that no single approach to documentation met each need in every case (Timms, 1972). This new approach stressed flexibility based on the client's situation and agency requirements.

Although no one recording formula will be effective in all cases, a systematic approach to documentation can be helpful, particularly for inexperienced workers and for seasoned professionals working with a new population. Despite a great deal of variety in today's documentation styles, one point remains clear: Documentation is essential to the effectiveness of social workers and the well-being of their clients.

HISTORY OF EFFORTS TO TEACH DOCUMENTATION

Three books were written about case documentation between 1920 and 1936 (Timms, 1972)—more titles than at any other time. Sheffield's (1920) *The Social Case History: Its Construction and Content* identified three purposes for documentation: improving client treatment, advancing and improving society, and enhancing the worker's critical thinking skills. Bristol's *Handbook on Social Case Recording* and Hamilton's *Social Case Recording* were published in 1936. Hamilton argued that standardization of record keeping was impossible: "There is no such thing as a model record, no routines which will make the case inevitably clear, accessible, and understandable. Records should be written to suit the case, not the case geared to a theoretical pattern" (Hamilton, 1936, p. 2). Hamilton predicted that practice and documentation skills would develop simultaneously, a notion that is also prevalent today.

More recent books were written by Timms in 1972 (*Recording in Social Work*) and by Wilson in 1980 (*Recording Guidelines for Social Workers*). Both offered practical guidelines on elements of recording. Kagle's *Social Work Records* followed in 1984; it is currently in its third edition (Kagle & Kopels, 2008). Although many social work practice texts include introductory material on documentation skills and methods (for example, Kirst-Ashman & Hull, 2011; Sheafor & Horejsi, 2012), practical recording guidelines are not included.

Documentation should matter to every practicing social worker and every student considering entry into the profession. It is a vital professional responsibility in which ongoing training is needed. This book provides specific training on documentation to help social workers prepare for and manage their record-keeping responsibilities.

SUMMARY

Wide disparity in note taking has been evident from the social work profession's beginnings. Today's documentation looks different from the notes written by early social work pioneers, and its importance is probably greater today than it was in the past. Both practitioners and their clients will benefit if social workers receive detailed instruction on the basic requirements of documentation.

CHAPTER 2

Documentation Today

"Recording is not an isolated part of social work practice. Effective recording goes hand in hand with effective interviewing/casework—it is impossible and undesirable to discuss one without the other" (Wilson, 1980, p. 3). Although documentation styles and expectations may have changed over the years, the importance of recording has not diminished. The case record is, first and foremost, a communication tool. Social workers must be prepared to document the services they provide, no matter what their education level or the setting in which they are employed. Today, as much as ever, effective social work requires accurate and responsible documentation.

It is understandable that new social workers are often confused about writing requirements and expectations. For example, academia is full of complaints about the poor writing skills of students (Bartlett, 2003; Richardson, 2008). Universities commonly require a first-year composition course, which is designed to raise students' writing skills to acceptable standards. It has been discovered, however, that when students are asked to complete an unfamiliar writing challenge, they are not necessarily able to adapt their writing skills to the new context. For example, a student who competently writes about the effects of global warming on coral reefs "might look like a much weaker writer when she tries her hand at a chemistry lab report for the first time" (Richardson, 2008, p. 48).

Similarly, a social work student may write an acceptable research paper on child abuse but may not be as skillful at writing his or her first case note during field education. Alternatively, a social work student may present a thorough process recording in graduate school but have difficulty producing the narrative notes required in an agency setting. Social work faculty members have expressed concerns about students' writing skills (Anderson, 2003; Simon & Soven, 1990; Waller, 2000). "Writing is an essential social work skill," said Falk and Ross (2001, p. 125), but "a significant proportion of BSW students lack the writing skills to carry out their social work responsibilities effectively" (p. 125). An informal survey of social work academicians revealed that educators must not only demand good writing but also convey its importance to success in practice. Social work educators "cannot sustain the notion that teaching writing is beyond their purview" (Waller, 2000, p. 166).

Although many have recognized their importance, documentation skills appear to be inconsistently taught and emphasized by schools of social work. For example, the current educational standards of the Council on Social Work Education (CSWE, 2008) do not directly address writing as a content area; however, they do require a liberal arts foundation, of which writing is an important component. The council's educational policy 2.1.3 addresses critical thinking skills and mentions writing skills: "Social workers demonstrate effective oral and written communication in working with individuals, families, groups, organizations, communities, and colleagues" (CSWE, 2008, p. 4).

How social work programs teach writing skills varies, according to the limited research that exists on the subject. A content analysis of social work syllabi from 15 Canadian universities (Paré & Allen, 1995) found no undergraduate or graduate courses devoted to writing in social work and little reference to writing in hundreds of course descriptions. Ames (2002) interviewed 20 full-time social work faculty members teaching direct practice courses in the Mid-Atlantic region of the United States. All agreed that documentation is important classroom content and indicated that they teach it in some form. A great deal of variation was reported in both the content and the manner in which recording content was delivered, however. Only five of 12 syllabi revealed specific assignments related to documentation.

Ames (2008) conducted another qualitative study regarding documentation, this time with 16 BSW field instructors. She found that respondents wanted students to know about recording before the students entered a field placement. They wanted students to be able "to pinpoint the important aspects of their observations and interactions with clients . . . to be able to discern 'what to write down' or to have the skills to pick out the pieces of the conversation that are pertinent" (Ames, 2008, p. 74). They described most students as writing too much and not having the ability to discriminate between what was important and what was not. Concise writing was noted as an important skill that students needed.

A third study investigated student perceptions of documentation in managed-care environments (Kane, 2002). This study found that over two-thirds of the participants learned documentation skills during their field education rather than in the classroom. "Most education about recording seems to take place in agencies, beginning with the field experience" (Ames, 1999, p. 232). New social workers should begin their positions prepared to document, but often they are unprepared.

"Educators of social workers have long recognized the importance of writing, yet little time is devoted to improving writing skills" (Szuchman & Thomlison, 2008, p. xi). Kagle (1984b) also found that a limited number of social work programs actually teach documentation skills in the classroom. Rather, the conventional wisdom seems to be that each agency is best suited to train its employees and interns on its documentation requirements. This situation is puzzling. Imagine if educators determined that other content areas in social work were best left to be taught by individual agencies!

Some educational programs are beginning to address the need to teach documentation skills. For example, Grise-Owens and Crum (2012) described one MSW program's efforts to improve writing skills using several strategies, one of which is a required professional writing course. The program director noted, "(a) I teach primarily social work practice courses, (b) professional writing is a key practice skill, (c), ergo, I teach writing" (Grise-Owens & Crum, 2012, p. 521). Similarly, Leon and Pepe (2010) described a required BSW course aimed at improving recording skills. Efforts such as these are encouraging but far from mainstream.

The critical importance of accurate and timely documentation is not often fully understood by new social workers, who are often anxious to work with clients but far less interested in the mundane tasks of documenting those services. "Social work students are often reminded that 'If it isn't written down, it didn't happen,' but how many actually understand the critical nature of documentation is yet another question" (Chase, 2008, p. 427).

There seems to be general agreement in the literature that, ideally, documentation training should occur in several locations: the classroom, the field education setting, and the workplace (Kagle & Kopels, 2008; Tebb, 1991). Professionals who have not been exposed to documentation concepts at all levels are at a distinct disadvantage. "Social workers who have not learned basic recording do not have a framework within which they can place theory, practice, and policy in the proper context" (Tebb, 1991, p. 430).

Clients are also affected by poor documentation. For example, outcomes of child and elder abuse cases often hinge on the accuracy, thoroughness, and precision of social work documentation. Clients' lives are influenced by social work recording: "Our reports and how clearly and precisely they are written often affect the clients we serve" (Glicken, 2008, p. xi).

Most agencies train new social workers on the job regarding their unique documentation requirements. Without a comprehensive classroom introduction to documentation, social workers may rely too heavily on the documentation style that they learn in this way, which may or may not be adequate as they progress through their careers (Kagle, 1993). Social workers who know only one method of documentation have problems switching to other required formats later, and the larger picture is often lost: "They do not understand the connection between actual practice and the recording process" (Tebb, 1991, p. 430). Also, many students spend a great deal of time in graduate school learning process recording, which they may not use at all in their practice experience (Kagle & Kopels, 2008).

"Recording need not be taught as a separate subject, but it certainly should be taught," Ames said (1999, p. 237). Ames suggested several content areas that students should learn: basic writing skills, information-gathering techniques, the importance of recording in practice, the variety of recording formats, application of recording skills, summary recording, and computer literacy. After additional research, Ames (2002) further recommended that the following information be taught in direct practice courses: basic writing skills; the purposes of documentation, including ethical and practical implications; the functions, forms, and components of recording; and the technical and ethical issues that surround computerized record keeping.

Kagle and Kopels (2008) suggested four ideal precepts for documentation training. First, it should occur throughout one's education, from classroom to fieldwork to entry-level practice. Second, it should progress from general concepts to specific applications. Next, skill development should move along a continuum, with advanced skills building on foundational ones. Last, education for practice and for recording should be linked and continuous. Documentation "should not be introduced as a necessary evil of agency practice but as an integral part of practice throughout the student's learning experience" (Kagle & Kopels, 2008, p. 118). These recommendations form the rationale of this book's approach to documentation education.

Kagle and Kopels (2008) have contributed important information about required content and legal issues related to documentation. Their work is not a step-by-step guide to learn how to document, however. Little practical help is available to train new practitioners in documentation. A how-to book on social work documentation guidelines was last published in 1980. Wilson's (1980) *Recording Guidelines for Social Workers* is currently out of print and obviously does not address the technological advances and increased demands for accountability that have emerged since its publication.

PURPOSES OF DOCUMENTATION

Wilson (1980) began her book with the interesting question, "What would it be like to have no records?" (p. 1). She portrayed a fictional medical social work department as it struggled through a day without records and provided an exercise for those wishing to experience the lack of documentation for themselves. The exercise invited the worker to pretend for two weeks that records did not exist in his or her agency. Cautioning that a supervisor's permission would be required to conduct this experiment, she asked the worker to refrain from consulting any case files and to neglect to record any service provision (Wilson, 1980, p. 212). It would be interesting to know how many days an agency would allow this experiment to continue. Wilson's point was that recording is necessary and useful to social workers on a practical, day-to-day basis.

Social work records serve many purposes. It was suggested by Sheffield as early as 1920 that the ultimate purpose of documentation was to better treat the client. Documentation is a form of clinical, ethical, and legal accountability (Ames, 1999). Such overarching purposes are not often fully comprehended by the social worker faced with daily client and agency demands. From a practical standpoint, the purposes of documentation, according to Wilson (1980), include the following:

- Creating and maintaining a record of social work activity and services performed
- Providing continuity of service in the event of worker illness or changeover
- Securing payment from third-party payers
- Maintaining quality of service provision through quality control efforts
- Providing the basis for statistical reporting requirements
- Assisting with supervisory review and feedback
- Organizing a worker's thoughts and actions

- Affording interdisciplinary communication
- Helping establish a client's eligibility for services
- Teaching new workers and interns about service provision
- Providing a baseline for research and evaluation
- Assisting with an agency's defense in legal actions
- Providing a therapeutic tool by sharing records with the client.

Although this remains a pertinent list today, additional reasons for social workers to keep records include these suggestions from Kagle (1984b):

- Assisting with consultation and peer review
- Supporting administrative decision making.

Today, it is generally agreed that social work records should do the following (Kagle & Kopels, 2008):

- Focus on service delivery.
- Include assessments that are objective, comprehensive, and fair.
- Focus on the information needed to provide services.
- Include the client's role in the process.
- Identify cultural factors that may influence outcomes.
- Be written as if the client and others involved in the case have access to it.
- Be organized, current, and well written.

ETHICS AND DOCUMENTATION

Ethical standards for social workers in the United States did not address documentation specifically until 1996, when a revised version of the NASW's *Code of Ethics* was adopted (NASW, 1996; Reamer, 2005); the most current version was last updated in 2008. The *Code of Ethics* charges social workers with the ethical duty "to accurately document the services they provide and protect private information contained in records, thus establishing national standards enforced by NASW committees on inquiry and by state licensing boards that choose to adopt NASW *Code of Ethics* guidelines" (NASW, 2008; Reamer, 2005, p. 327). The code also states the following:

3.04 Client Records

(a) Social workers should take reasonable steps to ensure that documentation in records is accurate and reflects the services provided.

(b) Social workers should include sufficient and timely documentation in records to facilitate the delivery of services and to ensure the continuity of services provided to clients in the future.

(c) Social workers' documentation should protect clients' privacy to the extent that it is possible and appropriate and should include only information that is directly relevant to the delivery of services.

(d) Social workers should store records following the termination of services to ensure reasonable future access. Records should be maintained for the number of years required by state statutes or relevant
contracts. (NASW, 2008, p. 20)

Records are also addressed in the code in the following sections:

1.07 Privacy and Confidentiality

(1) Social workers should protect the confidentiality of clients' written
and electronic records and other sensitive information. Social workers should take reasonable steps to ensure that clients' records are
stored in a secure location and that clients' records are not available
to others who are not authorized to have access.

1.08 Access to Records

(a) Social workers should provide clients with reasonable access to
records concerning clients. Social workers who are concerned that
clients' access to their records could cause serious misunderstanding or harm to the client should provide assistance in interpreting
the records and consultation with the client regarding the records.
Social workers should limit clients' access to their records, or por-
tions of their records, only in exceptional circumstances when
there is compelling evidence that such access would cause serious harm to the client. Both clients' requests and the rationale for
withholding some or all of the records should be documented in
clients' files.

(b) When providing clients with access to their records, social workers
should take steps to protect the confidentiality of other individuals
identified or discussed in such records. (NASW, 2008, pp. 10–12)

These standards provide general guidelines regarding documentation but cannot provide specific guidance in all matters. The code "does not provide a set of
rules that prescribe how social workers should act in all situations" (NASW, 2008,
p. 2). In comparison, the *Guidelines for Ethical Practice* of the Canadian Association
of Social Workers (CASW, 2005) provide more direction:

1.7 Maintenance and Handling of Client Records

Social workers maintain one written record of professional interventions and opinions, with due care to the obligation and standards of their
employer and relevant regulatory body. Social workers document information impartially and accurately and with an appreciation that the record

may be revealed to clients or disclosed during court proceedings. Social workers are encouraged to take care to

- report only essential and relevant details
- refrain from using emotive or derogatory language
- acknowledge the basis of professional opinions
- protect clients' privacy and that of others involved.

1.7.1   Social workers do not state a professional opinion unless it can be supported by their own assessment or by the documented assessment of another professional.

1.7.2   Where records are shared across professions or agencies, information is recorded only to the degree that it addresses clients' needs and meets the requirements of an employer or professional standards of practice.

1.7.3   Before using client records for any purpose beyond professional services, for example education, social workers obtain the informed consent of clients.

1.7.4   In some circumstances, access to client records may be officially authorized or required by statute. Where consent of clients is not required, social workers attempt to notify clients that such access has been granted, if such notification does not involve a risk to others.

1.7.5   Social workers ensure that clients have reasonable access to official social work records concerning them. However, if there are compelling professional, ethical or legal reasons for refusing access, social workers advise clients of their right to request a review of the decision through organizational or legal channels. . . . .

1.7.6   Social workers take due care to protect the confidences of others when providing clients with access to records. This may involve masking third party information in the record.

1.7.7   If clients are not satisfied with their records, social workers advise them regarding complaint mechanisms.

1.7.8   Social workers protect clients' records, store them securely and retain them for any required statutory period.

1.7.9   Social workers transfer or dispose of clients' records in a manner that protects clients' confidentiality and is consistent with provincial/territorial statutes governing records and social work regulation. Social workers also ensure that mechanical or electronic records are properly transferred and disposed of. (CASW, 2005, pp. 9–10)

In summary, both U.S. and Canadian ethical standards touch on documentation guidelines, with the Canadian guidelines providing more detail. Neither set, however, delves into the specifics of content or style. They cannot provide concrete guidance on how to record service delivery.

ACCESS TO CASE FILES

Social workers typically can assure clients that access to their records is limited. In the United States, the Privacy Act of 1974, effective from September 1975, guaranteed clients access to records maintained by government agencies. Although a great deal of fear was expressed that such knowledge would harm clients, the reality was that "clients turned out to be less vulnerable than had been assumed. They were able to listen to a frank assessment of their appearance, methods of coping, and characteristics without falling apart" (Houghkirk, 1977, p. 28). Today, it is accepted that clients have access to their own records. Both U.S. and Canadian ethical codes confirm that clients have the right to view their records.

Who, besides the client it concerns and the social worker who created it, has access to a social work record? The staff and affiliates of the agency at which services are received are also involved. "In reality, consumers are not just being served by their social worker—the setting employing the worker actually serves the client collectively" (Wilson, 1980, p. 185). It is commonly assumed that the social worker, his or her supervisor, and clerical staff have routine access to case files. However, the list of others who may also have access can be extensive: students, members of other disciplines who are with the same program, volunteers, computer technicians, researchers, consultants, agency attorneys, board members, staff conducting internal peer reviews, external licensing and accreditation bodies, parent organizations if the agency is part of a larger system, and third-party funding sources (Wilson, 1980). In those settings in which multidisciplinary records are kept, team members from a range of backgrounds chart concurrently with social workers.

Clients have the right to access their records, even if they are not considered competent:

> Although clients lack the capacity to provide informed consent (because of a permanent disability or a temporary incapacity), clients retain the right to receive information about themselves, which may be contained in their records, consistent with their level of understanding and comprehension. (Reamer, 2009, p. 60)

Thus, a client who is unable to give informed consent still has the right to receive information contained in his or her record.

Each agency should set clear guidelines regarding conditions under which records may be accessed and by whom. Everyone having access should receive training about confidentiality. Most agencies limit staff member access to those who need the information to perform a job function. This excludes the curious or those looking for gossip (Wilson, 1980).

IMPACT OF TECHNOLOGY

To say that technology is changing too quickly to keep pace with is no understatement. That it has changed the face of social work is also apparent (Belluomini,

2013). Since the first Internet connection was made in 1969, technology has emerged as a leading force in today's world (Leiner et al., 2000). Kurzweil (2001) noted that technological change occurs not linearly but exponentially. Rather than experiencing 100 years of progress in this century, people are more likely to experience 20,000 years of progress. Such massive change can be daunting, but it is instructive to read about the concerns of social workers practicing when the typewriter came into use. Sheffield (1920) compared handwritten and typed records and noted that "the typewriter is releasing time and energy in ways that count for the enrichment of our thinking upon our clients' problems" (pp. 79–80). Clearly, typewriters were seen as a time-saver, like computers are today.

Limited computer use for administrative functions began in agencies in the 1960s, and skyrocketing accountability demands in the 1970s dramatically increased computer applications (Finnegan & Ivanoff, 1991). Systems focused first on billing but later became more comprehensive. Networked and designed to meet multiple agency needs, these systems handled tasks from accounting to scheduling (Gingerich, 2002a). Schoech (1982) noted that computers were not seen as being useful to direct care staff but predicted that the computer was "destined to become the underlying communications tool" (p. 281). Concerns about client privacy issues and misuse of technology as expansion occurred were early themes of note.

Computer systems were slow to incorporate many functions that are increasingly seen today. Technology is now a mainstay in agencies and is used to organize, handle, collect, and retrieve information within organizations (Kagle, 2008). Software systems designed to help agencies become essentially paperless currently abound. The goal of many electronic systems is to capture client information from the time a client first applies for services through termination or discharge and beyond to follow-up. These Web-based systems allow for instant access to all forms of client documentation, in real time (Health Information Technology, n.d.). In addition to documenting service provision, these systems boast billing and scheduling features as well. Marketed as being compliant with the Health Insurance Portability and Accountability Act of 1996 (HIPAA) and fully secure, systems offer full encryption, security teams, and traffic-monitoring capabilities to the agencies purchasing them.

A review of several electronic record packages currently available reveals some common elements. These include client application information; electronic consent forms; appointment scheduling; client assessments; progress notes for individuals, couples, families, and groups; discharge and referral information; follow-up and outcomes tracking; revenue tracking and reporting; insurance forms and billing; and medication management. Pre-established forms can be used, or forms can be customized to fit an agency's special needs. Staff training on the use of the computer system is often one of the services offered. Generally, electronic records allow for documenting the same information contained in a paper case file.

Improving the quality of services provided and reducing costs associated with paperwork are two major benefits of electronic records. Another important emerging benefit is how intra-agency sharing of data as a way to improve communication flow about mutual clients is enabled (Swaminathan, 2012). With client consent, sharing information seamlessly is much more possible today than ever before. In addition, having real-time information with which to make decisions about a client is another benefit. Wireless tablets and portable laptops are increasingly used to instantly access a client's record by today's social worker. Social workers in the field can often interact with the office via smart phones. For example, a social worker may text a supervisor with a question he or she is unsure about, make brief notes on a smart phone application connected to a cloud server, and update a treatment plan using voice-recognition technology, all within minutes. Mobility contributes to the expectation for real-time, right-now responses, which can be a benefit or a curse.

Questions to consider before purchasing an electronic documentation product include the following:

- What features are available that are needed in my setting?
- How is client confidentiality ensured? What security measures exist? What about HIPAA compliance?
- Who has access to the records? Can clients access them if appropriate?
- How will this product help the staff? How will it hinder staff functions?
- Have other social workers in similar settings used this product? Can they be contacted to discuss important issues?
- What initial and ongoing training programs or classes are available to staff?
- How are problems addressed? For example, how have breaches of client information or system shutdowns been addressed?
- How much individual tailoring of forms is possible and at what cost?
- What are initial and ongoing product costs?
- How are new staff members provided with access to the product? When a staff member resigns, how does access end?
- How would the setting's current documentation practices fit into the product's capabilities?
- Are demonstrations or trial periods available to test the product?

As any technology matures and develops from its early uses, it becomes more dependable, as evidenced by other earlier technologies that improved over time (Kincaid, 2004). With that increased dependability comes an increase in benefits. The benefits of technology to social workers are clearly delineated by Kincaid (2004). There is no better way to access current, cutting-edge diagnostic and treatment information for clients or to remain current on new research trends. Increased online access to elected officials and grassroots opportunities to influence social policy can enable better client advocacy efforts. Professionals in rural settings can exchange ideas with peers in ways not seen before. Similarly, those with specific areas of expertise can locate like-minded professionals sharing similar interests with whom to share ideas. Online continuing education opportunities are readily available, less expensive to access, and in compliance with many jurisdictional licensure laws. Social work opportunities from home have expanded with technology, better meeting the personal needs of a predominantly female workforce. Fewer barriers related to ethnicity, gender, and other client characteristics arise when services are provided online. The mobility and ease with which information is accessed can translate into improved client services. Clearly, technology has had an impact on the world of social work in positive ways.

Of course, a downside to technology also exists. Technology can be dehumanizing and time consuming to learn and manage. It is unknown if technology frees up social workers' time and energy or requires more of it. Issues of confidentiality arise, as do contraindications of its use with certain types of clients. "When you have a computerized system, you have some likelihood of things going wrong" (Hoffman, as quoted in Putre, 2011, p. 30). Breaches in the system, system failure, and lack of client privacy of sensitive information are all possibilities with any system. In fact, computerized systems provide numerous opportunities for client privacy to be compromised. Information overload is also possible, with too many details available to too many people. Whether or not the benefits of technology use outweigh its drawbacks, it is clearly a force to be reckoned with.

Technology can simplify and improve the efficiency of social work documentation, but it also presents special challenges. One early study examined the recording habits of 88 social service agencies using computers for record keeping and found that 40 percent of them had increased, rather than decreased, the time spent on recording (Kagle, 1993). Besides the time it takes to install equipment, activate security features, and train employees to use the system, functional operation of the system took more time to achieve than anticipated. Agencies reported being additionally challenged by the impact of computer use on staff workload, time management, and security of sensitive information. More recently, Moellinger (2010) found that technology creates paradoxes in the workplace: Although technology use can generally result in more efficiencies, it concurrently creates a demand for increased productivity. Also, enhanced mobility is promoted as a benefit, but its constant use can result in increased isolation and avoidance of personal contact. These paradoxes represent trends that can be troubling for social workers managing documentation expectations in the technology-filled workplace.

Social workers should remember that clients are affected by technology, too. For example, clients often have smart phone access. "For many low-income families, their smart phone is a cheap computer—not an expensive phone" (Swaminathan, 2012, Mobility Matters section, para. 1). It can serve as a laptop, a landline, and a broadband connection. Social workers "should be aware of how much technology affects clients' lives" (Reardon, 2011, p. 11), in addition to being aware of how much technology influences their own lives.

Social work as a profession still has much to learn about technology. Being cautious about its use was offered as the most important piece of advice for those considering it (Reardon, 2011). One should fully explore the question of "whether embracing technology is simply a necessary business move or a trend that puts the profession's ethics in jeopardy" (Reardon, 2011, p. 11). Being clear about one's rationale for using technology is important when considering this complex issue.

However, social workers should strive to be on the cutting edge of technology, according to the *NASW & ASWB Standards for Technology and Social Work Practice*: "Social workers should keep themselves informed about technology that will advance quality program operations and service delivery" (NASW & Association of Social Work Boards [ASWB], 2005, p. 13). These standards are invaluable in helping one think through the impact of technology on social work practice, today and in the future.

SUMMARY AND EXERCISES

Documentation, although always important to social work practice, has grown in importance. Effective documentation is critical in social work, no matter what the setting. Creating a record of delivered services is important, as are the skills necessary to do so in a competent manner. Some training in documentation occurs in the classroom, but the majority appears to occur in agency settings. The purposes of documentation are myriad and speak to the complexities of social work practice. Technological advances have added to this complexity but have the potential to be a boon to social workers in managing their workload. Caution is necessary when considering the use of technology in social work settings.

These exercises are designed to help social workers think about the impact of technology on social work documentation, both today and in the future. Like many of the exercises in this book, many are most effective when two or more people work on them at the same time and then compare answers to give each other feedback.

Exercise 2.1: Reviewing Standards for Technology

Using your favorite search engine, type in "NASW and ASWB standards for technology." Open the PDF file and answer the following questions about the 2005 document:

1. Why do you believe these standards were developed? What is the most important reason for them?
2. Standard 3 (p. 6) addresses cultural competence and vulnerable populations. In your own words, what does this standard say? What is most important about it?
3. The issue of client privacy is addressed in Standard 7 (p. 9). Thinking of an agency with which you are familiar, how is technology used there and what steps are taken to protect client privacy?
4. Advocacy and community action (Standard 9.1) and community practice (Standard 9.2) are addressed on pages 11–12. What is most important about these sections?
5. Standard 9.3 (p. 13) says that social workers should keep themselves informed about technology. How do you see yourself doing this in your professional practice?

Compare your responses with those of a peer. What did you learn? Were there any surprises?

Exercise 2.2: Explore Electronic Record Systems

In your favorite search engine, type in "online mental health record system." Explore a few sites and select one software system to examine more closely. If an online demonstration is available, download and work with it. Using the list of questions to consider before purchasing an electronic documentation product that appears on page 18 of this chapter, assess this product for use at an agency with which you are familiar. Take notes and compare what you found with the findings of a peer who assessed a different software package. What did you learn that will help you in your future practice?

Exercise 2.3: Take a Test Run

Go back to your favorite search engine and type in "online mental health record." Find a system that offers a free 30-day trial. Ask a peer to enroll in the same 30-day trial period. Use it to document services you could provide to a well-known entertainment figure on whom you both agree or yourself if you were your client. At the end of the trial period, discuss the pros and cons of the product. Would you recommend its use at an agency in the future? Why or why not? How was your experience with the product similar to or different from your peer's experience?

Exercise 2.4: Technology Problems

How would you respond to each situation below? Make some notes about what you would do and ask a peer to separately do the same. Discuss each situation after you have both independently reviewed the scenarios. Do your responses differ? What did you learn?

1. A client asks for access to her electronic record, but the system has been shut down for maintenance. The client demands to see the notes now and has become highly agitated.
2. A community advocate wants to use technology to increase interest in and mobilize support for ending human trafficking. The advocate asks to use your name and your agency's name in a mass e-mail that she wants to send out to all residents of a very large city.
3. A patient who has attempted suicide is brought to an emergency department. You are the hospital social worker called in to help assess for inpatient treatment. You cannot access the patient's records because the electronic record system is denying you access. You need to make a recommendation soon, but the system administrator says you cannot access the system until tomorrow.
4. A noncustodial parent demands access to a child's electronic records, but no consent form is on file. The parent claims that consent was obtained

and should be in the electronic file. The parent produces a copy of what looks to be a signed consent form.

5. A group facilitator is killed in a car accident, and your agency assigns you to replace him. You do not have access to the group files but know the deceased facilitator's password, which you found on his desk.

6. You are current with your documentation in a client's electronic record but receive a call from a team member asking for an update on the client's progress. You refer the team member to the electronic record. You know the team member is not comfortable with technology and does not like to access the electronic record.

CHAPTER 3

Laying the Foundation

Begin at the beginning and go on till you come to the end.
—The King to Alice in *Alice in Wonderland* by Lewis Carroll

Documenting a case usually begins well before the social worker first meets the client, during the client's initial contact with the agency (Zuckerman, 2008). Because social workers are employed in so many settings (for example, schools, hospitals, nonprofits, and community-based programs), the word "agency" is used throughout this book to describe the work setting in a generic way. Some settings have unique documentation requirements. For example, based on accreditation standards, federal and state regulations, and legislative mandates, specific documentation guidelines exist in hospital settings (Smith, 2001). No matter what the setting, however, client information is typically entered into the agency's information management system during an intake screening or another similar procedure. Demographic information typically includes name, address, date of birth, contact information, reasons for seeking assistance, and billing information. Additional demographic data may also be collected, depending on the agency.

This information is typically gathered on a standardized sheet or screen, easily filled in, that can be accessed at the social worker's convenience and is usually available to the social worker by the time of the first client contact. In some agencies, it may be standard practice for the social worker to obtain or verify this information. The social worker is responsible for documenting services that are provided after the initial completion of the form.

Before social workers put pen to paper or fingers to keyboard, they should remember, as Borcherding (2000) said, that others will have to read and comprehend what is written, maybe even scrutinize it, and the client may exercise his or her right to read it. The writer's eyes are not the only ones viewing the record. Before beginning, the writer should think about who may access the document in the future and realize that unexpected eyes may read what is documented (Sormanti, 2012). For example, what would the next assigned worker appreciate reading about the case? If you were the next worker to assist community residents in advocacy efforts, what information would be helpful for you to know? Although it is the client's or clients' story being documented, the record is for the eyes of others who will need to understand that story in the future.

Sormanti (2012) reminded readers that professional documentation is both a responsibility and a privilege: "As such, it must be tended to with great skill, diligence, and care" (p. 129). Burack-Weiss (2012) echoed this sentiment. In addition to owing clients the full attention and benefits of social work skills, "we also owe our clients a full and thoughtful writing" (Burack-Weiss, 2012, p. 277). Sormanti (2012) suggested that the following principles serve as an underlying guide to telling the client's story:

- Keep the foundation's values and ethics as the basis for writing. The core values of social work and the ethical code should provide underpinning for all that is documented. Concepts of self-determination and confidentiality should be evident. "Remember that through your writing you are a spokesperson for the profession" (Sormanti, 2012, p. 129).
- Avoid using words that dehumanize or marginalize clients. Word choice should reflect basic respect for human dignity.
- Include strengths-based descriptors rather than focusing solely on client problems.
- Documentation has the power to facilitate understanding and human connectedness.

FINDING INFORMATION

The primary source of information is usually the client, although there may be other ways to obtain information. With the consent of the client, the worker may contact family members as well as practitioners and agencies that have served the client. Past records may be a source of information, along with reports from referring workers or agencies. All reports are maintained in a confidential manner, according to agency policy.

CONFIDENTIALITY

Confidentiality is defined by the *Social Work Dictionary* as "a principle of *ethics* according to which the social worker or other professional may not disclose information about a client without the client's consent" (Barker, 2014, p. 87). Except for compelling professional reasons, such as foreseeable harm to another, social workers must keep information obtained while providing services confidential. The NASW *Code of Ethics* (2008) states that social workers have an obligation to protect written and electronic client records: "Social workers should take reasonable steps to ensure that clients' records are stored in a secure location and that clients' records are not available to others who are not authorized to have access" (section 1.07[l], pp. 11–12).

It is the responsibility of the social worker to ensure that the client's record is physically secure. Wilson (1980) reminded readers that precautions must be taken to physically safeguard a case file: "Records are usually something physical. . . . Certain precautions must be taken in everyday storage and handling to prevent unauthorized disclosures and high-risk carelessness" (p. 185). Wilson also offered the following guidelines:

- Records should be kept in a locked desk, file cabinet, or storage area when not in use.
- Unattended records should not be left lying on a desk for any length of time.
- Records should not be taken home, although this presents difficulties if the worker conducts home visits or works from a mobile location. Agency policy should be followed regarding removing files from the agency setting.
- A client's record should not be on a social worker's desk during an interview, as its presence can cause unease or invite unauthorized review if the worker is called away.
- A system should be in place that tracks the location of a record within an agency.
- Unauthorized photocopying of records should not occur.
- Materials used for teaching, such as process recordings or supervisory notes, should be kept separate from the client's file.
- A policy should exist that indicates how long files are maintained after case closure and offers guidance on record retention.
- When records are not physical papers but maintained electronically, care must also be taken to safeguard the files. Chapter 9 provides more detail regarding electronic records and their safety.

Clients have the right of access to their social work records. The NASW *Code of Ethics* (2008) indicates that "reasonable access" to records must be provided to a client. Client access may be limited "in exceptional circumstances when there is compelling evidence that such access would cause serious harm to the client" (section 1.08[a], p. 12).

INFORMED CONSENT

Consent is informed when the client understands all risks and possible outcomes of receiving services. The NASW *Code of Ethics* (2008) states,

> Social workers should use clear and understandable language to inform clients of the purpose of the services, . . . limits to services because of the requirements of a third-party payer, relevant costs, reasonable alternatives, clients' right to refuse or withdraw consent, and the time frame covered by the consent. Social workers should provide clients with an opportunity to ask questions. (section 1.03, pp. 7–8)

The only person able to give informed consent is a competent client. The *Social Work Dictionary* defined *competence* in the legal system as "the capacity to understand and act reasonably" (Barker, 2014, p. 84). A client is typically determined to be incompetent by a court via a legal process that varies across jurisdictions. A child is not typically considered legally competent, although the age of competency also may vary across jurisdictions. A social worker should be educated on jurisdictional requirements regarding client legal competency. If a client is not considered legally competent and lacks the capacity to provide informed consent, an appropriate third party must provide it. Consent forms are typically part of the client's case file and are covered in more depth in chapter 6.

AGENCY REQUIREMENTS

Any agency employing social workers has a unique set of documentation requirements; it is impossible to cover them all in this book. New interns and social workers should ask questions about the agency's documentation policy until they understand exactly what is required. They should not assume that because one agency documented in a certain manner, all agencies do so in that way. Questions that are appropriate for an intern or social worker to ask any agency regarding documentation requirements include the following:

- Which types of documentation will I be responsible for?
- Can I view completed case files so I can learn about specific documentation expectations?
- In what time frame is documentation expected to be completed?
- Is scheduled time made available for completion of documentation requirements?
- How is electronic documentation used?
- What safeguards are in place to ensure confidentiality of documentation?
- What supervisory assistance and feedback will be provided to help me improve my documentation?

WHEN TO DOCUMENT

Section 3.04 of the NASW *Code of Ethics* (2008) states that documentation should occur in a timely way, to ensure appropriate delivery of services. The shorter the time between service provision and documentation, the better. Details are remembered most clearly soon after the contact. However, immediate documentation is often a luxury that busy social workers cannot afford. "Practitioners must find time to record when there is insufficient time even to respond to real and emergent client needs" (Kagle & Kopels, 2008, p. 28). Taking a few minutes after each client contact to document is often not possible. For example, a wilderness social worker providing group therapy in the woods often cannot document immediately after a group session ends. A neighborhood advocate cannot always document about a rally at its conclusion. A mental health therapist cannot often record between tightly scheduled sessions. However, social workers should strive to keep as current in documentation as possible. Ways this may be accomplished should be discussed with one's supervisor.

NOTE TAKING

Notes should not be taken during interviews if at all possible. It is too easy to hide behind note taking, focusing on the paper and pencil or the computer screen and keyboard rather than on the client. The exception is when the client is providing information that will be difficult to recall without a written reminder (Wilson, 1980)—for example, dates of birth or family names and addresses. In such cases, it is best to simply say, "May I take a few notes? I want to remember these dates accurately." Make sure the client is comfortable with how you will be taking these minimal notes. For example, explain the use of a note-taking application on a tablet or smart phone, if that is acceptable practice at the agency.

If the client does not appear comfortable with this, do not take notes. Recall what is possible from memory once the session is over. Make a few quick notes immediately after the client's session to preserve important facts and feelings. These personal notes often are useful aids when formally documenting and are sometimes called *shadow records,* or psychotherapy notes kept separate from the client's record. Voice recognition technology is being increasingly used to create personal notes. This technology involves speaking into a device that translates one's spoken voice into written words by using a computer application. This technology is imperfect in transcribing accurately, but it can provide enough detail to jog one's memory between a session and a later time when documentation can occur. Voice recognition technology will likely continue to evolve, but care should be exercised regarding who has access to the transcribed notes and how security can be maintained.

Hard copies of electronic informal or shadow notes should not be maintained in the case file and are not a substitute for formal records. "If such notes are placed in the agency record, they become part of the client's permanent file, and are subject to access and disclosure" (Kagle & Kopels, 2008, p. 90). Personal notes not filed in the permanent record may also be subpoenaed during court proceedings (Kagle & Kopels, 2008). Destroying personal notes after formal recording is considered the safest method of dealing with these informal notes, whether hard copy or electronic ones.

HIPAA AND PSYCHOTHERAPY NOTES

HIPAA regulations give psychotherapy notes separate from a client's record special consideration: These notes are not generally open to disclosure to the client or anyone else. The regulations define these as notes recorded by a mental health professional "documenting or analyzing the contents of a conversation during a private counseling session or a group, joint, or family counseling session and that are separate from the rest of the patient's medical record" (U.S. Department of Health and Human Services, 2014). These are the professional's notes, created for his or her own personal use. Social workers must establish a clear system that demonstrates the intent to keep the notes separate and distinct from the rest of the client record. These notes provide an opportunity to record personal reactions, doubts, or interpretations and supervisory questions in a form most useful to the clinician (NASW, 2013). Although separate from the formal record, these notes must also be maintained confidentially.

WHAT TO DOCUMENT

One of the most important challenges a new worker faces is deciding how much or how little to document.

> On the one hand, records should be concise to save resources and to protect the client's privacy. On the other hand, they must be inclusive enough to facilitate service delivery, meet accountability standards, and afford legal protection to the practitioner and the agency. (Kagle, 1984b, p. 12)

Balancing these requirements is difficult without experience and training.

Good documentation requires making "complex professional judgments" (Kagle & Kopels, 2008, p. 30). Critical thinking is an important component of effective documentation. "Critical thinking requires an ability to distinguish between a fact, an assumption, an opinion and a value" (Sheafor & Horejsi, 2012, p. 86). It also requires an ability to question what one thinks is known and to be open to other truths and possibilities. One must think critically to understand a client situation and to document it. New social workers often err on the side of recording everything that transpires during an interview—a phenomenon sometimes referred to as *overdocumentation* (Kagle, 1993). The ability to summarize the important information and leave out extraneous detail is important. Kane, Houston-Vega, and Nuehring (2002) referred to this as *walking a tightrope*: recording adequately yet with an eye toward others who may need to examine the record, such as the client or the court system.

Just as interviewing skills must be developed in a series of small steps practiced over time, so too must the skill of selecting what to document. A first step is understanding the purpose for which services are provided (Kagle, 1984a). Items should be selected for documentation on the basis of whether they are directly related to that purpose. For example, if a client is being seen for couples counseling, coping skills would seem more important to document than information about a work situation. If a grassroots organizer's goal is to build a community coalition, relationship building would seem more important to document than information about upcoming political elections. In addition, Kagle (1984a) suggested that the therapeutic interventions used in the interaction will also provide guidance in choosing items to record. The modality used directs the social worker to focus on particular areas in the client's treatment. For example, a social worker using solution-focused brief therapy would be guided by the treatment choice to document exceptions to client problems. This can be a helpful basis for selection of appropriate documentation content.

Skills such as choosing what to document, writing with clarity and conciseness, and demonstrating self-confidence will grow with practice. Working through the exercises that appear at the end of this and subsequent chapters will help build documentation skills that will highlight and complement high-quality social work services.

WHAT NOT TO DOCUMENT

Moline, Williams, and Austin (1998) suggested that the following material should not be included in case records:

- Information that could be embarrassing to the client or the worker
- Extraneous material that has no impact on services
- Information that could be misinterpreted by other readers such as relatives, attorneys, and other professionals.

This includes discussion of other people or topics not pertinent to services, sensitive information (such as sexual fantasies), and past behaviors that have no bearing on present services. In addition, the social worker's personal opinions and feelings about the client or clients or the topic under discussion should not be noted. The record's focus is the client, not the social worker.

WHEN TO WRITE MORE

Freedheim and Shapiro (1999) offered guidelines on when to document a lot or a little: "The question is not whether to keep records but, rather, how lengthy and detailed those records should be" (p. 8). They suggested that the helping professional's notes be more extensive and detailed in the following situations:

- When something unusual or complex occurs
- When new plans or decisions about treatment are made
- When important or new information is obtained
- When situations that are potentially dangerous (to either the client, the social worker, or another person or living creature) are discussed
- When an emergency exists
- When there is reason to anticipate legal action
- When difficulties in providing optimal treatment occur (such as failure to keep appointments).

WHEN TO WRITE LESS

A brief summary is acceptable when a session is routine—"characterized by relatively low levels of new information or change from the ongoing direction" of services (Freedheim & Shapiro, 1999, p. 28). Knowing when a session is routine can be confusing to a new practitioner, however, and making such a judgment requires practice and experience. Supervision can help lessen this confusion.

Irrelevant facts about how the social worker has spent his or her day are not considered appropriate items for the record. The purpose of a record is not to provide evidence of the social worker's busy schedule to his or her supervisor. Sheffield (1920) referred to these as "behold-me-busy" details (p. 93). An example is documenting a string of unsuccessful telephone calls individually rather than writing "six telephone calls were placed to the client's home before she was reached."

Recording items that appear elsewhere in the case file is also a time waster, as is the use of flowery language. These are not new problems in social work, however, as both were noted nearly 100 years ago: "Take up at random almost any history in any office and on a single page one will find words, phrases, clauses, whole sentences that either repeat the thought or stretch it out through ten words where five would do" (Sheffield, 1920, p. 113). Sheffield suggested that when one is unsure of whether to document a particular fact, one should ask, "Is this . . . of relative importance for treatment or has it only a slight or a temporary bearing?" (pp. 92–93). This suggestion remains helpful today.

HOW TO KNOW IF THE DOCUMENTATION AMOUNT IS ADEQUATE

New practitioners often wonder if what has been documented is "enough" or "too much." It may be helpful to ask a supervisor or peer for feedback on the amount of detail contained in the case record. If a new worker sits in on a session with a supervisor or experienced coworker, it may be beneficial for both to write case notes separately and compare the content afterward. This method will help a new social worker become more confident in his or her documentation adequacy.

GUIDELINES FOR CASE NOTES

Formal notes may be handwritten or produced on a computer. Either way, certain considerations apply. Each note should begin with the full date (month, day, year) and end with the worker's full signature (or a shorter format, if acceptable in that setting) and credential (such as license or last degree obtained). Only those abbreviations approved by the agency should be used. If in doubt about the acceptability of an abbreviation, spell it out. Attention should always be paid to spelling and grammar, which will be covered in chapter 4.

When handwriting case notes, these rules should also be kept in mind:

- Black ink is best. Some agencies allow the use of blue ink, but pencil or other colored inks should never be used. Pencil can be erased and is not considered permanent, and colored inks often do not photocopy well. To present oneself as professionally as possible, use black ink, which is the standard across settings.
- An error should never be totally obscured. One line should be drawn through it, the word "error" and the date written above, and the correction added next to that. Correction fluid should never be used; it suggests that the writer is hiding something, and its use cannot be defended in court.
- Legibility is critical, as a note that cannot be read is worthless. If cursive handwriting is not legible, printed notes are acceptable.

When typing notes electronically, the following should be kept in mind:

- Boldface, italics, and underlining should be avoided, along with capitalizing entire words to emphasize them.
- Exclamation marks should not be used in professional writing except in rare instances.
- The spell-checking or auto-correct functions should not be used to replace proofreading. It remains the social worker's responsibility to make sure that the correct words, correctly spelled, are used.
- Security of all electronic documents must be ensured. (NASW & ASWB, 2005)

SUMMARY AND EXERCISES

The process of documenting services begins before a client's first meeting with a social worker. In addition to technical considerations, it is essential to use critical thinking skills.

The exercises in this and subsequent chapters are designed to help social workers develop these important skills. Many of the exercises are most effective when two or more people work through them at the same time, compare answers, and give each other feedback.

Exercise 3.1: Documentation Skills Self-Assessment

Honestly rate yourself on each statement below, with 1 = strongly disagree, 2 = disagree, 3 = agree, and 4 = strongly agree.

1. I can usually select the best words to express myself.
2. I can usually write in a focused way.
3. My writing is usually well organized and logical in sequence.

4. I am highly skilled at expressing myself in writing.
5. I am highly skilled at comprehending what I have read.
6. I have confidence that I know how to write about a client.
7. I have a good memory for details.
8. I know the difference between objective and subjective information.
9. I know the difference between a summary and a SOAP note.
10. I can tell what is important about a client session and what is not.
11. I am highly skilled at homing in on what is important in a conversation.
12. I know the difference between a complete and an incomplete sentence.
13. I know the difference between "your" and "you're."
14. I know the difference between "its" and "it's."
15. I know when to use commas, periods, semicolons, and colons.
16. I understand what is meant by subject and verb agreement.
17. I know the difference between writing in the first, second, and third person.

Total your score and see where you fall in the following scale:

0–17:   Your skills are poor but can be improved with hard work and diligence with these exercises.
18–35: Your skills are fair, with plenty of room for improvement through these exercises.
36–53: Your skills are good, with room for improvement through these exercises.
54–68: Your skills are excellent, and these exercises will be a good refresher.

Complete each sentence with a short phrase.

1. Areas in which I am most confident about documenting are . . .
2. I think my documentation strengths are . . .
3. I am least confident about documenting . . .
4. Areas in which I think I need the most help are . . .

Save this exercise. You will be asked to refer to it again in chapter 12.

Exercise 3.2: A Note about Today

Write a detailed note about your day, as if you were an outsider observing it rather than experiencing it. Refer to yourself as "he" or "she." Include as much detail as you can. Use the following example to get you started:

> Today she got up after sleeping in. Her alarm went off, but she didn't feel like getting up right away. She dozed off and on for over 15 minutes. When she finally decided that she had better get moving, she showered and had a quick breakfast that consisted of an eight-ounce glass of orange juice and a large cinnamon roll. She checked her e-mail messages and found that she

had several to return. She took a few minutes to do that but couldn't get to all of them because she was running out of time. She packed up and headed out the door.

Next, critically analyze what you just wrote. Name three things you like about your note. Name three things you don't like.

Save this exercise. You will be asked to refer to it again in chapter 12.

Exercise 3.3: Summarizing

Summarize the note you wrote in exercise 3.2. Cover the important points but shorten it as much as possible.

Critically analyze the notes from exercises 3.2 and 3.3. How are they different? Similar? Which one was easier to write? Why?

Save this exercise. You will be asked to refer to it again in chapter 8.

Exercise 3.4: Television Interview Case Note

Listen to a television talk show personality or late-night host interview a guest. The topic of the interview is not important. Listen without taking notes. Once the interview is completed, write a case note about the contact, as if you were the interviewer.

Critically analyze the note. What do you like about the note? What do you feel was well done?

Save what you wrote during this exercise; you will use it again in chapter 8.

Exercise 3.5: Can This Note Be Improved?

Read the sample case note below.

January 28. The new client came to see me and looked like she hadn't gotten very much sleep lately. Her hair was uncombed and she had dark rings around her eyes. Her shirt was dirty and I don't think she had any makeup on. She's overweight, so I don't think she's having a problem getting food. She says she needs some advice on what to do with her life. She lives with her mom in her mom's apartment, and her son lives there, too. He's two and she's 22.

She just got fired from her part-time job working at the local grocery store and is worried about her finances. She got fired because she had a hard time getting up in the mornings and coming in on time. Her boss didn't understand what it's like to have a young boy to take care of and a mom to help out too, and he just fired her all of a sudden, last week. It wasn't a great job anyway, but it was the only one that she had found after looking for over a year.

Before this job, she worked at a convenience store but quit because she didn't like it and didn't see a future there. She finished high school at least.

Her mom is on disability, so the household doesn't have much money coming in. Her son is a handful and doesn't like to listen to her, she said. He threw a tantrum last night and she had to listen to him cry most of the night. It helped to calm her after she had a few drinks, and she shared some of her last drink with her son. That helped him sleep finally but by then it was pretty late.

She was worried about coming here but knows she needs help. She says she's stuck in a rut and doesn't see any way out. I asked her about college and she laughed, saying that she had a mouth to feed and that was more important right now. I was only trying to suggest ways to improve her life, which is what she said she wanted. She's going to come back to see me next week, and I said that would give me some time to check out some resources for her. It seems like she needs an awful lot of help though, and not just with getting her life together.

Critically analyze this note. Name three things you like about it and three things you don't like. Then rewrite the note to improve it.

Critically analyze what you just wrote. Name three things you like and three things you dislike about it.

Share your work with a peer and ask for feedback.

Exercise 3.6: Choosing the Right Details

A client is being seen for the first time in a mental health clinic for depression. Consider how appropriate it would be to include each item below in a client's case note. If you're not certain, note that.

1. Details of the client's sexual encounter last night
2. How long the client has felt depressed
3. Family history of depression
4. The client's age and marital status
5. The client's statement "sometimes I feel like ending it all"
6. Recent losses that the client has experienced
7. What the client was wearing
8. The client's weight
9. Names of medications the client is taking
10. The client's difficulty in finding the clinic.

Ask a peer to complete the same exercise, and discuss your answers. Are there any differences in responses?

Complete the next task while working alone. For each item that you considered appropriate to document, describe a setting in which you think the same information would not be important to document. For each item that you considered inappropriate to document, describe a setting in which you think this information would be important to document. For each item about which you were unsure, describe a setting in which you are sure this information should be documented. For example, if you believe that the client's weight is not important to document in the context described earlier, in what setting would it be important? (For example, you may believe that it would be critical information in a program treating eating disorders.)

If you believe an item should be documented in all settings, note that as well.

Again compare responses with your peer. How did your responses differ? How were they similar? What is the most important thing you have learned from this exercise?

Exercise 3.7: Writing More or Writing Less

This exercise is designed to help you begin thinking about those instances in which detailed, longer notes are better than short notes.

For each item below, decide whether you think the item should be longer or shorter. Write down the reasons you believe this to be the case. Be as specific in your reasoning as you can.

1. The client is making steady progress on her treatment plan goals.
2. The policy presentation by the committee went very well.
3. The client has just experienced the death of a close friend.
4. After weeks of meetings, the client shares details of a traumatic event.
5. The client threatens you with a lawsuit for not helping him enough.
6. The group is meeting with you for the last time, as all goals have been met.
7. The client is motivated to complete a homework assignment you have given.
8. The client explains the reasons for missing several appointments.
9. The task force agrees to a referral that you feel is important to make.
10. The adult client's mother wishes to review her daughter's file with you.

Exercise 3.8: Analyzing Notes

Critically analyze the following two case notes, both describing the same session.

Note 1

February 1, 2015. I met with a client today for the first time, a 42-year-old referred for grief counseling by her doctor. The client had blotches on her face and red eyes from crying. She seemed pretty worked up and it was hard to get her to talk much at first, she was crying so much. I finally got out of her that her mom died a while back in a house fire. She was sleeping when a cigarette she had been smoking lit the curtains up. She never had a chance to get out, and neither did her cat, Blackie.

The client says she can't sleep and can't concentrate when she's at home, and at work it's even worse. She works as a computer technician and knows a lot about computer problems. I self-disclosed that I needed her last week when my computer wasn't working and she seemed to pull herself together when I said that. I asked what meds she takes and she said she's taking something, she can't really remember, but it's not helping her very much and makes her feel funny. All she can think about is fire and the pain of being burned alive like her mom. She says her husband doesn't know what to do and is getting frustrated with her. He tells her to get over it and move on. The client, she's never seen a social worker before so didn't really know what to expect. I had to go over some basic stuff like what I can do and what I can't do. She kept saying "I'm not crazy, you know," almost like she thought she was. I tried to listen as best as I could, but the tears were getting to me. I think it's just normal reaction to a pretty nasty loss, but it's hard for her to see that what she's feeling is normal in any sense of the word.

We started to talk about goals and what she wanted to accomplish. I'm going to see her again next week, same time as today. She said she'd do some homework to bring in with her next time, but I doubt that she'll follow through, she seemed pretty unreliable to me. J. Moreno

What do you like about this note? Dislike? Be as specific as possible.

Note 2

February 1, 2015. This social worker met with the client today for the first time. The client is a 42-year-old female who was referred by her physician for grief counseling. The client reports having lost her mother six months ago in a house fire. The client is having problems sleeping and states that she cannot concentrate at home or at her full-time computer technician job. She is on medication but reports that it is not helping her. She is consumed with thoughts of fire and the pain her mother must have experienced. Her husband reports being at a loss for helping her and is becoming increasingly frustrated with her inability to "get over this and move on." The client has never met with a social worker before and shares some hesitancy in seeking help. "I'm not crazy, you know," she repeated several times. This worker offered reassurance and reflective listening. The client was encouraged to know that she is not "crazy" but experiencing a normal reaction to a horrible loss.

Goals were set and an appointment scheduled for 2/9/2014 at 4:00 p.m. The client agreed to jot down brief notes of times when she is feeling less consumed by thoughts of fire and pain. She will bring these with her to the next session. [Name], BSW

What do you like and dislike about this note? Be as specific as possible.

How is this note different from the previous one? Which note would you be more proud to sign your name to?

What is the most important thing you learned in this exercise?

Exercise 3.9: Comparing Notes

Go to http://www.youtube.com and search for either "community organizing" or "social work interview," on the basis of your interests. Select a video to watch with a peer, not taking any notes while watching it. When you have finished viewing the video, you and the peer independently write a note about its contents. Compare the two notes and answer the following questions:

1. What was similar between the two notes?
2. What was different?
3. Decide on which note is better. Why did you select this note over the other?
4. What did you learn that you can apply to practice?

CHAPTER 4

Special Issues in Documentation

Writing competently is an important skill that many lack. "I've come across far too many who, in the words of *The American President*'s protagonist, Andrew Shepherd, 'couldn't find a coherent sentence with two hands and a flashlight'" (Drozdowski, 2003, p. 1). Simon and Soven (1990) reminded their social work readership that "our profession suffers from as severe a shortage of competent writers as do other professions and the nation at large" (p. 48). One can blame primary and secondary schools for not doing a better job of teaching basic spelling and grammar or colleges for not producing better writers, but the end result is that many social workers enter the field without well-honed written communication skills.

Good writing is important. Documenting factually, objectively, and accurately involves writing well. Lengthy writing is often not better writing. Instead of writing longer, it is better to write smarter and more succinctly (Berner, 1998). This, however, takes practice. Clearly, the ability to communicate well in writing can be the difference between a social work professional who is taken seriously and one who is not.

> Obvious misspellings, incorrect tenses, and other writing errors typical of the uneducated will cause the reader to question not just the writer's knowledge of English but the content of the recorded entry. . . . If a worker consistently produces poorly organized, vague, and unclear recordings, the supervisor will wonder how he can communicate clearly with his clients during interviews. (Wilson, 1980, p. 116)

Several special considerations should be kept in mind when documenting work with clients. Writing about clients requires a different set of skills than writing a book report or responding to a friend's e-mail. A well-written case file is a reflection of the social worker composing it. Some social workers express themselves in writing better than others do. Even a poor writer, however, can take steps to improve his or her writing skills. Writing well should be a goal of every social worker—and, like any skill, writing improves with practice. This chapter focuses on the basic writing skills necessary for good practice, and it includes risk management guidelines that social workers need to be aware of when writing about clients. The chapter addresses grammar, spelling, the importance of precise and nondiscriminatory language, and protecting oneself from risk through the written word.

GRAMMAR AND USAGE

Sentence Fragments

Social work documentation should be written in complete sentences—in other words, sentences with both a subject and a verb. The following are examples of sentence fragments: "states she does not feel well today" (no subject) and "client not well today" (no verb). To make either fragment a complete sentence, one could write, "The client states that she does not feel well today."

Run-On Sentences

The two types of run-on sentences (Hacker, 1996) both lack a coordinating conjunction (such as "and," "but," "or," or "yet"). The first type also lacks punctuation—for example, "The client has a little girl she does not live with her." To improve this sentence, one would write, "The client has a little girl, but she does not live with her." In the second type, called a *comma splice*, two or more independent clauses are joined by a comma without a coordinating conjunction—for example, "The client has a girl, she does not live with her." These types of run-on sentences can be rewritten as two separate sentences or improved by adding a coordinating conjunction.

Subject–Verb Disagreement

The subject of a sentence should always agree with the verb; both should be either singular or plural. For example, in the sentence "The client is a woman," there is one client and the verb "is" is singular. The sentence "The clients are women" has both a plural subject (clients) and a plural verb (are). This can become confusing when word groups modify the subject. For example, in the problem sentence "The client who is a member of Weight Watchers need help," the subject is the client, not Weight Watchers, so "need" should be changed to "needs." By identifying the subject (client) and verb (needs), one can eliminate the confusion.

Indefinite Use of "They," "It," and "You"

The sentence "They said that the client cannot live there" is unclear, because the reader does not know who "they" are. Clarify by stating, "The landlord says that the client cannot live there." Similarly, in the sentence "In the psychological report, it says that the client has major depression," the word "it" is indefinite. It is clearer to write, "The report says that the client has major depression."

Point of View

Social work documentation should be written in the third person, a concept that can be confusing. "The point of view of a piece of writing is the perspective from which it is written: first person (I or we), second person (you), or third person (he/she/it/one or they)" (Hacker, 1996, p. 116).

Hacker pointed out that the first-person point of view is a good choice for informal writing, as it emphasizes the writer. The second-person point of view emphasizes the reader and works well for giving advice or explaining how to do something. Client records, however, are written from the perspective of the third person or subject, who is, in this case, the client. Therefore, "I met with the client" should be written instead as "This social worker met with the client." Similarly, "I set up an appointment for next week" should be written as "This worker set up an appointment for next week."

The words "you" and "I" should never be used in a formal social work record except when directly quoting, as in "The client replied, 'I don't think like you do.'"

Active versus Passive Voice

Whenever possible, use the active voice instead of the passive one. In an active voice, the subject is doing the action (Fogarty, 2010). For example, in the sentence "The client felt she was hurried through the intake process," "was hurried" is passive. The active voice is "The client felt hurried through the intake process." In another example, "Once a week, the client will clean the house," is better than writing "Once a week, the client's house will be cleaned." Whenever actions can be made active, they should be, as it strengthens the writing and makes the point of the sentence more clear.

Who, Whom, Whose, That, Which

In most situations, the words "who," "whom," and "whose" refer to people, whereas "that" and "which" refer to animals or things (Hacker, 1996). "Although *that* is occasionally used to refer to persons, it is more polite to use a form of *who*" (Hacker, 1996, p. 182).

When to use "who" and "whom" can be a much stickier question to answer. A quick tip is to remember that both "whom" and "him" end with the letter "m." When trying to decide whether to use "who" or "whom," ask if an equivalent phrase would use "he" or "him." If the answer is "him," use "whom" (Fogarty, 2007). "Whom do I love? I love him. Who loves me? He loves me."

Sometimes, a better option is to rephrase the sentence to eliminate the problem. If you are struggling with "the team member who/whom was assigned to work with the client," you can write "the team member assigned to work with the client" instead.

Punctuation

Because punctuation can affect a document's readability and precision, it is important to get it right.

Quotation Marks. Using a client's words in the official record lends authenticity to documentation and can be a powerful addition to case notes. This is done through the use of quotation marks. "The client said, 'It doesn't matter to me one way or another what happens,'" is more powerful and precise than "The client indicated he does not care what happens."

Periods. A period is used to mark the end of a sentence, except when a question mark or exclamation point ends it. Exclamation points should rarely be used in social work recording. They should be saved to express truly exceptional feeling or emphasis (Hacker, 1996)—for example, "The client repeatedly yelled at the group members, 'I'm so angry with you all!'"

Commas. The complete rules governing the use of commas are complex, and books have been written just about this small punctuation mark. According to a T-shirt, "Commas save lives. Let's eat Grandma. Let's eat, Grandma." It's obvious that these two sentences convey very different meanings and a misplaced comma is dangerous! It is not that difficult to get the basics right. The most common uses are noted below with examples (Straus, 2008).

- Use commas to separate words and word groups in a series of three or more. *Example:* The client indicated that she is in need of food, housing, transportation, and employment after her discharge.
- Use a comma to separate two adjectives when the word "and" can be inserted between them. *Example:* The client presented as a thoughtful, engaged person.
- Use a comma to set off the year in a month–date–year phrase. *Example:* The couple was married on February 9, 1980, at noon.
- Use a comma to set off the state in a city–state phrase. *Example:* They met in December 1976 in Fremont, Ohio, and married in 1980.
- Use commas around degrees or titles used after names. *Example:* Emily Dare, MD, referred the client for services.
- Use commas to set off expressions that interrupt sentence flow. *Example:* The client appears, on the basis of her nervousness, unwilling to confront her spouse.
- Use commas after phrases of three or more words that begin a sentence. *Example:* To qualify for benefits, the client must complete this application.
- Use a comma to separate two clauses joined by a conjunction (for example, "and," "or," "but," "for," "nor"). *Example:* The client expressed willingness to this social worker on several occasions to attend a support group, but he has not attended yet.
- Use a comma to introduce direct quotations. *Example:* The client's mother said, "My daughter has been a nightmare to raise."

- Use commas before and after words such as "therefore" and "however."
  Example: The client, therefore, is being terminated from services.

When in doubt about the need for a comma, read the sentence out loud. If, at the point where you are considering a comma, taking a breath or a pause is necessary, a comma may be useful.

Semicolons and Colons. Although often confused, semicolons and colons function quite differently. A semicolon connects major sentence elements of equal grammatical rank, whereas a colon calls attention to the words that follow it (Hacker, 1996). The need for semicolons can be lessened by writing shorter sentences. For example, the sentence "The client and his family are very motivated; this worker is impressed with their level of commitment" can be easily expressed in two separate sentences: "The client and his family are very motivated. This social worker is impressed with their level of commitment."

Colons are used frequently in social work documentation. For example, "The client agreed to the following: completion of an unannounced home visit, a psychological evaluation, and attendance at parenting classes." Use of the colon is appropriate to highlight a phrase—for example, "The client's stated goals are simple: to reunite his family and to be a better father." A colon also can introduce a quotation. "The client's stated goals are clear: 'I want to get my family back together and learn how to be a better dad.'"

Apostrophes. Apostrophes are used to show that a noun is possessive, indicating ownership (Hacker, 1996). Improper use of the apostrophe can dramatically change the writer's meaning. The phrase "a client's needs," for example, refers to the needs of a single client, whereas the phrase "clients' needs" indicates that several clients have needs (Straus, 2008). Several common rules about apostrophe usage follow:

- Use an apostrophe followed by an "s" to show possession by one person—for example, "the group member's feelings" refers to the feelings of one group member. Although styles vary, this rule generally holds true even if the word ends in "s" ("Mrs. Jones's son").
- To create the possessive form of a plural noun ending in "s," place an apostrophe after the "s"—for example, "the group members' feelings" refers to the feelings of all group members.
- To create the possessive form of a plural noun that does not end in "s," add an apostrophe followed by "s"—for example, "the children's toys."
- Do not use an apostrophe with possessive pronouns such as "his," "her," "its," "theirs," "ours," "yours," or "whose." An example is "The case file is hers, not yours." Another example is the letter closing "Sincerely yours." It is not correct to write "Sincerely your's."
- Apostrophes are also used to form contractions, which combine two words into a shorter form with the apostrophe standing in for the missing letters. For example, "it is" becomes "it's." Other common contractions

are "don't" (do not), "can't" (cannot), "you're" (you are), "we'll" (we will), and "she's" (she is). Contractions should not be used in social work documentation, as they are not considered appropriate in formal writing. They can, however, be used in a direct quote. For example, it is acceptable to write, The client stated, 'I feel terrible, and it's not getting any better.'

Question Marks and Exclamation Points. Question marks should be used only after writing direct questions and should be used one at time. "Should the client's therapy really be terminated???" is not an appropriate use of question marks, for example.

One exclamation point is often used to denote emphasis or surprise but should rarely be used in formal kinds of writing (Straus, 2008). "The therapist is really impressed by the group's motivation!" is not an appropriate use, for example. "The group's motivation is impressive" is adequate, written in the active voice and more professional in tone.

Use of Capital Letters and Numbers

Straus (2008) spelled out simple rules for using capital letters. An example follows each rule.

- Capitalize the first word of a sentence. "The client discussed her concerns."
- Capitalize the first word of a quoted sentence. "The community leader said, 'We only want to be treated fairly.'"
- Capitalize a proper noun. "Memorial Hospital is located there."
- Capitalize a person's title when it follows the name in a signature line. "Sincerely, Nancy Sidell, Social Worker"
- Capitalize the first word of a salutation and the first word of a complimentary close. "Dear Mr. Smith" and "Truly yours."
- Capitalize all words in publication titles (articles and prepositions are *not* capitalized). *The Social Work Dictionary* and *The Encyclopedia of Social Work.*

The use of numbers is less complicated. Straus (2008) suggested spelling out single-digit numbers, such as "five" and "six," and using numerals for other numbers, such as "10" and "139." Spell out simple fractions, such as "one-half of the audience held up picket signs." Do not use numerals to begin a sentence but write out the number. For example, instead of "20 percent recidivism rates are typical," write "Twenty percent recidivism rates are typical."

SPELLING

Correct spelling is a reflection of the social worker's knowledge and abilities. A social worker can be very skilled at providing social work services, but if he or she cannot spell correctly, that skill may not be clear to readers of the record. What impression is made by the following text, written by an undergraduate social work student? "It don't matter weather I can writ good or not—the main thing is that I be able to help my clients—they is really in need of my serfices" (quoted in Wilson, 1980, p. 116). No one should be proud to claim authorship of such a phrase.

Spelling skills can be learned by paying attention to words that frequently cause problems. A word processing program's spell-check function cannot replace a writer's ability to spell. Spell-check programs cannot identify words that are spelled correctly but used inappropriately. For example, the lines of the poem "Candidate for a Pullet Surprise" underscore this point (Zar, 1994): "It plane lee marks four my revue / Miss Steaks aye can knot sea" (p. 13). Each word is spelled correctly, but what impression would a writer create by using the wrong words in this way? The following list was compiled from several lists of commonly misspelled words (Gillett, 2010; Hacker, 1996, p. 304; Strunk, 2006, pp. 48–49). Review it and make note of those words that you find difficult to spell.

absence	definite	latter
acceptable	definitely	liaison
accidentally	describe	license
accommodate	develop	maintenance
achievement	disappoint	memento
acknowledge	discipline	mischievous
acquire	eligible	misspell
advice	embarrass	necessary
all right	emphasize	neighbor
analyze	entirely	noticeable
answer	especially	occasion
apparent	exaggerated	occasionally
appearance	exceed	occurred
argument	existence	occurrence
basically	experience	opportunity
believe	familiar	perseverance
benefit	foreign	personnel
benefited	government	physically
bureau	grateful	possession
business	harass	precede
category	height	preference
changeable	ignorance	preferred
commitment	immediate	prejudice
committed	immediately	prevalent
conceivable	incident	privilege
conscience	incidentally	probably
conscientious	independent	proceed
conscious	indispensable	publicly
criticism	irrelevant	pursue
criticize	judgment	questionnaire
decision	knowledge	quiet

quite	separate	undoubtedly
receive	similar	unnecessarily
referred	sincerely	until
relevant	succeed	usually
repetition	thorough	vengeance
schedule	transferred	whether

There are several other lists of commonly misspelled words (Oxford Dictionaries, 2014; Weisman & Zornado, 2013). The following are additional problematic words often found in social work documentation:

aggressive	foreseeable	unfortunately
colleague	process	unforeseen
dilemma	resistance	

Homophones

Homophones—words that sound similar but have different meanings—can be a challenge. Knowing the difference between homophones is important in social work recording (Hacker, 1996). Several books and other publications have provided lists of commonly confused words (Glicken, 2008; Hacker, 1996, p. 301; "Homophones," 2010). The following list contains homophones that can be important for a social worker to distinguish:

accept (to receive) / except (to exclude)

affect (to exert an influence) / effect (to accomplish a result)

aid (assistance) / aide (an assistant) / -ade (a fruit drink)

a lot (many, an empty space) / allot (to allocate) / alot (not a word)

all ready (completely prepared) / already (before the time specified)

allude (hint at) / elude (avoid or evade)

ante- (before or in front of) / anti- (hostile to or opposing)

are (a form of the verb "to be") / our (belonging to us) / hour (unit of time)

capital (city) / capitol (legislative building)

complement (to complete) / compliment (to express praise)

counsel (to advise) / council (committee or work group)

have / of ("they must have been," not "they must of been")

here (this place) / hear (to perceive sound)

incite (to urge or set in motion) / insight (awareness)

insure (insures a car) / ensure (one ensures health by taking vitamins)

its (of or belonging to it) / it's (it is)

passed (moved by) / past (in a earlier time)

patience (ability to wait) / patients (people served in care settings) principal (head of a school) / principle (general or fundamental truth)

residents (occupants) / residence (home)

role (activities related to a position or job / roll (to tumble or a small bread)

than (in comparison with) / then (at that time)

their (belonging to them) / they're (they are) / there (at that place)

threw (hurled) / through (went by or done with) / thru (not a word)

to (in the direction of) / too (also) / two (2)

who's (who is) / whose (belonging to whom)

your (belonging to you) / you're (you are)

Commonly Misused Words

Some commonly misused words have been identified by Weisman and Zornado (2013):

Among and amongst: Both are correct, but "among" is more commonly used in American English.

I and E: The old grade school rhyme applies: "I before E, except after C, and when sounding like A, as in neighbor and weigh."

Irregardless: This is not a word. The correct word is "regardless."

Lay and lie: Lay is to place somewhere. Lie is to place oneself down and also to deceive or tell an untruth. To add to the potential confusion, the past tense of "lie" is "lay," and the past tense of "lay" is "laid."

Lose and loose: Lose is to suffer loss. Loose is free, not securely attached.

Raise and rise: Raise is to move something to a higher position. Rise is to get up from lying, sitting, or kneeling posture.

Set and sit: Set is to put something somewhere. Sit is to be seated.

Toward and towards: Both are correct, although "toward" is used more often in American English.

Unnecessary Words

Writing simply will be easier if these phrases are not used (Dorn, 2007):

"Please do not hesitate to contact me." Instead, use "Please contact me."

"I am very appreciative of. . . ." Instead, use "I appreciate."

"Very unique." This is redundant—use "unique."

"Truly," "really," "actually," "literally." These are unnecessary.

"Could be possible." Either something is possible or it is not.

ABBREVIATIONS

Because a client's record may be seen by several different people, care must be taken to make it easily understood. The excessive use of abbreviations can be confusing. Even though the social work profession has used abbreviations through-out its history, the practitioner should use them sparingly. Hospitals often have a list of abbreviations that are acceptable for use in case file recording, but most agencies do not. In the absence of a specific agency policy, it is best to spell out any word for which the abbreviation could be confusing (Wilson, 1980).

SIGNATURES

A social work assessment or case note is not considered complete without the author's signature. If the signature is not legible, the name should be printed below it (Wilson, 1980, p. 113). Initials should not be substituted for a full signature. In most instances, one's full name should be used, followed by one's highest degree (Sharon Jones, PhD), credential (Sharon Jones, LSW), or job title (Sharon Jones, Clinical Social Worker). Agency policy often specifies the preferred format.

NONDISCRIMINATORY AND PEOPLE-FIRST LANGUAGE

Language used in case records should be nondiscriminatory unless the ques-tionable language is pertinent to the case and can be directly attributed to a specific source (Staniforth & Larkin, 2006). For example, it may be appropriate to write, "The client's mother stated that she 'will not tolerate having a redneck for a son.'"

People-first language aims to avoid dehumanizing people with a disability or medical condition (Texas Council for Developmental Disabilities, 2007). An exam-ple of a people-first phrase would be "person with a disability" rather than "disa-bled person." Similarly, a cancer patient would be referred to as "an individual with cancer." The emphasis is on the individual first and his or her condition second. The concept also favors a focus on having rather than being—for example, "she has a learning disability" rather than "she is learning disabled" (Snow, 2009). See Table 4.1 for more examples.

SPECIFIC, CONCRETE LANGUAGE

How one speaks is often different from how one writes. Speaking informally is usually acceptable, but when writing in a case file, extra care should be taken to select the words that best convey the intended meaning (Glicken, 2008). Stani-forth and Larkin (2006) suggested the helpful acronym FACTS—that is, records should be factual, accurate, complete, timely, and systematic (pp. 16, 17). They should also be as precise as possible. Strunk (2006) advised writers to "prefer the specific to the general, the definite to the vague, the concrete to the abstract" (p. 22).

Instead of "Several employment interviews completed by the client have resulted in no job prospects," it is more precise to write, "The client has had

TABLE 4.1 Examples of People-First Language

Say:	Instead of:
People with disabilities.	The handicapped or disabled.
He has a cognitive disability or diagnosis.	He's mentally retarded.
She has autism (or a diagnosis of . . .).	She's autistic.
He has Down syndrome (or a diagnosis of . . .).	He's Down's; a mongoloid.
She has a learning disability (diagnosis).	She's learning disabled.
He has a physical disability (diagnosis).	He's a quadriplegic or is crippled.
She's of short stature or she's a little person.	She's a dwarf or midget.
He has a mental health condition or diagnosis.	He's emotionally disturbed or mentally ill.
She uses a wheelchair or mobility chair.	She's confined to a wheelchair or is wheelchair bound.
He receives special ed services.	He's in special ed.
She has a developmental delay.	She's developmentally delayed.
Children without disabilities.	Normal or healthy kids.
Communicates with her eyes, device, or the like.	Is nonverbal.
Client.	Customer, consumer, recipient, and so forth.
Congenital disability.	Birth defect.
Brain injury.	Brain damaged.
Accessible parking, hotel room, and so on.	Handicapped parking, hotel room, and so on.
She needs . . . or she uses. . . .	She has problems with . . . has special needs.

Source: K. Snow (2001), *Disability Is Natural* (Woodland Park, CO: BraveHeart Press). Copyright 2009 Kathie Snow, All Rights Reserved. Reprinted with permission.

three job interviews but no offers." Instead of "She looked like she had just won the lottery," it is more concrete to write, "She smiled broadly and clapped her hands."

It is usually best to avoid unnecessary words and to shorten lengthy phrases when this can be done without loss of meaning. Being precise and stating thoughts simply are better than long sentences, repetition, and wordiness. Examples are given in Table 4.2.

A commitment to continuing to learn words is a helpful strategy. As with any new skill, "the only way to build your vocabulary is through practice and repetition" (Young, 2014, p. 321). Ways to help build a personal vocabulary are suggested in exercise 4.16.

Slang should be avoided in case file documentation, unless it appears in a direct quote. For example, it would be acceptable to write, "The client indicated that she feels 'really pissed off' today." It would not acceptable to write, "This worker is angry that the client blew off attending her court hearing." The slang words "dude," "ballistic," and "radical" are also inappropriate except in quotations. When in doubt about the appropriateness of a word, do not use it.

TABLE 4.2 Simple and Concise Language

Inflated Language	Simpler Alternative
Absolutely necessary	Necessary
Along the lines of	Like
As a matter of fact	In fact
As well as	And
At all times	Always
At the present time	Now or currently
Because of the fact that	Because
By means of	By
Due to the fact that	Because
For the purpose of	For
For the reason that	Because
Have the ability to	Be able to
Her sister, who is a member of the police force	Her sister, a police officer
His story is a strange one.	His story is strange.
In light of the fact that	Because
In order to	To
In spite of the fact that	Although
In the event that	If
In the neighborhood of	About
Make use of	Use
Totally unanimous	Unanimous
Until such time as	Until
Upon	On
Utilize	Use

Sources: Glicken, 2008; Hacker, 1996; Strunk, 2006.

LEGAL ISSUES

All social workers face the possibility that a lawsuit or other legal action could be filed against them. Proper documentation is one way in which social workers can help protect themselves and their clients. "Recordkeeping is especially critical in situations that involve the potential for social worker liability" (Robertson & Jackson, 1991, p. 13). Although all social workers know that risk exists, some may be less informed than others about ways in which they can reduce that risk (Houston-Vega & Nuehring, 1997). For example, Kane (2002) found that only one-third of MSW students in his study believed that they had the documentation skills and knowledge to protect themselves in a lawsuit.

Reamer (2005) divided risk management issues related to documentation into four categories: content, terminology, credibility, and access (p. 328). Regarding content, he identified several guidelines:

- Serve and protect. Sufficient detail should be documented so that appropriate client services can occur.
- Strike a balance. Knowing how to write neither too much nor too little is often a matter of experience.
- Avoid overdocumentation in a crisis. Excessive detail in a crisis can serve as a red flag during an ethics hearing or in a courtroom. A social worker should not suggest that a case was handled in manner that is not typical.
- Use caution with personal notes. These can quickly become the property of the courts if subpoenaed. Information in personal notes can pose a risk to both the social worker and the client.
- Be cautious in documenting services for families and couples. Keeping separate records for sensitive information may be better, so that each client can be protected in the event of a dispute. For example, the social worker may document relationship issues in a couple's joint file but document private issues about one individual's struggle with sexual orientation in a separate file. In this way, risk may be diminished.
- Do not air agency "dirty laundry." Never put sensitive details and personal opinions about the agency or individual staff members in client files.

Reamer's second category involves the use of language and terminology. Risk can be reduced if the words used are clear, precise, and specific. The use of jargon, slang, and abbreviations can cause confusion and misunderstanding. It is also risky to document conclusions without supporting details. A statement that "the client was hostile" should be followed by the evidence for the conclusion—for example, "as shown by his angry outburst and refusal to answer any questions." Protection is also afforded by avoiding defamatory language. Avoiding libel (a written untruth about someone) and slander (a spoken untruth about someone) can decrease one's risk of being legally liable for defamation of a client's character (Reamer, 2001). It is also helpful to keep in mind that one is writing for an audience: Supervisors, third-party payers, the court, and the client are all potential readers of the file.

Reamer's third category is credibility. Written documents help social workers maintain their credibility. Ways to minimize risk related to credibility include the following:

- Document in a timely fashion. Failure to do so can challenge credibility and negatively affect client services.
- Avoid prognostic documentation. Do not record planned interventions and anticipated events until they take place. Prematurely recording notes can lead to inaccuracies and harm credibility.
- Write or print legibly, using proper grammar and spelling. Paying attention to detail helps establish credibility.
- Acknowledge errors. Clearly mark each error by drawing one line through it, initialing and dating it, and labeling it "error." This should occur as

soon as the error is found. Never change, hide, lose, or destroy records. Do not use correction fluid or an eraser to hide errors.

Reamer's final category for managing risk related to records is access to documentation. To help protect oneself and one's clients, Reamer suggested the following:

- Acquire legal know-how. Understand the differences between a subpoena to appear with documents and a court order to disclose file contents.
- Know relevant statutes and regulations. Know the laws and regulations that pertain to the agency and the population it serves. A supervisor can help by explaining the unique requirements of relevant laws before this knowledge is needed.
- Secure records. Store records in secure locations to prevent unauthorized access.

SUMMARY AND EXERCISES

This chapter has covered several special issues in social work documentation. Although not a glamorous aspect of documentation, proper grammar and spelling are important aspects of professional practice.

The following exercises offer an opportunity to practice these skills. It can be helpful to work through them with a peer and ask for feedback. All exercises provide either a sample within the exercise itself or an answer key at the end of the chapter.

Exercise 4.1: Incomplete and Run-on Sentences

Read the sample notes below. What questions do they raise in your mind?

Note 1

Client sad. Not sure why. Unable to figure it out, she seems so down. Suspect it's about her mom, need to find out for sure next time.

Note 2

Met with client today, little progress on goals noted. She said she didn't care to work on them today. Suggested rescheduling she agreed. Next meeting tomorrow same time same place as today.

Note 3

Made 3 calls to referral agencies today. No one answered just left message cause plan has to be finalized soon if discharge date is still on target. Did find out housing info, passed along to client who seemed excited to have it though he can't apply for housing until assistance has been approved which could take 4–6 weeks yet or longer given the special circumstances of this crazy case.

Note 4

Case closed today. Referrals for home care assistance and homemaker services completed. Client happy with outcome.

Note 5

Met for couples counseling today. Unsure if long-term commitment exists, too much distrust, too little patience, separate expectations that don't match up.

Using the example below as a guide, respond to each sample note by listing the questions that it raised and rewriting the note, using complete sentences and adding information if needed.

Sample Response to Note 1

Questions: Who isn't sure why? What does "seems so down" mean? When is next time? Why didn't the worker find out this time?

Revision: Today, the client seemed very sad and said she was "so down." When questioned, she said she did not wish to talk about it. This worker pressed her to make sure she was not suicidal. She indicated she is very sad about her mother's upcoming marriage. Her reactions to this were discussed. The next visit was planned for Thursday at 8:00 a.m.

Exercise 4.2: Subject–Verb Agreement

Read each sentence below and identify the subject and verb of each statement. Do the subject and verb agree? If not, rewrite to improve. Use the response under sentence 1 as an example.

1. Group members was referred by the court system.

    Subject = members. Verb = was. Agreement? No.

    Rewrite: Group members were referred by the court system.

2. The client, a practicing Baptist, request agency services.

    _____

    _____

    _____

3. Each family member were very quiet at the beginning of the session.

    _____

    _____

    _____

4. The community program's volunteer coordinators attempted to explain their position to the news media.

    _____

    _____

    _____

5. The two daughters still living at home is being abused by the stepparent.

    _____

    _____

    _____

6. Suggestions for ways to better manage money was made to the client.

    _____

    _____

    _____

7. The treatment team members was not confident that the client would succeed without further intervention.

    _____

    _____

    _____

8. The client who is battling several addictions need a social worker who will not be easily manipulated.

    _____

    _____

    _____

9. The client's complex problems means inpatient treatment will last at least six months.

    _____

    _____

    _____

10. The concerned teachers need to know that their students' safety has not been compromised.

    _____

    _____

    _____

Exercise 4.3: Proper Use of "You," "It," and "They"

In each sentence below, indicate whether the word in boldface is used properly and clearly. If not, correct the sentence.

1. In the referring documents, **it** indicates that past services have been refused.
2. The clients said **they** were not happy with how slowly change has occurred.
3. "**You** aren't the only child in the family **who** has experienced physical abuse," the sister pointed out.
4. This worker stated, "**It** only means that your parents care very much."
5. The doctors **they** say the client is a good candidate for hospice care.
6. "**You** sound very frustrated with your spouse," this social worker reflected.
7. Even though the client feels that **it is** the end of the world, things will get better.
8. This social worker was told, "**You** are being bull-headed."
9. **He** told this worker that **they** were not continuing treatment after next week.
10. The client's parents **they** feel, from their perspective, that progress is being made.

Exercise 4.4: Third-Person Point of View (I)

In each example below, rewrite the following statements in the third person.

1. I met the client at 10:00 a.m. at her home.
2. We made a follow-up appointment for next Wednesday at 2:30 p.m.
3. I believe that no additional services are needed at this time.
4. The clients and I are in agreement that family interventions are on target.
5. The community organizer told me that she needed the mailing list by next week at the latest.
6. The group agreed to allow me to bring in a cofacilitator for future meetings.
7. My supervisor and I are meeting this afternoon to discuss the matter further.
8. The client confided to me that he wishes to end his engagement.
9. My client is a talented seamstress and knitter.
10. "You have a safety issue regarding your children," I said.
11. I stated, "You have made wonderful progress so far."
12. I explained that I will be unable to meet next week because of my vacation.
13. My thought, I explained, was to try a behavioral rehearsal technique.
14. The client, her mother, and I are all in agreement about the plan.
15. I encouraged the client to think about her pregnancy and her health.
16. "You can't be serious about moving out," I said to the daughter.
17. The home visit went very well, my supervisor agreed.
18. This social worker met with the client and we terminated services today.
19. "The physical therapist said you were ready for a new challenge," I told her.
20. The play group moms met with me for a half hour this morning.

Exercise 4.5: Third-Person Point of View (II)

In this exercise, decide whether the statement is written from the third-person point of view and rewrite it if necessary.

1. This social worker explained the ethical responsibility of confidentiality to her.

    Correct?   Rewrite if needed:

    _____

    _____

2. You can tell me anything because what we talk about will stay here in this office.

    Correct?   Rewrite if needed:

    _____

    _____

3. I am confused and need help in understanding what is going on with you, I said.

    Correct?   Rewrite if needed:

    _____

    _____

4. "How do you think you are going to handle this divorce?" this worker asked.

    Correct?   Rewrite if needed:

    _____

    _____

5. My supervisor would like permission to sit in on our next session, so she can give me feedback," I explained to the client.

    Correct?   Rewrite if needed:

    _____

    _____

6. This worker and my colleague conducted the home visit to assess the safety of the home environment for the children.

    Correct?   Rewrite if needed:

    _____

    _____

7. My client and I are probably going to terminate our relationship this week, because the boundary crossing is making me uncomfortable.

    Correct?   Rewrite if needed:

    _____

    _____

8. Her mom and dad were both very pleased with her progress, and I told her I was very proud of her hard work too.

    Correct?   Rewrite if needed:

    _____

    _____

9. I am referring her for medication adjustment to Dr. Wolfe.

    Correct?   Rewrite if needed:

    _____

    _____

10. This worker explained to him how the court hearing would progress.

    Correct?   Rewrite if needed:

    _____

    _____

Exercise 4.6: Who, Whom, Whose, Who's, That, Which

In each example below, indicate whether the word in bold type is appropriate. If not, note the correct word.

1. The client's significant other, **that** refuses to attend sessions, is not helping at this point.

2. The house **who** burned last week must be torn down for safety reasons.
3. A conflict of interest **that** could be a problem was explained to the client.
4. The client, **whom** is an immigrant from India, teaches math at the local college.
5. The case manager **who** had been working with the client moved.
6. The client is very attached to her dog, **who** is a schnauzer.
7. The written contract **whom** the client signed is considered valid, according to the attorney.
8. The nursing home assessment **who** was completed last week was very thorough.
9. The school administrator **that** was concerned about the weather closed school early yesterday.
10. The workshop at **which** the client is employed provides his transportation to and from work daily.
11. The client cares deeply about her mother, **who** she loves unconditionally.
12. The client's cousin, **whom** is also his best friend, does not seem to be a very good role model.
13. The child **that** was allegedly abused by her father is in foster care.
14. The group facilitator **who** has been in charge for the past year is sick today.
15. The referral, **which** was made last week, was preapproved for insurance coverage.
16. The mental health staff meeting, **whom** had been postponed due to scheduling problems, was held today.
17. The shelter's budget, **which** the director sent to the board last week, has been cut.
18. This worker wonders if the client **that** seemed uneasy had been discriminated against.
19. The people **that** said they were coming never showed up at the community action meeting.
20. "**Who's** side are you on anyway?" the client asked this social worker.

Exercise 4.7: Punctuation

Correct the punctuation in the sentences below.

1. The client stated I am so angry I could spit!
2. The interview participants were the mom the dad their 17 year old daughter and their 12 year old son
3. The social work plan was amended to include the following—biweekly sessions weekly support group attendance and AA meetings
4. The client dislikes her children she has a hard time connecting with them
5. Following the suicide threat this worker discussed the matter with her supervisor.
6. What I'm trying to tell you is that my mom kicked me out of the house yesterday the client said

7. The comatose patient's family his minister his doctor and this social worker all met discussed the options and decided to discontinue further treatment.
8. The disaster victims needed food; water; shelter; and a listening ear
9. The emergency room referred the client to this worker after the disturbance caused by the client the EMS personnel and the sister were unclear about what had happened
10. In summary the client met all of his goals is pleased with his progress and is looking forward to years of drug-free living.

Exercise 4.8: Punctuation in Case Notes

Correct the punctuation in the following case notes, as well as any other problems you find. A sample response is provided for Note 1 at the end of the chapter. (You may want to photocopy the pages and work on the copies.)

Note 1

This social worker conducted an initial assessment of a 31 year old female who was referred by her physician because of problems coping with her life. She said I have my hands full and have no energy and now my daughter decides to run away I need a break or I'll break. When asked what that meant she confided that sometimes she feels like breaking something further discussion revealed that the client is very angry with her significant other; the jerk is a hazard to my health. She stated that sometimes she feels unsafe and at risk of him harming her; her friends feel that he controls her; and she does not really care about him anymore.

Note 2

The client met with this social worker and continued to work on goals. He indicated that his significant other however is not pleased with the changes that he has been making in his life and prefers that things not change because he feels like he has to make changes too in order to keep up with client who is increasing his self-confidence daily he says. I think that he needs to do what's best for him and so does the significant other and if that means this relationship doesn't work out in the long run then so be it. This social worker congratulated him on the strides he is making and assisted him in thinking through his next steps.

Note 3

The family canceled their appointment today they said it was because his car broke down; and there is no public transportation in their small community. Their appointment was rescheduled for next week when they hoped to have the car fixed; in the meantime this worker will explore housing resources for them because living so far out of town poses problems for not only this kind of thing but lots of other activities end up getting canceled as well they are very motivated.

Exercise 4.9: Contractions and Apostrophes

Review the following sentences for appropriate punctuation and make changes as needed. (You may want to photocopy this exercise and mark up the copy.)

1. "It's a problem that I can't solve alone," the client said.
2. The group members' chairs' were facing in a circle.
3. When this worker arrived at the house, a dog holding it's bone came to the door.
4. "Yours isn't the first case I've seen like this," this social worker stated.
5. The clients' yelled at their peers' all the way back to their room's.
6. In her fathers opinion, the client should have an abortion instead of keeping her baby.
7. The clients needs include tutoring and medication assessment.
8. New Yorks eligibility requirements' have confused clients' for year's
9. This social worker assured the clients' that more options were available to them than they realized.
10. The supervisors' agreed to discuss the sisters' cases at the staff meeting tomorrow.
11. The community resource councils attention was focused on the housing proposals under consideration.
12. The families feelings about the client being discharged home were complex.
13. Its impossible to know if the client is being truthful.
14. Most elders contracted the flu in the last ten days, as its spread across the area was unchecked.
15. The clients feelings were spared when one group member finally said "I think your okay."

16. She feels underappreciated and is hurt by her families attitude of indifference toward's her.

17. Theres an opening for the client to be treated tomorrow at the doctors office.

18. The progress reports did not indicate any suicidal ideation.

19. The client cannot seem to understand that this workers hands are tied by regulations' that do not always make sense.

20. Its a shame that the clients mother isn't being supportive.

Review the following case notes and correct the use of contractions and abbreviations.

Note 1

This active 81 year old client is hoping to be chosen for the Senior Olympic's tennis team. He's raising his 16 year old grandson and is concerned about who'll look after him when he's traveling with the team, should he be selected. The grandson isn't a problem at school or at his part time job at the local grocery store but "he's 16 years old after all," the client laughed. There's a chance that the client wont be selected but this worker commended him for thinking ahead. When asked, he said he's got a gay friend who'd be willing to step up and help out but there both leery about this, wondering if they'd be problems' with the friend's being gay.

Note 2

The couple lost their only child two months ago in a freak car accident. They're referred for grief counseling and its a shame how upset they both seem. Attending a support group was discussed; they can't imagine anyone they're being helpful because of the unique circumstances' surrounding their loss. This worker's listening skills were used to explore their feeling's about this painful loss.

Exercise 4.10: Spelling

Correct the misspellings in the following sentences.

1. The client prolly had good intentions of following through but was not motivated.

2. This worker encouraged the client to keep her journal til the next appointment.
3. The parents were adviced to attend the parenting program this evening.
4. The family was defenitley open to examineing their biazes.
5. The questionare was not entirely completed.
6. The boy seemed very conscience of the problems that are occuring in his life rite now.
7. The client exageratted when he said, "U r my favorite staff member."
8. She seemed embarased about having to dissappoint the naybors by not attending.
9. The judgement of the court was recieved without emotion.
10. The buro was greatful to the maintainence staff for clearing sidewalks after the storm.
11. The cleint harrassed this worker, saying, "Ignerance is bliss."
12. The couple was refferred to apear before the family service liason.
13. "I'm dissappointed in myself for not criticising the desicion before now," she stated.
14. This social worker feels there was not a very strong committment for imediate change.
15. The client did not understand pubic elegebility requirments.

Exercise 4.11: Homophones

Select the correct homophone in each sentence.

1. "(Our, Are) family is a mess," the mother stated.
2. This worker (complimented/complemented) the group members on their honest feedback to one another.
3. They must (of, have) been living in filth for weeks, from the looks of the apartment.
4. "(Your, You're) not alone in this struggle," the client reminded her spouse.
5. "(Your, You're) struggle is the same as mine," the client reminded her spouse.
6. It is apparent that the client does not (accept, except) his role in the situation.
7. (Accept, Except) for one cat, the animals have been removed from the home.
8. The client said that the shelter felt much safer (then, than) her previous living situation.
9. The client has (accepted, excepted) that she is going to have custody of her children after the hearing.
10. "(Its, It's) the (principal, principle) of the thing," the client argued.
11. The judge spoke to the child privately in her (ante, anti)chamber.
12. Growing up in a series of foster homes must (have, of) been hard for the client.
13. "(They're, Their, There) is no harder work than admitting one's mistakes and growing from them," this worker told the client.

14. "My biggest problem is sitting out (they're, their, there) in the waiting room, waiting to take me home," she said.
15. "(They're, Their, There) going to tease me for being pulled out of class to meet with you," the adolescent stated.
16. "(Who's, Whose) toy is this?" this social worker asked the children.
17. It had to (of, have) been a strength of (there's, theirs, they'res) to care for the difficult child.
18. The home and (its, it's) furnishings received a thorough cleaning.
19. The client cried for a few minutes, (then, than) was (already, all ready) to start over.
20. The single parent believed it was (too, to, two) late to start over again in a new town.

Exercise 4.12: Nondiscriminatory and People-First Language

Read the following statements and rewrite those in which you feel the language is discriminatory or does not put people first.

1. The client arrived, dressed in bright clothing and pink nail polish.
2. The dwarf was married to a normal-sized person.
3. The autistic child was noncommunicative and unable to make eye contact.
4. The cancer patient was struggling with her chemotherapy treatment today.
5. The special ed class was on a field trip today to the local museum.
6. The old woman looked and smelled like death warmed over.
7. The client and his mentally retarded brother were living two blocks away.
8. The client wears glasses for her nearsightedness, she indicated.
9. The client with major depression was assigned to this worker today.
10. She reminded this worker of his mother, and not in a good way.
11. The fat man had a hard time fitting in the office chair, he was so obese.
12. The infected couple looked emaciated and sickly.
13. She said that she gets along just as well in her wheelchair as her classmates do on their feet.
14. The blind man and his seeing-eye dog attended the assessment interview.
15. The client stated, "I'm not sure why you care about what this silly old woman thinks. No one else does and half the time, I don't either."

Exercise 4.13: Specific, Concrete Language

Read the following statements and rewrite each to be more precise or concrete.

1. In spite of the fact that he laughed, it was apparent that he was upset by his mother's criticism.

2. The client has the ability to accomplish her goals if she decides she truly desires to reach them.
3. She refused to attend the support group for the stated reason that she found it a waste of time.
4. The educational session planned for this evening was canceled in light of the fact that the weather was deteriorating and the forecast suggested it would only get worse.
5. The client described himself as a reformed Catholic until such time as he finds another faith that is more suited to his beliefs and his current lifestyle.
6. Informed consent documents were explained and signed for the purpose of covering agency policies and procedures along the lines of proper case file review.
7. Her father, who belongs to the local volunteer firefighter association, also has an interesting history of having been raised along the lines of having to live on the streets to survive.
8. The hospice staff noted that, in the event of an emergency that would result in the client's death, the client's husband would need support in the form of immediate assistance with coping.
9. Until such time that the prison is less crowded, the group members will be forced to continue to meet in the small, cramped room that has limited seating space.
10. At the present time, the client can no longer stay at the shelter due to the fact that she has stayed longer than the program allows already and has not made progress on goals that were mutually set by the staff of the shelter and her.
11. The session ended in the neighborhood of 11:15 a.m. by means of this social worker indicating that the time had run over by quite a bit.
12. At all times is the client to be observed for her own safety.

Exercise 4.14: Legal Risk Management Issues

Decide whether the following statements are true or false.

1. It is acceptable to write in the case file, "This social worker is furious with the client for acting so stupidly," so long as it is accurate.
2. Errors in the case file can be corrected using correction fluid.
3. The statement "The client is a horrible parent" is libelous.
4. Documenting in a timely manner means completing notes within six months after case closure.
5. It is reasonable to write in the case file, "The client was angry, as evidenced by her red face, shaking hands, and raised voice."
6. If a worker has time to write a case note about a session with a client before the session occurs, she should do so because it will save her time later.

7. It is important to understand the laws governing social work services before a crisis with a client occurs.
8. A client's record should not be left up on a computer screen when the social worker leaves the office for lunch.
9. If a social worker loses a record, the loss should be reported to the supervisor immediately.
10. Anyplace in a social worker's office is considered a secure location in which to store records.
11. If an automated spell-checker finds no mistakes in a note, it is probably acceptable.
12. It is not necessary to pay close attention to the accuracy of details in a case file, because very few people will have access to it.
13. It is acceptable to write in a case file, "The assessment is incomplete because the worker did not have time to complete it."
14. It is acceptable to write in a case file, "The transferring social worker's records were very shoddy and not helpful to this worker."
15. It is acceptable to write in a case file, "The client's spouse requested a joint meeting, but the client refused, indicating that she was not ready yet."

Exercise 4.15: Active versus Passive Voice

Rewrite these sentences in the active voice.

1. The work of this case has all been done by the client.
2. The client's case will be closed this Friday.
3. The community meeting had been scheduled already.
4. The family is in love with their pet snake.
5. The supervisor had been contacted by the attorney.
6. The situation will be resolved when the couple adopts.
7. A better safety plan will be developed by this worker before the client's discharge.
8. The budget used to be managed by the agency director.
9. Discipline would always be handled by the child's grandfather.
10. The discharge will need to occur once a physician has seen the patient.

Exercise 4.16: Building Your Vocabulary

Take these steps to help build your vocabulary

- Sign up for a free "word a day" e-mail through http://www.wordsmith.org or download to your desktop the "word of the day" widget if you are a Mac user. A "word of the day" app is available on some phones as well. Any of these programs will provide a daily word and its definition. Even if a particular day's offering is not a word you would use in professional practice, building your general vocabulary will boost your confidence and spelling skills.

- In your favorite search engine, type in "vocabulary words for social workers." Explore the lists that result and make a note of those words with which you are unfamiliar.
- Choose one list from a previous search and count how many words you know and would feel comfortable using in documentation. Share your list with a peer who is completing the same exercise.
- Start your own social work vocabulary list, either on paper or electronically. There are free apps for creating electronic flash cards that are easy to use and access via smart phone, tablet, or computer. Dedicate yourself to creating a set of flash cards for words you find difficult to spell or remember.
- Develop a personal plan on ways you will continue to develop your social work vocabulary. Make a commitment to improving your vocabulary daily. Share your plan with a peer, and make an appointment in four weeks to discuss how your plan is working.
- Keep reading! Reading how others use written words well can help in building your own vocabulary. What you choose to read does not have to be related to social work but should be just well written and enjoyable. Pay attention to words you are not familiar with and look them up in a search engine or online dictionary if you are not sure of their meanings.

EXERCISE ANSWER KEY

Exercise 4.2

No.	Subject	Verb	Agreement
1	members	was	no
2	client	request	no
3	member	were	no
4	coordinators	attempted	yes
5	daughters	is	no
6	suggestions	was	no
7	members	was	no
8	client	need	no
9	problems	means	no
10	teachers	need	yes

Exercise 4.3

1 = no (they indicate); 2 = yes; 3 = yes; 4 = yes; 5 = no (doctors say); 6 = yes; 7 = yes; 8 = yes; 9 = yes; 10 = no (parents feel).

Exercise 4.4

1. This worker met the client at 10:00 a.m. at her home.
2. The client and this social worker made a follow-up appointment for next Wednesday at 2:30 p.m.
3. No additional services are needed at this time.
4. There is agreement that family interventions are on target.
5. The community organizer indicated she needed the mailing list by next week at the latest.
6. The group agreed to allow a cofacilitator for future meetings.
7. This social worker and his supervisor are meeting this afternoon to discuss the matter further.
8. The client confided that he wishes to end his engagement.
9. This client is a talented seamstress and knitter.
10. "You have a safety issue regarding your children," this worker said.
11. This social worker told the judge, "The client has made wonderful progress so far."
12. This social worker cannot meet next week because of vacation plans.
13. This worker provided an explanation of a behavioral rehearsal technique.
14. The client, her mother, and this worker are all in agreement about the plan.
15. This worker encouraged the client to think about her pregnancy and health.
16. "You can't be serious about moving out," this worker said to the daughter.
17. The home visit went very well, the supervisor agreed.
18. This social worker met with the client and terminated services today.
19. The physical therapist said the client was ready for a new challenge.
20. The play group moms met with this social worker for a half hour this morning.

Exercise 4.5

1. (No change is needed.)
2. This worker assured the client that what is discussed in session will stay in this office.
3. "I am confused and need help in understanding what is going on with you," this social worker stated.
4. (No change is needed.)
5. "My supervisor would like permission to sit in on our next session, so she can give me feedback," this clinician explained.
6. This worker and her colleague conducted the home visit to assess the safety of the home environment for the children.
7. This client and worker will likely terminate the relationship this week, because of boundary-crossing issues.
8. Her mom and dad were very pleased with her progress, and this social worker expressed pride at her hard work too.

9.   This worker referred the client to Dr. Wolfe for medication adjustment.
10.   (No change is needed.)

Exercise 4.6

1 = no (who); 2 = no (that); 3 = yes; 4 = no (who); 5 = yes; 6 = no (which); 7 = no (that); 8 = no (that); 9 = no (who); 10 = yes; 11 = no (whom); 12 = no (who); 13 = no (who); 14 = yes; 15 = yes; 16 = no (which); 17 = yes; 18 = no (who); 19 = no (who); 20 = no (Whose).

Exercise 4.7

1.   The client stated, "I am so angry I could spit!"
2.   The interview participants were the mom, the dad, their 17-year-old daughter, and their 12-year-old son.
3.   The social work plan was amended to include the following: biweekly sessions, weekly support group attendance, and AA meetings.
4.   The client dislikes her children; she has a hard time connecting with them.
5.   Following the suicide threat, this worker discussed the matter with her supervisor.
6.   "What I'm trying to tell you is that my mom kicked me out of the house yesterday," the client said.
7.   The comatose patient's family, his minister, his doctor, and this social worker all met, discussed the options, and decided to discontinue further treatment.
8.   The disaster victims needed food, water, shelter, and a listening ear.
9.   The emergency room referred the client to this worker after the disturbance caused by the client. The EMS personnel and the sister were unclear about what had happened.
10.   In summary, the client met all his goals, is pleased with his progress, and is looking forward to years of drug-free living.

Exercise 4.8

Note 1: This social worker assessed a 31-year-old woman, referred by her physician because of coping issues. She indicated she is stressed, is without energy, and is dealing with her daughter's running away. She stated, "I need a break or I'll break." With further probing, she confided that sometimes she feels like "breaking something." She admitted to being angry with her significant other and reported that "the jerk is a hazard to my health." She indicated that sometimes she feels unsafe and at risk of harm from him. Her friends reportedly feel that he controls her. The client noted that she does not really care about him anymore.

Exercise 4.9

1. (No change is needed.)
2. The group members' chairs were facing in a circle.
3. When this worker arrived at the house, a dog holding its bone came to the door.
4. (No change is needed.)
5. The clients yelled at their peers all the way back to their rooms.
6. In her father's opinion, the client should have an abortion instead of keeping her baby.
7. The client's needs include tutoring and medication assessment.
8. New York's eligibility requirements have confused clients for years.
9. This social worker assured the clients that more options were available to them than they realized.
10. The supervisors agreed to discuss the sisters' cases at the staff meeting tomorrow.
11. The community resource council's attention was focused on the housing proposals under consideration.
12. The family's feelings about the client being discharged home were complex.
13. It is impossible to know if the client is being truthful. (*Avoid contractions in formal writing.*)
14. (No change is needed.)
15. The client's feelings were spared when one group member finally said, "I think you're okay."
16. She feels underappreciated and is hurt by her family's attitude of indifference toward her.
17. There is an opening for the client to be treated tomorrow at the doctor's office.
18. (No change is needed.)
19. The client cannot seem to understand that this worker's hands are tied by regulations that do not always make sense.
20. It is a shame that the client's mother is not being supportive.

Exercise 4.10

1. The client probably had good intentions of following through but was not motivated.
2. This worker encouraged the client to keep her journal until the next appointment.
3. The parents were advised to attend the parenting program this evening.
4. The family was definitely open to examining their biases.
5. The questionnaire was not entirely completed.
6. The boy seemed very conscious of the problems that are occurring in his life right now.
7. The client exaggerated when he said, "You are my favorite staff member."

8. She seemed embarrassed about having to disappoint the neighbors by not attending.
9. The judgment of the court was received without emotion.
10. The bureau was grateful to the maintenance staff for clearing sidewalks after the storm.
11. The client harassed this worker, saying, "Ignorance is bliss."
12. The couple was referred to appear before the family service liaison.
13. "I'm disappointed in myself for not criticizing the decision before now," she stated.
14. This social worker feels there was not a very strong commitment for immediate change.
15. The client did not understand public eligibility requirements.

Exercise 4.11

1 = Our; 2 = complimented; 3 = have; 4 = You're; 5 = Your; 6 = accept; 7 = Except; 8 = than; 9 = accepted; 10 = It's, principle; 11 = ante; 12 = have; 13 = There; 14 = there; 15 = They're; 16 = Whose; 17 = have, theirs; 18 = its; 19 = then, all ready; 20 = too.

Exercise 4.12

1. (No change is needed.)
2. The client of short stature was married to a person of average size.
3. The child with autism was noncommunicative and unable to make eye contract.
4. The patient with cancer was struggling with her chemotherapy treatment today.
5. The class of students with special needs was on a field trip today to the local museum.
6. The woman looked pale and sickly.
7. The client and his brother who has a cognitive disability were living two blocks away.
8. (No change is needed.)
9. (No change is needed.)
10. (No change is needed.)
11. The man had a difficult time fitting into the office chair.
12. The couple appeared emaciated.
13. (No change is needed.)
14. The man and his guide dog attended the assessment interview.
15. (No change is needed.)

Exercise 4.13

1. He laughed, but it was apparent that his mother's criticism upset him.
2. The client can accomplish her goals if she chooses to do so.
3. She refused to attend the support group because it was a "waste of time."

4. This evening's educational session was canceled because of the poor weather forecast.
5. The client described himself as a reformed Catholic for now.
6. Informed consent documents were explained and signed.
7. Her father, a local volunteer firefighter, had a very difficult childhood.
8. The hospice staff noted that the patient's husband would need support in dealing with the client's death.
9. The group will continue to meet in a small room with limited seating until a better option is available.
10. The client must vacate the shelter because she has exceeded the length-of-stay policy and has not made progress on meeting her goals.
11. The session ended late, around 11:15 a.m.
12. The client is to be observed around the clock.

Exercise 4.14

1 = F; 2 = F; 3 = T; 4 = F; 5 = T; 6 = F; 7 = T; 8 = T; 9 = T; 10 = F; 11 = F; 12 = F; 13 = F; 14 = F; 15 = T.

Exercise 4.15

1. The client has been doing the work.
2. The case is closing this Friday.
3. The community meeting is scheduled.
4. The family loves their pet snake.
5. The attorney contacted the supervisor.
6. The couple's adoption will resolve the situation.
7. This worker will develop a better safety plan before discharge.
8. The agency director used to manage the budget.
9. The child's grandfather always handled discipline.
10. The physician will discharge the patient after seeing him.

PART II

Sections of a Case Record

Many case record features are common across settings. A key feature of all records is that professional activity is evidenced throughout, from the first interaction with a client through termination and aftercare follow-up, if appropriate (Houston-Vega & Nuehring, 1997). Traditionally, records are organized in folders, with information organized by tabs or dividers and fixed together with a prong or binder. Computerized records are rapidly replacing hard-copy files, however. In any format, a case file may be written by one social worker, a group of social workers, or a variety of professionals working in a multidisciplinary setting. It may be written about a single client, a couple, a family, a group, or a community.

Case files vary on the basis of agency needs and requirements, but they usually include the following documents: an information summary sheet; confidentiality, informed consent, and release forms; assessment information and service or treatment plans; progress notes and contact logs; and communication about clients, such as correspondence sent or received and referral information. Chapters 5 to 9 cover basic sections of a case file and provide examples and exercises related to each.

CHAPTER 5

Information Summary Sheets

"Most social work professionals would agree that good record-keeping protects and benefits clients, whereas poorly written records can harm clients" (Ames, 2008, p. 70). Information summary sheets are typically the first piece of a record whereby social workers can begin good recording-keeping practices.

When a client initially contacts a social worker or agency, demographic information is typically collected and organized in one location, usually on a form called a "face sheet," a "demographic sheet," an "initial intake form," or an "information summary sheet." Whatever its name, it is typically the first form one finds in a case file. This information is collected at the point of intake, immediately prior to the first appointment, or at the beginning of the initial meeting.

WHAT BELONGS ON A SUMMARY SHEET

Moline et al. (1998) recommended putting down certain information on the summary sheet, including the following:

- Full name
- Telephone number (work and home)
- Date of birth and age
- Physical description
- Marital status
- Occupation
- Education
- Children living with the client (names and ages)
- Other people living with the client (names, ages, relationship to the client)
- Special interests or hobbies
- Health insurance company, policy number, and telephone number.

When deciding what information to include on a summary sheet, caution is urged. First, unnecessary information should not be requested. For example, it may not be important for an agency to know that a 50-year-old client attended a particular grade school or collects model cars for a hobby. Also, caution should be exercised if the agency requires clients to provide Social Security numbers or other sensitive identifiers. It is generally considered much safer if clients are assigned case numbers by the agency, distinct from their Social Security numbers. In addition, cell phone numbers are important in today's mobile society; an increasing number of people are disconnecting landlines and using mobile telephones exclusively.

The following details may be important to record on a demographic sheet:

- Referral source (who referred the client for services)
- Referral status (open, closed, referred)
- Reason for contact (presenting problem)
- Annual income
- Current involvement with other agencies
- Race
- Religion.

It is up to each agency staff member or private practitioner to determine what information is necessary to include, but these guidelines should be followed:

- Collect only the information that is needed to provide services efficiently and effectively.
- Do not assume that clients can complete a sheet asking for this information in advance. This could be difficult, for example, for a client who cannot read or write or for a family dealing with immediate stress. Prompting and assistance may be needed to obtain the information.
- Each space on the form should be filled out. Leaving items blank suggests that one did not ask for the information. Instead, note the reason for the lack of information—for example, that the question is not applicable or the client chose to not disclose the information.
- Explain to the client the reason for requesting any sensitive information. For example, income information may be necessary to evaluate eligibility for services.

SUMMARY AND EXERCISES

Demographic data are generally collected from a client wishing to be served by an agency or social worker. Clients should be asked only for information that is directly related to the purpose of the service delivery. Agencies and staff should be sensitive when asking clients for information of a personal nature.

The following exercises are designed to explore these and related issues. It can be helpful to work through them with a peer.

Exercise 5.1: Analyzing Information Summary Sheets

Ask a local social service agency for a blank copy of the form used to collect demographic data. Ask a peer to do the same with a different agency. With your peer, review the two blank forms and discuss the following questions.

1. What are the forms' similarities and differences?
2. What information is requested? What information seems to be missing, given the list of typically requested information that appears earlier in this chapter? Why do you think that is?
3. How could having demographic information before meeting with the client help or hinder the helping process?
4. Are there any questions on the forms that you would have difficulty completing? Why or why not?
5. If you could redesign the form, what would you ask differently? What would you not ask? Why?
6. What is the most important thing you have learned from this exercise?

Exercise 5.2: Completing Information Summary Sheets (I)

Complete the information sheet below as if you were a client seeking services.

Client Information Summary

Name:		Case number:	Admission date:
Address:		Home phone:	Work phone:
		Cell phone:	E-mail:
Date of birth:	Age:	Gender:	Race:
Occupation:		Education:	
Marital status:		Religion:	
Referral status:			
Gross family income:		Number of people living on income:	
Medical assistance number:		Other insurance:	
Household members:			

Name:	Relationship:	Date of birth:	Age:

Reason for admission:	
Prognosis at discharge:	
Referred to:	

Then, using the sheet you just completed, answer the following questions:

1. What information was easy for you to provide? What was difficult? Why?
2. What information did you hesitate to provide, if any? Why?
3. Do you think clients would react the same way you did? Explain your thoughts.
4. If the form asked for your annual income or your Social Security number, would you provide it? Why or why not?
5. What other sensitive information would you not wish to share with someone you do not know? What would make you more willing to share it?
6. Critically analyze the information form you completed. What are its strengths and weaknesses? What information is missing that you would like to see added?
7. What is the most important thing you have learned from completing this exercise?

Exercise 5.3: Completing Information Summary Sheets (II)

Fill out the same information form for a pet or other favorite animal. Imagine the animal needs to see a social worker because it is bored at home and feels that life is worthless. Add additional information as needed.

Exercise 5.4: Completing Information Summary Sheets (III)

Using the alternate form below, ask your peer to assume the role of a client who cannot read or write. Complete the information summary sheet by asking him or her the questions necessary to complete the form. Switch roles and repeat the exercise.

Client Face Sheet

Name:	Case number:	Today's date:
Address:	Date of birth:	Gender:
Telephone 1:	Telephone 2:	Telephone 3:
Referred for:	Referred by:	Referral status:
Occupation:	Insurance 1:	Insurance 2:
Race:	Religion:	Marital status:
Living with:		Assigned worker:

Discuss the following questions:

1. What made this exercise difficult or easy?
2. How would completing the form with a client differ from filling out your own?
3. Critically analyze this face sheet. What are its strengths and weaknesses?

CHAPTER 6

Confidentiality, Release Forms, and Informed Consent Forms

It is important to note to whom recorded information belongs. "Technically, the information recorded in a case record belongs to the client. His existence is what makes the data possible and most of what is recorded comes from the client directly or indirectly" (Wilson, 1980, p. 189). Confidentiality, release forms, and informed consent documents help safeguard the information that belongs to the client.

Legal and ethical problems can be minimized by educating new clients about services that the social worker will provide and the policies that outline those services. The most effective method is a spoken explanation and discussion with the client, followed by written and signed documentation (Reamer, 1998). The information should take into account such factors as the client's literacy level, primary language, and vision capability (that is, whether the client can read the form with or without glasses or other corrective lenses). Written materials should be at the sixth-grade reading level (Houston-Vega & Nuehring, 1997). The overarching goal is to "reduce malpractice risks while avoiding discouraging clients with an overly legalistic, procedural impression of the practice setting" (Houston-Vega & Nuehring, 1997, p. 28).

Several formats can be used to convey this information to clients; variations exist between agency settings. Some agencies do not need each of these forms, whereas others may have developed additional forms that fit their requirements. Generally, however, all forms are explained to, discussed with, and signed and dated by the client. A witness generally signs the forms to verify that the client signed them, not to verify that the client understands them. One set of all signed forms should be provided to the client, and another complete set should be filed in the case record. In instances in which clients have consented to sharing information with third parties, a copy of the consent form should accompany the documents.

CONFIDENTIALITY

Confidentiality is "a principle of *ethics* according to which the social worker or other professional may not disclose information about a client without the client's consent" (Barker, 2014, p. 87). The NASW (2008) *Code of Ethics* states that confidential information about clients can be disclosed only with "valid consent from a client or a person legally authorized to consent on behalf of a client" (p. 10) and that disclosure without authorized consent may occur only when "necessary to prevent serious, foreseeable, and imminent harm to a client or other identifiable person" (p. 10).

The NASW (2008) *Code of Ethics* also says that social workers have an ethical responsibility to

> discuss with clients and other interested parties the nature of the confidentiality and limitations of clients' right to confidentiality. Social workers should review with clients those circumstances where confidential information may be requested and where disclosure of confidential information may be legally required. (NASW, 2008, p. 11)

Examples of such instances, such as the possibility of harm to the client or a request by a third-party payer, should be provided. The NASW (2008) *Code of Ethics* specifies that this discussion should occur as early as possible in the social worker–client relationship and continue throughout the course of service provision as needed. When more than one person is involved in treatment (for example, in group or family treatment), it is the responsibility of the social worker to inform and seek agreement among the parties regarding confidentiality of information shared. The standards found in the CASW's (2005) *Guidelines for Ethical Practice* closely parallel the NASW standards.

In addition to providing evidence that the information was shared orally, a written summary can further help a client retain these important concepts. Agency policy should stipulate the ways in which confidentiality is explained and documented. Reamer (1998) suggested that the following topics be included in a discussion of confidentiality, depending on agency setting and need:

- A brief statement of why confidentiality is considered important
- Relevant jurisdictional requirements and ethical standards of confidentiality
- How records will be stored and access to documents will be limited
- Circumstances in which information must be disclosed
- How consent will be obtained to release information
- Procedures for sharing information in supervision and consultation
- Access by insurers, managed care companies, or employee assistance programs
- Disclosure of information by telephone, fax, or other electronic means
- Access to agency facilities by outside parties
- Processes for audiotaping and videotaping.

INFORMATIONAL HANDOUTS

Informational handouts can help orient clients to the helping process. These handouts often include information about the social worker's qualifications, the code of ethics under which the social worker practices, and the agency setting.

Social Worker's Background Statement

Clients should be aware of a social worker's qualifications to work with them. Informing the client in a written statement about one's degrees, professional licenses, and experience in working with similar clients is considered good practice (Moline et al., 1998). What is important is that the client learns and feels confident about the social worker's professional background and expertise. A sample background statement might look like this:

> I am [Name], a licensed social worker specializing in gerontology social work. I have worked at this agency for 12 years and have prior work experience in medical and mental health settings. I am a member of the National Association of Social Workers and am committed to their code of ethics. I received my social work degree in 1998 from the Ohio State University. I am licensed to practice social work in the state of Pennsylvania. I have received specialized training in aging and health care issues. I have also been active with the Association of Social Work Boards and CSWE.

Code of Ethics

A copy of the professional ethical code to which the social worker adheres is often shared with the client. It is important for the client to understand the ethical guidelines the social worker follows and to have a copy of the code as a reference tool if there are future questions.

Agency Description

Background information about the setting in which services will be provided can help clients feel more comfortable and educate them about the agency's purposes. A few sentences about the agency and its mission, its staff, and the range of services provided are typically included in an agency description. A practice-setting statement (Houston-Vega & Nuehring, 1997) might look like this:

> ### About the Mountain Laurel Homeless Shelter
>
> The Mountain Laurel Homeless Shelter was established in 1984 with the mission of providing short-term housing to residents of the Mountain Laurel region who need a temporary place to live. The shelter's board of directors and staff believe that everyone needs help at some point in their lives.

Our mission is to provide that assistance and improve the quality of life for all residents of the area.

The shelter employs two licensed social workers and four paraprofessionals with a wide range of experience in helping children and families cope with the challenges of inadequate housing. Comprehensive services include individual assessment and counseling, group treatment, information and referral, and employment counseling.

Consent to Treat

The term *informed consent* implies not merely that consent was given but also that the client understood and was fully informed about the actions to which he or she consented. The *Social Work Dictionary* defines informed consent as

> the granting of permission by the client to the social worker and agency . . . to use specific intervention, including diagnosis, treatment, follow-up, and research. This permission must be based on full disclosure of the facts needed to make the decision intelligently. Informed consent must be based on knowledge of the risks and alternatives. (Barker, 2014, p. 216)

Consent is truly informed when the client "understands all risks and outcome possibilities that can occur" (Moline et al., 1998, p. 35). It is important to remember that informed consent is voluntary. When a client is not able to provide informed consent (in the case of a minor, prisoner, or person incapable of understanding), a parent, legal guardian, or legal representative must provide consent. Braaten (2007) said that the informed consent process should be incorporated into any client's treatment, regardless of age or capacity: "Solicit consent even from those who are not competent (or of age) to consent" (p. 18). Information provided to children should be explained in an age-appropriate manner.

Houston-Vega and Nuehring (1997) described informed consent as a two-tiered process. First, clients are oriented to the general operating procedures of the agency. Then, social workers provide a working agreement for a client to give his or her informed consent to begin services. Informed consent forms are typically one page long and are explained and signed prior to the beginning of treatment (Moline et al., 1998). They usually include the following:

- Type of services provided
- Length of time sessions can be expected to last
- Limits of confidentiality
- Benefits and risks of life changes as a result of services.

Social workers are cautioned against using blanket forms that ask the client to consent to all services that the agency provides (Kagle, 2002). In this situation, the client cannot give true informed consent. A new consent form should be signed when there is a major change in the treatment plan or contract.

Informed consent takes on special significance when services are provided electronically. Reamer (2009) reminded social workers that clients need to be aware that services received electronically may be more superficial than those delivered in person. For example, a client should be informed that an e-mail explanation of a complicated matter may not be as detailed or helpful as one provided in a face-to-face discussion. Nonverbal communication clues are lacking in most forms of electronic communication. This can result in a less valuable clinical experience. Electronic privacy risks should be explained fully to clients.

FEE AGREEMENTS

Clients should give written consent, after discussion, to any fee agreement with the social worker. The consent form should spell out acceptable forms of payment, how third-party payment is handled, sliding fee scales (if applicable), charges for missed meetings, payment schedules, and consequences of nonpayment (Houston-Vega & Nuehring, 1997).

WORKING AGREEMENTS

A working agreement is a written document that explains how services will be provided. It indicates that a client understands such issues as how and by whom services will be provided, how a treatment plan will be established, what to do in case of an emergency, and how termination will occur. In addition, it typically states that the client understands both the risks and the benefits of treatment (Houston-Vega & Nuehring, 1997). Working agreements are unique to each setting and are usually signed by the client(s), the social worker, and a witness.

CONSENT FOR RELEASE OF CONFIDENTIAL INFORMATION

A number of situations require a client's informed consent to release confidential information. For example, a third-party payer may request information about treatment, an agency to which the client wishes to be referred may ask for information, or a worker may want to videotape a session for supervisory purposes. In all cases, the client must authorize any release of information (Wilson, 1980, p. 189). Agencies typically have developed standardized forms for this. They usually include an expiration date, at which point the consent ends (Sheafor & Horejsi, 2012). Consent has a time limit, rather than being granted forever.

As with consent for treatment, a client's consent to release information must be informed. This means that "the client knows what's going on when information is released so he can determine intelligently if he wants it given out" (Wilson, 1980, pp. 189–190). The client must fulfill 10 conditions for consent to be informed:

1. Know that a request for information has been made.
2. Understand exactly what information is to be disclosed.
3. Actually see the material that is requested for release.
4. Know to whom the information is to be released—name, position, and affiliation.
5. Know why the information is being requested and how it will be used.
6. Have a way to correct or amend the information to ensure it is accurate and complete before its release.
7. Specify whether the receiving party has a right to release the information to a third party.
8. Be aware of the ramifications of granting or denying permission.
9. Understand that permission has a time limit and is revocable.
10. Give consent in writing.

Reamer (2001) added these four important items to the informed consent list:

1. Forms should be available in the client's primary language, and interpreters should be available to answer questions.
2. No information can be added to the form once the client has signed it.
3. Coercion or undue influence must be avoided.
4. A hold-harmless clause should be considered that releases the worker from any liability connected with a confidentiality breach by a third-party payer.

Copies of the consent form should be provided to the client and the receiving party. One complete set should also be kept in the case file.

Kagle (2002) warned social workers not to ask a client to sign a blanket release form. A separate form should be signed for every request to release information.

Additional sample forms can be found in Braaten's (2007) *The Child Clinician's Report-Writing Handbook*, Houston-Vega and Nuehring's (1997) *Prudent Practice: A Guide for Managing Malpractice Risk*, and Zuckerman's (2008) *The Paper Office*.

HIPAA REQUIREMENTS

HIPAA is a federal law that addresses client privacy. Effective April 2003, it created national minimum standards for protecting client privacy that supersede most state laws (Kagle & Kopels, 2008).

HIPAA concerns how client information is kept safe and private. "It is the information in the record that is protected by this law, and so it not only applies to electronic records (for example, word processor documents, faxes, data entry) but also to paper records and even oral communications" (Zuckerman, 2008, p. 27). Examples of oral communications include face-to-face conversations and telephone calls about clients. A social worker should consider safety and privacy issues during all types of communications about clients.

HIPAA guidelines must be followed by health care providers, and social workers are considered health care providers. The guidelines are clear about this: "Almost all social workers or the agencies they work for are considered health care providers because they furnish, bill, or are paid for health care" (Kagle & Kopels, 2008, p. 237). A few exceptions exist. For example, a provider who does not transmit health information electronically is not required to comply with HIPAA.

Protected health information covered by HIPAA "includes information about a person's health care, mental or behavioral health information, or the payment for those services" (Kagle & Kopels, 2008, p. 238). The general rule is that a patient or personal representative must authorize the release of protected information, except in situations that could result in serious risk or harm, such as child abuse or neglect.

Sheafor and Horejsi (2012) reported that the following HIPAA rules are particularly relevant to social workers:

- At the beginning of the relationship, the client must be educated about his or her privacy rights and informed of how the provider intends to use and disclose health information.
- The client has a right to view, copy, and correct records. Access can be denied in certain situations, if it is believed that the access may result in harm.
- Procedures must be in place to guard client information, including information stored electronically.
- Health information cannot be disclosed to a client's employer.
- Release of information requires informed consent, with exceptions such as when information is needed to conduct an audit or to arrange care.
- Mental health providers can refuse to disclose notes to the client's health insurance company without first obtaining the client's consent.
- Enrolling in health plans or receiving benefits cannot depend on a client's authorization to release information.
- A hospitalized client has the right not to have his or her identity or health status shared with others.
- Records must be shredded when destroyed.

Revisions to HIPAA in 2013 provided additional guidelines regarding storing and transmitting electronic protected health information and closed loopholes in the original rules. Compliance requirements were expanded to include subcontracting entities, and privacy protections will not apply to records 50 years after a patient's death. In addition, notices of privacy practices must now include information about the right to notice of a privacy breach; the right to restrict disclosure if self-paying; fundraising communications and the right to opt out of receiving those communications; and the right to allow disclosures of therapy notes, sales of protected information, and marketing disclosures only on the basis of a signed authorization (Morgan, 2013).

Even though some social workers may not be required by law to comply with HIPAA, it is recommended that they comply anyway, for reasons related to financial incentives and best practices (Kagle & Kopels, 2008; Zuckerman, 2006). Non-HIPAA-compliant social workers may have problems becoming approved providers for certain insurers. They may also have difficulty accessing client information from HIPAA-compliant providers who may not know that exemptions exist. Many of HIPAA's requirements are consistent with what are considered best practices of protecting a client's right to privacy (Zuckerman, 2006). Regardless of HIPPA's requirements, it is every social worker's responsibility to learn about HIPAA and the protections it offers the public.

Additional details about HIPAA can be found at the Health Information Privacy Web site of the U.S. Department of Health and Human Services (http://www.hhs.gov/ocr/privacy/).

SUMMARY AND EXERCISES

Social workers use several forms to ensure that their policies on confidentiality and informed consent are understood by clients. Each agency has its own forms, tailored to the special needs of the population it serves. It is important for a social worker to be aware of these forms and to be able to explain issues surrounding confidentiality and informed consent to clients.

The following exercises are designed to familiarize readers with some of the most important forms. As in other chapters, they are most effective when carried out by peers who can compare responses and offer each other feedback.

Exercise 6.1: Analyzing Background Statements

Read and critically analyze the statements below. What are the strengths of each statement? What areas could be improved? Rewrite the statements, adding additional facts if necessary.

Statement 1

My name is Patrick O'Grady. I'm licensed to practice social work and have been employed at this mental health agency for just a few months. My experience is limited, although I'm really eager to learn all that I can to help you with your issues. I received my BSW earlier this year and my GPA was 3.569. My internship was spent working in a domestic violence shelter and I learned so much there.

Statement 2

Thank you for selecting our agency to provide you with group counseling. My name is Ani M. Shibata and I have been working with groups at this agency since 2008. Prior to that, I have over 12 years of experience in the field. I hold a BA in psychology and an MSW, and I am a proud member of NASW. I'm a LCSW, ACSW, CAC, and YMCA board member. I am CEU compliant and trained in EMDR and SFBT.

Exercise 6.2: Writing a Background Statement

Write a brief statement about yourself that could be used when working with clients. Use the sample provided in this chapter to guide you. Then review it with a peer. What are its strengths? How might it be improved?

Exercise 6.3: Analyzing an Agency Description

Read the agency description below. What do you like about it? What are its problems? Rewrite it to improve it. Add additional information if you think it is necessary.

> You can expect to be treated like family at the Family Counseling Center of Greater Tioga! Our committed and dedicated staff looks forward to working to strengthen your family, however loosely you define it. Established in 2003, our mission is to strengthen our community by strengthening families! Working at the center are several folks who will encourage and assist you and your family in ways you may never have thought possible. You can put your trust in us to provide you with assessment, counseling, information, and education.

Exercise 6.4: Analyzing Informed Consent Forms

Do an Internet search for sample informed consent forms. Print out and review three different forms, then answer the following questions.

1. What do the three sample forms have in common?
2. In what ways are they different?
3. Which form would you be most comfortable signing? Why?
4. Highlight any phrases in the forms that a client might not understand. How many did each form contain? How many did your preferred form contain? Do you understand all of the highlighted phrases?
5. An agency supervisor is considering recommending that your organization use the form you identified as being the least understandable of the three. What advice would you give to the supervisor about this?
6. Imagine that you are a client who is asked to sign the least understandable of the three forms. What questions would you need to have answered before signing?
7. What have you learned from this exercise?

Exercise 6.5: Other Agency Forms

Ask an agency employing social workers for copies of blank forms used with clients. Review them and answer the following questions:

1. What are the strengths of the forms?
2. In what ways could the forms be improved? Be as specific as possible.

3. If you were the administrator of the agency, would you recommend that any of the forms be revised? If so, why? How would you go about revising them?
4. Do any of the forms cover issues that were not addressed in this chapter? If so, what is their purpose? Do you agree that they are important in that agency setting?
5. How understandable are the forms for clients? Do you think they are written at a sixth-grade reading level?
6. Highlight phrases that may not be easily understood. How many are there? Do you understand them well enough to explain them to a client?
7. How could any confusing terminology be improved?

Exercise 6.6: Consent-to-Treat Scenarios

Consider the four scenarios below. In each case, what would you do? Why?

Scenario 1

You have been offered a position with a well-respected agency in your community. In the course of the interview, you learned that the agency has no policies or procedures for obtaining client informed consent to treat. The supervisor indicated that the agency does not see a need for this. The agency also does not routinely obtain client consent to release confidential information, because the agency attorney has indicated that doing so opens the agency up to potential legal problems.

Scenario 2

Your supervisor has transferred an open case to you. The previous social worker left the agency suddenly. A review of the file reveals that the client did not sign a working agreement or consent-for-treatment form. It also appears that the worker released information to two other agencies, but there are no release forms in the file.

Scenario 3

A 16-year-old client does not wish to have his treatment information released to his school, although his parents have signed a form giving their consent to do so. You have explained that the parents have the right to sign this form, as the client is not legally able to do so. The client is very angry and upset and threatens you physically.

Scenario 4

You remember the client signing forms at the beginning of treatment, and you recall having witnessed them. You believe you probably made a copy of all the forms for the client, as that is your standard practice, but you cannot find your copies in the file anywhere. You have thoroughly searched your office and cannot locate the forms.

CHAPTER 7

Assessments and Treatment Plans

Before meaningful services can be extended, social workers must assess a client's needs and plan for necessary types of services. "Your job is to find out who that person really is, and the information in a file is only as useful and accurate as the competence and insight of the people reporting it" (Lukas, 1993, p. 3). Ways of documenting the assessment and treatment plan processes are covered in this chapter.

WRITING ASSESSMENTS

Assessment has been defined as the "process of determining the nature, cause, progression, and prognosis of a problem and the personalities and situations involved therein" and "the social work function of acquiring an understanding of a problem, what causes it, and what can be changed to minimize or resolve it" (Barker, 2014, p. 29). Assessments may be called "psychosocial assessments," "biopsychosocial assessments," "social histories," or some other name specific to an agency.

Critical thinking skills are certainly involved in the assessment process. Sheafor and Horejsi (2012) described it as a "thinking process by which a worker reasons from the information gathered to arrive at tentative conclusions" (p. 171). It is necessary to organize the gathered information into a usable format. "During assessment, the available information is organized and studied to make sense of the client's situation and lay a foundation for a plan of action" (Sheafor & Horejsi, 2012, p. 171).

An assessment serves several purposes, which include helping the social worker and client better understand the client's problems and strengths, guiding the development of an intervention or treatment plan, and providing a foundation from which to monitor progress and the effectiveness of the helping process (O'Hare, 2009). A thorough social work assessment attends to all dimensions of a client, including his or her strengths and issues that impede optimal functioning. It may be compiled from a variety of sources in addition to client interviews. It may involve observations, the use of referral documents, client-completed surveys, personal interactions between the social worker and client, and collateral information from others whom the client has given the social worker permission to consult (Hepworth, Rooney, Rooney, & Strom-Gottfried, 2012).

The organization of assessments varies tremendously, as does the term used to describe the report. Its purpose is consistent, however: It provides an organizational framework for better understanding the client's situation, assists with treatment planning, and helps communicate the client's circumstances to other involved professionals. It is a client's story.

Sheafor and Horejsi (2008) wrote that a good assessment includes eight features:

1. It is brief and provides only necessary information.
2. It is clear and simple, using jargon-free terms and understandable language.
3. It is useful. The purpose of the report should be kept in mind when preparing it.
4. It should be organized with logical headings and categories.
5. It should be respectful of the client's privacy.
6. It should be objective, accurate, and nonjudgmental.
7. It should include only information that is relevant and clearly connected to the client's involvement with the social worker or agency.
8. It should focus on client strengths whenever possible. A report that focuses only on the client's presenting problem, weaknesses, and limitations is inconsistent with good social work practice and undermines the importance of basing change on the client's abilities.

Kagle (2002) also argued that cultural factors and their influence on a client's situation should be addressed in an assessment and plan.

Although the organization of the assessment report varies, the following commonly used headings were identified by Wilson (1980, pp. 120–122):

- Date and reason for referral
- Medical situation
- Family situation
- Living arrangements
- Economic situation
- Background information
- Worker's impressions
- Casework goals (treatment plan).

Nearly 30 years after Wilson wrote them, the headings remain fairly consistent with what is recommended today. Sheafor and Horejsi (2012, p. 179) listed the following as the current most commonly used headings:

- Identifying information (name, date of birth, address, and so on)
- Reason for report
- Reason for social work or agency involvement
- Statement of client's problem or concern

- Client's family background
- Current family composition, household membership, or both
- Relationships to significant others
- Ethnicity, religion, and spirituality
- Physical functioning, health concerns, nutrition, home safety, illness, disabilities, medications
- Intellectual functioning, education, school performance
- Psychological and emotional functioning
- Strengths, ways of coping, and problem-solving capacities
- Employment, income, work experience, and skills
- Housing, neighborhood, and transportation
- Recent use of community and professional services
- Social worker's impressions and assessment
- Proposed intervention and service plan.

Lukas (1993, pp. 169–171) collapsed several headings into a smaller number of categories:

- Identifying information
- Presenting problem
- Household description
- Historical and developmental data
- Client contact
- Diagnostic information.

In comparing the categories, one notices differences in format but similarities in content. A comparison of assessment reports used by several agencies will reveal differences, too. Each agency's format may feature different categories, but the content is usually quite similar.

It is generally considered optimal to organize the information chronologically. For example, in discussing a client's work experiences, write about the earliest employment first (Lukas, 1993). Similarly, note a client's family of origin before writing about his or her current family situation. Sticking to chronological order will make it easier to keep the information organized and understandable.

A social worker's opinions appear in only one section of the assessment, typically labeled "social worker's impressions and assessment." This is often the most difficult section for new social workers to complete, as it requires a thoughtful analysis of the information. It calls for a succinct professional opinion—not a restatement of the facts but an objective interpretation and analysis of those facts (Wilson, 1980). This section often includes answers to the following questions:

- What problems and needs does the client see?
- What problems and needs does the social worker see?
- How does the client feel about his or her situation?
- How appropriate are the client's feelings and behaviors?
- What efforts has the client made to solve his or her problems?

The social worker's opinions should be explained. For example, if a worker writes, "The client needs educational testing," an explanation of why the worker feels this is necessary should follow: "because he is testing two levels below his grade and reports having difficulty reading" (Braaten, 2007).

The report should be dated and conclude with the full signature and credentials of the author. It should be written using complete sentences and grammatically correct language. The author should refer to himself or herself in third person. The report, typically typed, may be written in paragraph style or a fill-in-the-blank format, depending on agency protocol.

DIAGRAMING CLIENT INFORMATION

Sometimes it can be helpful to visually map client information. The most common forms of diagrams to help with assessment are the genogram, the cultural genogram, and the ecomap (Sheafor & Horejsi, 2012). All of these methods use symbols to portray relationships. The genogram is frequently used to show family relationships over three generations (Barker, 2014), whereas the cultural genogram is used to depict the client's cultural background (Sheafor & Horejsi, 2012). An ecomap shows "a variety of reciprocal influences between the client, relevant social institutions, and environmental influences" (Barker, 2014, p. 134).

SPECIALIZED ASSESSMENTS

Some practice situations require specialized assessments; these vary on the basis of agency and client need. Below are some common specialized assessments with which social workers should be familiar.

Mental Status Examination (MSE)

The MSE is a widely used tool that helps organize observations about the client. Whereas the general assessment is based on client-provided information, the MSE is a record of the social worker's observations (Lukas, 1993). Used with adults, it can also be adapted for use with children. It provides a standardized way to assess the client over time, providing snapshots of change in the client. The tool is a way to understand three questions: "What has changed? When did it change? Has it changed for the better or for the worse?" (Lukas, 1993, p. 14). Lukas (1993) provided essential areas to address in the MSE (p. 15):

- Appearance: how the client looks and behaves
- Speech: how the client speaks
- Emotions: the client's mood most of the time and how the client appears to be feeling
- Thought process and content: how the client thinks and what the client thinks about

- Sensory perceptions: indications of illusions or hallucinations
- Mental capacities: orientation of the client to person, place, and time; an estimate of the client's intelligence; the ability to remember and concentrate; and the extent of judgment and insight
- Attitude toward the social worker: how the client behaves toward the worker.

An MSE may be in the form of a standard checklist, a form with blanks to complete, or a narrative in paragraph format. Regardless of the format, it is important to use the client's own words when possible.

Mini-MSE (MMSE)

The MMSE is a tool developed in 1975 that tests cognitive functioning. It is used most commonly to evaluate older adults for dementia, using 30 items that assess orientation, word registration, attention, word recall, language, and visuospatial abilities. It can be quickly administered—in less than 15 minutes—and has a body of research supporting its validity. However, it relies on verbal responsiveness and the client's ability to read and write. It has also been suggested that culture and gender may bias scoring (Warchol, 2010).

Developmental Assessment

When working with children, it is important to understand their earliest environment and experiences (Lukas, 1993). A development assessment or developmental history will guide this process. In this assessment, the social worker obtains information from one or both primary caregivers, without the child present. Most information focuses on the time period just before the child's birth to approximately the age of five years. The developmental history allows a view of the child's functioning over time, from the perspective of the caregiver. Typically, an outline of possible questions helps prompt the social worker in acquiring this information.

Diagnostic Assessment

Social workers should be familiar with ways in which clients receive diagnoses for mental health issues. The *Diagnostic and Statistical Manual of Mental Disorders*, first published in 1952, is now in its fifth edition and is commonly referred to as DSM-5 (American Psychiatric Association, 2013). The manual notes that "reliable diagnoses are essential for guiding treatment recommendations, identifying prevalence rates for mental health service planning, identifying patient groups for clinical and basic research, and documenting important public health information" (American Psychiatric Association, 2013, p. 5). Although the ability of a social worker to assign a mental health diagnosis to a client varies across jurisdictions and use of the DSM-5 remains controversial, this guide is nonetheless widely used by social workers. It is important to know that diagnostic information that may appear on client assessments can be further researched in the DSM-5.

Trauma Assessment

Barker (2014) defined trauma as "an injury to the body or psyche by some type of shock, violence, or unanticipated situation. Symptoms of psychological trauma include numbness of feeling, withdrawal, helplessness, depression, anxiety, and fear" (p. 436). Trauma-informed practitioners recognize the following issues (CSWE, 2012, p. 5):

- The nature of trauma and traumatic experiences are inherently complex.
- Trauma affects children, adolescents, adults, and families in specific ways . . . [with] a wide range of reactions.
- Trauma recovery is possible but presents specific challenges.

It is important to accurately assess the impact of trauma on a client to effectively work with him or her. The following factors are important to include in a trauma assessment (National Child Traumatic Stress Network, n.d.):

- Prevalence of type of trauma
- Associated types and rates of mental distress and associated behavioral and functional impairment
- Cultural background and cultural meanings of the traumatic event
- Developmental factors, including age and cognitive and social functioning
- Socioeconomic factors
- Logistical barriers to receiving help
- Strength-based resources.

The National Center for Social Work Trauma Education and Workforce Development Web site lists 36 trauma measures that can be useful in assessing clients for trauma (http://www.ncswtraumaed.org/resources); this is explored in an exercise at the end of this chapter.

Suicide Assessment

It is likely that at some point in any social worker's career, clients at risk for suicide will be encountered (Sheafor & Horejsi, 2012). Although suicide risk can be assessed in many ways, a useful five-step evaluation and triage model (SAFE-T) has been developed (Substance Abuse and Mental Health Services Administration, 2009). The five steps are as follows:

1. Identify risk factors, including suicidal behavior, current and past psychiatric disorders, key symptoms, family history, precipitants or stressors, changes in treatment, and access to firearms.
2. Identify protective factors, determining internal abilities to manage stress and external factors, such as responsibility for others, positive relationships, and social supports.

3. Conduct a suicide inquiry, asking specific questions about thoughts, plans, behaviors, and intent.
4. Determine risk level and intervention need, on the basis of clinical judgment.
5. Document. The following elements should be documented clearly: risk level and rationale, a treatment plan to address or reduce current risk, firearms instruction if relevant, and follow-up plans. For youths, treatment planning should include a role for the parent or guardian.

In addition to suicide risk, it is important to assess a client's risk to others, including the social worker (Lukas, 1993). Examining any existing records in advance may help in evaluating a client's potential for violent behavior. Factors to look for include the following (Lukas, 1993, p. 104):

- Diagnosis that includes violent or impulsive behavior
- Previous history of violent behavior
- History of substance abuse
- Head injury or injury to the central nervous system
- Previous history of physical abuse by others
- Previous history of suicidal behavior
- Previous history of delusions or hallucinations, especially command hallucinations.

Although the presence of these indicators cannot accurately predict future violence, awareness of them can provide helpful background data. They are also important to determine when meeting a client about whom little is known. Concerns should be documented and discussed with a supervisor so that the social worker can find ways to feel safe with clients and the client can obtain the assistance he or she needs.

Couple and Family Assessment

Assessing the complex social structure of a family can be challenging. No matter how "family" is defined, assessing one accurately and completely helps inform treatment planning. Sheafor and Horejsi (2012, pp. 199–202) suggested addressing the following dimensions when assessing a family unit:

- How is family membership defined? Definitions may be based on biological, legal, functional, and perceived factors.
- What facts and realities describe the family?
- Is the family's functioning supported by the community?
- What boundaries and subsystems describe the family?
- What rules and roles govern family interaction?
- How do family members balance separateness and togetherness?
- How well does each member fit within the family system?
- How do family members handle differences?

- What communication patterns exist within the family?
- How does the family make decisions?
- What is the mood of the family?
- What are the moral, ethical, and spiritual aspects of the family's functioning?
- To what tasks and activities do the adults and older children devote their time?
- Who supports and who opposes change?

Group Assessment

Clients are typically assessed individually before being referred to or placed in a therapeutic group setting. However, it is important to recognize that social workers are involved with many different groups, not just the ones they lead therapeutically. Small working committees, interagency planning groups, community action groups, and self-help groups are examples of other types of groups that are part of a social worker's work life. Groups can be well functioning, in which all members work toward a common goal, or dysfunctional, in which members are frustrated and goals are not achieved (Sheafor & Horejsi, 2012). A social worker should continuously assess group functioning in an effort to increase the group's effectiveness and efficiency. To accomplish this, it may be helpful to take informal notes that record the following features of a group (Sheafor & Horejsi, 2012, p. 203):

- What are the observable actions of the group?
- What is the emotional mood of the meetings?
- How do members interact with one another?
- Who influences other members?
- Who are the formal and informal leaders?
- Who moves the group forward?
- What forces impede progress?
- How are decisions made?
- How invested are members in the group?

In addition, it is important to assess the cultural awareness and sensitivity of the group and how confrontation is handled (Ephross & Greif, 2009).

Community Assessment

In some settings, social workers must document community-level assessment activities. Similar to assessment reports for small client groups, agency policy will dictate the specifics of what is to be included in community assessments. Typically, data are collected, analyzed, and organized into a report that needs to be written with the end user in mind (Sheafor & Horejsi, 2012). Community needs assessments usually include the following information: an overview of the existing problem or problems being focused upon; the goals, objectives, and methodology used in collecting and analyzing data; a review of existing policies and current programs available; the views of those directly affected by the issue; how other communities may have approached the problem; unmet service needs; and suggested solutions and recommendations (Beer & Leonard, 2001; Sheafor & Horejsi, 2012). Community asset mapping is a useful activity that focuses on the community's potential resources in predicting change effort success (Kirst-Ashman & Hull, 2015). Asset mapping provides a visual depiction of abilities of individual community members, membership organizations and associations, and community-based institutions. A force field analysis is another type of assessment used in macro practice. It is "a review of the barriers to accomplishing your goal and the factors likely to help you achieve it" (Kirst-Ashman & Hull, 2015, p. 316). Examining the opposing and supporting forces for change in a community setting can assist in realistically planning for change. Another way to organize community assessment is through recording activities associated with the three tasks outlined by Netting, Kettner, McMurtry, and Thomas (2012): focusing on the target population, determining community characteristics, and identifying community structure may provide a framework for organizing documentation efforts when assessing community. It is important, no matter how the record is organized, to base needs assessment recommendations on data and to be able to explain the data that support the decisions (Shea, Santos, & Byrnes, 2012). Maintaining the data used to make decisions makes good practice sense.

CULTURAL ISSUES IN ASSESSMENT

With any assessment, it is important to consider and document issues related to culture. According to the DSM-5 (American Psychiatric Association, 2013), *culture* refers to "systems of knowledge, concepts, rules, and practices that are learned and transmitted across generations. Culture includes language, religion and spirituality, family structures, life-cycle stages, ceremonial rituals, and customs, as well as moral and legal systems" (p. 749). These identities can be sources of strength and support, but they may also present difficulties. The concept of intersectionality is helpful to keep in mind when documenting issues related to culture. Intersectionality suggests that group members hold several statuses based on factors such as gender, sexuality, social class, age, disability, and race. "These multiple social locations are experienced simultaneously, are mutually reinforcing, and therefore must be considered in tandem rather than independently" (Sears, 2012, p. 546). They intersect and combine to form the foundation of discrimination and to influence life chances to receive valued resources, such as education and wealth. Viewing culture through an intersectional lens can be helpful when documenting the impact of perceived difference on clients and client groups.

The DSM-5 features the Cultural Formulation Interview (CFI), a tool composed of 16 questions to explore with clients to better understand the impacts of culture (American Psychiatric Association, 2013, pp. 752–754). The questions are as follows:

1. What brings you here today?
2. How would you describe your problem to family, friends, or others in the community?

3. What troubles you most about your problem?
4. Why do you think this is happening to you?
5. What do others in your family, your friends, or others in your community think is causing your problem?
6. Are there any kinds of support that make your problem better, such as support from family, friends, and others?
7. Are there any kinds of stresses that make your problem worse?
8. For you, what are the most important aspects of your background or identity?
9. Are there any aspects of your background or identity that make a difference to your problem?
10. Are there any aspects of your background or identity that are causing other concerns or difficulties for you?
11. What have you done on your own to cope with your problem?
12. In the past, what kinds of treatment, help, advice, or healing have you sought for your problem?
13. Has anything prevented you from getting the help you need?
14. What kinds of help do you think would be most useful to you at this time for your problem?
15. Are there other kinds of help that your family, friends, or other people have suggested would be helpful for you now?
16. Have you been concerned about this and is there anything that we can do to provide you with the care you need?

An informant tool allows the same questions to be asked of a knowledgeable collateral contact (American Psychiatric Association, 2013, pp. 755–757). Both tools are designed to obtain information related to the impact of one's culture on current issues. Similarly, culture affects groups and communities and should be a consideration when attempting to understand the client system.

WRITING TREATMENT PLANS

The treatment plan may be described differently from agency to agency. It may be called the "goals and objectives," "service contract," "therapeutic contract," "initial plan," or another term. No matter what its name, it "specifies the desired outcome of the service(s) to be provided, the key actions that will be taken to achieve this outcome, the major roles and responsibilities of those involved in this effort, and the relevant timelines" (Sheafor & Horejsi, 2012, p. 233).

Treatment plans are completed after the assessment and are based on it. They have been described as "the backbone of every progress note" and a "road map to get to the end of treatment" (Ward & Mama, 2010, p. 82). Rothman (2002) called them the "blueprints for the change process that will occur" (p. 305). They are considered the legal contract or formal agreement on which services will be based. The contract, Rothman (2002) said, is between the client and the agency: "They are not between a client and a specific worker. The client has come to the agency for service, and the initial relationship is defined in this way" (p. 304).

Sheafor and Horejsi (2012, p. 226) recommended that, at a minimum, the following elements be included in a treatment plan:

- Problems or concerns to be addressed
- Goals and objectives of intervention
- Activities the client will undertake
- Activities to be performed by the social worker
- Expected duration of the intervention (in weeks or months)
- Probable location and number of sessions or meetings
- Identification of additional people, agencies, or organizations expected to participate and their role in the change process.

Rothman (2002) said that having a way to review and evaluate the plan is also essential.

Treatment plans typically consist of goals and objectives, two distinct elements. A *goal* is a desired end toward which an activity is directed (Sheafor & Horejsi, 2012), whereas *objectives* are measurable action steps aimed at achieving the goal.

A goal is a preferred outcome toward which all service activities are focused, the end result sought by the social worker and client—for example, to learn a skill or acquire knowledge, make an important decision, change a behavior, alter an attitude, or rebuild a damaged relationship (Sheafor & Horejsi, 2012). Rothman (2002) recommended setting one overarching goal, so as not to overwhelm or diffuse intervention.

A goal is usually not concretely measurable (Ward & Mama, 2010). It is typically a problem statement written in a way that suggests a solution. For example, if the problem is that the client drinks alcohol excessively, the goal might be to decrease alcohol consumption. Garvin (2002) offered the following additional guidelines for establishing goals:

- If the goal is attainable, the amount of time it would take should be measurable. It should be clear to everyone involved when a goal has been accomplished. For example, if a goal is to change a specific behavior, the client and social worker should know when that behavior has changed.
- The goal should be stated in terms of the client's behavior, not the worker's. Starting a goal statement with "help the client" is not client oriented but rather focused on what the social worker will do.
- The feasibility of meeting the goal should be considered. It may not be reasonable to accomplish a particular goal, given the client's particular strengths and challenges. Care should be taken to not set the client up for failure.
- The goal should be legal and ethical, and achieving it should not result in harm to someone else.
- The skills of the worker should be adequate to assist the client in reaching the goal.
- Goals should be phrased positively, as a means of encouraging growth.

Braaten (2007) agreed with the importance of positive phrasing, further suggesting that the goal should focus on presence rather than absence. For example, a goal of improving communication with one's spouse is better and more affirming than a goal of stopping dysfunctional communication patterns.

According to Braaten (2007), a goal must be important to the client. It will be very difficult to accomplish if it is not personally meaningful and worthwhile to the client.

Vandiver and Corcoran (2009) added that focusing on the client's strengths when setting a goal will make the goal easier to attain. Ways to do this include helping the client remember how successes have been accomplished previously, affirming those successes and abilities, and determining which skills and behaviors can be transferred to the current situation.

As mentioned earlier, objectives are different than goals: They are measurable actions aimed at achieving a given goal. "An objective is more specific and written in a manner that allows for measurement and evaluation" (Sheafor & Horejsi, 2012, p. 231). An objective consists of three related elements, according to Rothman (2002): an action statement, a time frame, and evidence of achievement (that is, it should be apparent when an objective is reached). If the goal, for example, is to reduce excess drinking, the objectives may be to attend weekly meetings of Alcoholics Anonymous, to drive past the bar after work each day instead of stopping, to develop alternate socialization strategies, and to attend weekly counseling sessions.

Objectives are the step-by-step actions by which goals are met. They are detailed, not subjective, and measurable—the action plan for how the goal will be accomplished. They should be realistic and should feature actions that can be accomplished: "If someone is having financial difficulty, you would not list winning this week's state lottery as an objective" (Ward & Mama, 2010, pp. 109–110). Each goal should be accompanied by at least two objectives, more if necessary (Jongsma & Peterson, 2003).

Sheafor and Horejsi (2012) stated that a well-written objective "describes who will do what, by when and under what conditions" (p. 231). Objectives typically start with the word "to" and involve action verbs that describe observable actions. Phrasing objectives of what the client will do, rather than what the client will not do, is considered best practice. The following are examples of appropriate action verbs commonly used in objectives (Sheafor & Horejsi, 2012, p. 232):

arrange	demonstrate	plan
attend	discuss	practice
conduct	learn	select
decide	obtain	visit

Rothman (2002) suggested that objectives should always reflect what the client wants and be written in the client's own words. Simple and specific objectives are most effective. Objectives should indicate both social worker and client responsibilities, unlike goals, which should be client focused: "If all the defined tasks are for the client, the worker–client alliance will be minimized" (Rothman,

2002, p. 307). Conversely, dependence will result if all objectives are for the social worker to complete.

Some service plans include categories for problems, goals, objectives, interventions (what approaches will be used), and assessment and evaluation (how progress will be tracked) (O'Hare, 2009). Others include only problems, goals, and objectives. Still others are more detailed and specify criteria used to decide whether acceptable levels of change have occurred (Sheafor & Horejsi, 2012). Places for client and worker signatures and dates are standard, however.

Treatment plans are just that: plans. Even the most well-designed plans often change. "A willingness to revise objectives in response to changing circumstances is critical to effective helping" (Sheafor & Horejsi, 2012, p. 233). In addition, revisions can be a sign of progress. Most agency policies require that social workers update or revise plans periodically.

INDIVIDUAL SERVICE PLANS

An individual service plan (ISP) is a specific type of document used by and with people with disabilities. It may also be called an individual program plan or habilitation plan, but regardless of the name, it generally provides "written detail of the supports, activities and resources required for the individual to achieve personal goals" (Illinois Department of Human Services, 2013, p. 3). Such plans may be updated annually or as needed, when major life changes occur. True and MacDougall (n.d.) noted that "it is a history, a list of things to do, and a plan for making future hopes and dreams a reality" (para. 1). The individual and team are responsible for its development, and it features the following points: It is unique to the individual, it is goal oriented, it is structured for success, it is supported by the team and staff working with the person, it is outcome oriented, it is reinforced across systems, and it provides the supports necessary for success (True & MacDougall, n.d., para. 4–10).

Although the ISP is an individualized document, the following common elements are generally contained in one (Illinois Department of Human Services, 2013, pp. 41–42):

Personal description	Strengths and needs
Medical, dental, and nutritional information	Vocation
Background or history	Education
Social relationships	Financial situation
Goals and objectives	Communication style
Interests and activities	Learning style
Personal values	Personal rights
Personality, feelings, and emotions	Recent life changes
Sources of comfort and discomfort	Vision for the future
Assessment	

The ISP is signed by the client or guardian and all service providers.

INDIVIDUALIZED EDUCATION PLANS

Barker (2014) defined an *individualized education plan* (IEP) as "a legal requirement, based on provisions in the Individual Disabilities Education Act (IDEA) (P.L. 101-474), that each identified child with disabilities must be evaluated and that a plan to meet his or her unique needs must be developed before placement in any education program" (p. 214). Thus, school social workers and those working with children in other settings must be familiar with the IEP.

Each public school child receiving special education and related services must have an IEP, an individualized document that "creates an opportunity for teachers, parents, school administrators, related service personnel and students (when appropriate) to work together to improve education results for children with disabilities" (U.S. Department of Education, Office of Special Education and Rehabilitative Services, 2000, p. 1). Certain information must be included in an IEP, such as current performance, annual goals, special education services, accommodations required, participation in state- and districtwide tests, needed transition services, and measured progress. Copies of the completed plan must be provided to the child's parents or guardian, and everyone involved in implementing the plan must have access to it.

OTHER TYPES OF PLANS

Social workers are often involved in planning for a variety of other kinds of situations and clients. These are unique to the agency setting and the population being served. For example, nursing homes have requirements for care plans that are very specific to that population. Community planning to tackle a specific issue may involve documentation requirements. It is important to ask these questions about expectations of treatment planning in any new social work setting:

- Which types of formal service planning occur in this setting?
- What are the minimum documentation requirements for service planning in this setting?
- Are a few service plans available for review, to enable better understanding of the expectations?
- Are observation opportunities available for additional exposure to service planning development?
- Where can more be learned about service planning in this setting?

SUMMARY AND EXERCISES

Writing an assessment requires a social worker to gather and process a large amount of information into a coherent document that guides the treatment planning process. Writing skills are essential when formulating both assessments and treatment plans, regardless of the service setting involved.

The following exercises offer an opportunity to become more familiar with both assessments and planning documents. Similar to exercises in other chapters, they can be especially effective when carried out with a peer.

Exercise 7.1: Analyzing Assessment Formats

Ask for a local social service agency's assessment and treatment plan forms. Review them with the following questions in mind:

1. What are the similarities and differences between the two sets of forms?
2. Why do you think certain information is requested and other information is not, given what you have learned in this chapter?
3. If you could redesign the form or ask different questions, what would you do?
4. What is the most important thing you have learned from this exercise?

Exercise 7.2: Self-Assessment

Photocopy the following assessment form and fill it out as if you were the client. Write at least a few sentences in each category.

Assessment Report

Client name: _____

Date: _____

Data source: _____

Reason for seeking assistance: _____

Family background: _____

Current living situation: _____

Physical functioning: _____

Interpersonal relationships: _____

Religion and spirituality: _____

Economics and transportation: _____

Current community connections: _____

Social work impressions and assessment: _____

_____

Social worker
_____

Exercise 7.3: Objectivity

Read the following statements as if they were found in an assessment. Determine if the language used is appropriate. If it is inappropriate, rewrite it to be more acceptable. Use statement number 1 as an example.

1. It is apparent to this social worker that the client is a cold, unfeeling, unhappy person who cannot even begin to manage her chaotic life or that of her child.

   Appropriate? No. **Why or why not?** Contains judgmental language.

   Rewrite: On the basis of the client's statements that she is "miserable and numb to anything going on around me," this worker's impression is that the client is having difficulties coping with her child's demands.

2. This worker concludes that this welfare mother and her absent boyfriend are trying to cheat the system.

   _____

   _____

   _____

3. The client claims he completed high school but is not sure of the year.

   _____

   _____

   _____

4. This social worker was surprised at the intensity of the anger in the client's response when she said, "I am divorced and the details don't matter. My marriage has been over a very long time. Can we just leave it at that?"

   _____

   _____

   _____

5. The family seems to have a careless attitude when it comes to clothing selection or how its members present themselves in public.

   _____

   _____

   _____

6. This 78-year-old seems to be cognitively intact and very insightful about her diminished physical abilities. Her strengths include knowing that her son, who lives with her, is untrustworthy and can manipulate agencies to help them get their basic needs met.

Exercise 7.4: Recording Social Worker's Impressions

Read the following statements and determine if the language used is appropriate. If it is inappropriate, rewrite it to be more acceptable. Use the first statement as an example.

1. Going to be a great client, is likable and friendly, very enjoyable interview

    Appropriate? No. **Why or why not?** Incomplete sentences, judgmental.

    Rewrite: The client appeared outgoing and friendly, two strengths that will assist her in working through her issues.

2. I am positive that the client was honest with me and is committed to improving her life by enrolling in parenting classes.

    _____

    _____

    _____

3. The client is a very pretty young lady who is struggling with her cultural identity. While she respects her family's traditions, she also wants to be more like her peer group.

    _____

    _____

    _____

4. It is this worker's impression that the client's anxiety over finding another job is influencing other spheres of her life. Her self-esteem has taken a beating, and her marriage appears to have suffered as a result. She is motivated, however, and appears capable of change.

    _____

    _____

    _____

5. This social worker is impressed by the client's strength in seeking assistance in managing her caregiving responsibilities. She is torn between

demands of her job, caring for her children, and caring for her mother, who is 84 years old. She could be a poster child for the sandwich generation.

_____

_____

_____

6. This client has very poor hygiene (smells bad, torn clothes, dirty face) but seems oblivious to how he comes across. He needs to lose weight, which he admitted, but he really needs to improve his lifestyle, for which he has limited insight.

_____

_____

_____

7. This client's depression appears to be worsening. A referral to a psychiatrist for medication adjustment seems warranted, as does enrollment in a support group.

_____

_____

_____

Exercise 7.5: Critiquing an Assessment

Read the following assessment report and critique it. What do you like about it? What needs to be changed before you would agree to sign it?

Sample Assessment

Kansas Family Service Agency	
Name of client:	Dorothy Gale
Case number:	4111958
Date of birth:	March 9, 1995
Address:	R.R. 3, Oakdale, KS 33231
Date of report:	October 29, 2010
Social worker:	[Name], BSW
Reason for report:	This report was prepared to assist in understanding Dorothy and her situation.

(*continued*)

Sample Assessment (*continued*)

Reason for social work involvement:	Dorothy was referred to this agency by her aunt, who expressed concern about her niece's mood swings and hysterical state since a tornado touched down at the family farm. Dorothy agreed to come to this agency for assistance, although she appears to be firm in her delusions of having traveled to a faraway land during the tornado.
Source of data:	This report is based on two one-hour interviews with Dorothy (October 21 and 28) and a telephone conversation with her aunt.
Family background and situation:	Dorothy is a 15-year-old female who is being raised by her aunt and uncle on a nearby farm. She has lived with them for as long as she can remember. She has no memories of her parents, who died in a tragic accident when she was a year old. Prior to the tornado, she appeared well adjusted, according to her aunt. Dorothy indicates a close relationship with her aunt and a more distant relationship with her uncle. She, her aunt and uncle, and three farmworkers are the sole occupants of the farm. She repeatedly stated "there's no place like home" when asked how she enjoyed living on the farm. She appears visibly anxious when asked about the tornado.
Physical functioning and health:	Dorothy appears to be physically fit and she says she is in good health. She is 5 feet 3 inches tall and weighs 110 pounds. Neither she nor her aunt reports any health concerns prior to the tornado. She was hit on the head during the tornado, however, and was unconscious for several hours. Since then, she insists that she has traveled to a land she refers to as Oz. She has reportedly been consistent in her detailed descriptions of Oz and the people who inhabit the area. Her family doctor reports that physically she is fine.
Educational background, school performance, cognitive functioning:	Dorothy attends the local public school and achieves average grades. She is a hard worker when she is interested in a subject, according to her aunt, but has historically been given to periods of daydreaming. These periods have recently increased in frequency and length.
Psychological and emotional functioning:	Dorothy describes herself as "moody" but fun loving and playful. She denies any suicidal thoughts and says she is rarely depressed. She described an instance when she was faced with the removal of her dog as one that depressed her. She finds great comfort in her pet. She exhibited a great deal of excitement (flushed face, increased voice tone, more animation) when describing, in detail, her experiences in Oz.
Interpersonal and social relationships:	Dorothy reports having no close friends but her dog, Toto, with whom she has a very close relationship. She expressed disappointment at not being able to bring her dog with her to the agency.

(*continued*)

Sample Assessment (*continued*)

Ethnicity:	Dorothy is Caucasian and of German descent.
Religion and spirituality:	Dorothy is of the Baptist faith and states that she attends church weekly with her aunt and uncle. She believes in God, she states, and in world peace. She also indicated that she has recently come to believe in witchcraft, something that she did not believe in before the tornado struck.
Strengths and problem-solving capacity:	Dorothy has a great deal of musical talent and enjoys singing to herself and her dog. She describes coping with adversity through "believing in myself. I have the ability to solve my own problems." When asked for an example of good problem-solving skills, she responded with "I got home from Oz, didn't I? I was forced to be strong and persevere, and I made it home again."
Employment, income, work experience, and skills:	Dorothy's work history consists of helping her aunt around the farm, assisting the hired hands with light farm duties, and gardening.
Use of community resources:	This is Dorothy's first use of community resources.
Impressions and assessment:	This 15-year-old seems to living in a fantasy world, following being hit in the head when a tornado touched down at her family farm. She appears flushed and excited when describing her journey to and from Oz. She appears to find comfort in dwelling on this experience and seems to want to be taken seriously and to be believed.
Intervention and service plan:	This worker hopes to engage Dorothy in weekly sessions, in an attempt to work through her issues. She will need emotional support and reassurance as she faces the truth that her experiences in Oz were only the result of her head injury. Referrals to a neurologist for further assessment, as well as to a psychiatrist, are planned. A suggestion for family therapy will also be made to her aunt.
Signature of social worker:	

Exercise 7.6: Writing an Assessment

You are a social worker in a mental health clinic who has made the following notes about a client. Compile the notes into an assessment report, using a copy of the blank assessment form provided at the end of the exercise.

> Client is 24-year-old woman, Sanja Latha
> Raised by immigrant Indian parents in New York City; moved from NYC to this town when took job
> Practicing Muslim; unmarried
> Math teacher in local high school

Five siblings, all older and married through arranged matches

Doesn't feel close to any siblings—sister closest in age is eight years older

Closer to mother, except not lately due to pressure

Small network of teacher friends from school that she goes out with after work

Enjoys math puzzles, knitting, working out, reading in spare time

Feeling increasing pressure from parents who wish to arrange her marriage

Refusing to meet man parents have selected

Depressive symptoms: excessive sleeping, no interest in anything, sad all the time

Symptoms for two months, worse over time

Rents apartment, has car payment, one credit card bill—finances not problem

Proud of being able to support herself

Wants to get married someday, but not in arranged marriage

No medication currently; complains of headaches, menstrual cramping

First anxiety attack two days ago; second one this morning

Called in sick from work for third day, only days missed in four years of employment

Visit expected from parents and an older sibling this weekend

Consequences of disappointing family very upsetting—tearful when discussing

Honor student in high school; graduated summa cum laude from college with degree in math education

Describes college roommate as closest friend, but she has moved across the country to take a job

Consequences of refusing match: "too awful to think about"

Parents paid for education and down payment on car

Muslim faith very important to her—"It defines who I am"

Does not recall disobeying parents in past

Describes self as usually optimistic and thoughtful person

First visit with social worker ever, hasn't accessed community services before

Referred by principal at school who is "very worried" about her.

Assessment Report

Name of client:	
Case number:	
Date of birth:	
Address:	
Date of report:	
Social worker:	
Reason for report:	
Reason for social work involvement:	
Source of data:	

(*continued*)

Assessment Report (*continued*)

Family background and situation:	
Physical functioning and health:	
Educational background, school performance, cognitive functioning:	
Psychological and emotional functioning:	
Interpersonal and social relationships:	
Ethnicity:	
Religion and spirituality:	
Strengths and problem-solving capacity:	
Employment, income, work experience, and skills:	
Use of community resources:	
Impressions and assessment:	
Intervention and service plan:	
Signature of social worker:	

Exercise 7.7: Recognizing Goals and Objectives

Determine if each statement below is a goal or an objective.

1. Improve timeliness of service delivery to clients.
2. To meet once weekly with a family support aide.
3. To improve coping skills.
4. To apply for college admission by January 1.
5. To seek an end to childhood poverty in the agency's service area.
6. To expose her, in structured activities, to small groups of people.
7. Social worker will research nursing home options in the area.
8. Spouse will watch children for one evening a week.
9. Client will attend supervised visits with her children twice weekly.
10. To write a list of five things of which she is most proud.

Exercise 7.8: Critiquing Objectives

Read the following objectives and rewrite them to improve them, if necessary.

1. Increase client's communication skills in four weeks.
2. By next week, contact agencies that can help with all of these problems.
3. Attend weekly meetings with the interdisciplinary treatment team.
4. Practice behavioral rehearsal techniques until comfortable with telling mom about pregnancy.
5. Demonstrate the ability to accurately pay the bill when buying breakfast.
6. Select new day care, arrange for reliable transportation, meet new people.
7. To make a list of strengths and problems with the current living situation.

Treatment Plan

Name of client:		
Date:	Problem statement:	
Date:	Goal statement:	
Date:	Objective:	Completion date:
	1.	
	2.	
	3.	
	4.	
	5.	
	6.	
	7.	
	8.	
Signature of client:	Date:	
Signature of social worker:	Date:	

Exercise 7.9: Formulating Goals and Objectives

Photocopy the form that follows and use it to write a treatment plan for the client described in Exercise 7.6.

Exercise 7.10: Critiquing a Client–Social Worker Contract

The following treatment plan is based on that found in Sheafor and Horejsi (2008, p. 335). Critique it and improve it where you feel this is necessary.

Client–Social Worker Contract

This agreement is between Stella Gabel and Nancy Sidell, who is employed at Mountain View Clinic.

The goal of this contract is to assist Stella with grieving the loss of her spouse of 40 years.

To achieve this goal, the following objectives will be met:

1. Stella to meet weekly with Nancy for at least four weeks.
2. Stella to journal feelings each week and bring them to weekly sessions for discussion.
3. Stella to recall positive memories about spouse.
4. Stella to attend a widows' support group that meets monthly at the hospital.
5. Nancy to explore financial resources to assist with income loss.
6. Nancy to explore better ways of coping than have been used so far.

Progress will be reviewed and evaluated by both the client and the social worker. Both will know that things are better once that happens.

The consequences of not reaching the objectives are that Stella will continue to feel terrible and be unable to manage activities of daily living.

This plan will be renegotiated in six weeks.

Client's signature:

Date:

Social worker's signature:

Date:

Exercise 7.11: Writing a Treatment Plan (I)

Imagine that you are a client seeking services from a social worker. Select one of the following problems:

1. You do not have the knowledge, skills, or abilities to pass a required college course.

2. You do not have the knowledge, skills, or abilities to pass a social work licensing examination.
3. You scored poorly on your annual performance evaluation.

Now imagine you are the social worker. For the goal selected earlier, construct a treatment plan using the blank treatment plan form introduced earlier.

Exercise 7.12: Writing a Treatment Plan (II)

Using the blank treatment plan form introduced earlier, complete a treatment plan for Dorothy Gale, using the information from exercise 7.5.

Exercise 7.13: Exploring Genograms

1. Type "symbols for genograms" into your favorite search engine and explore the results.
2. Next, type "sample genogram." Select a model genogram.
3. Using standard symbols and a sample model genogram, create a genogram for yourself, using at least three generations of your family.
4. Share your genogram with a peer who has also completed this exercise.
5. Discuss what you found easy about this tool and what was difficult.
6. Give one another feedback on the genogram. Were the appropriate symbols used? What might have made the genogram easier to understand?
7. Think of a client problem for which using this tool during an assessment might be helpful. Discuss with your peer how this could be useful. In what ways might it not be useful?
8. What have you learned about genograms related to your personal practice?

Exercise 7.14: MSE

1. Critique the following MSE. What do you like about it? In what ways could it be improved?

Em Gale is a neatly dressed Caucasian female who appeared older than her stated age of 56 years. She seemed distressed during the interview and made infrequent eye contact. She seemed uncomfortable and wrung her hands for the entire interview. Her speech was high-pitched and she seemed very nervous. She stated, "Since the tornado, I'm not sleeping and can't turn off my brain. We almost lost my niece Dorothy during the tornado and I was so worried. I'm still worried." She described her thoughts as constantly racing and worrying. She is preoccupied with fears of losing her niece to another tornado. She denies suicidal or homicidal thoughts and shows no evidence of hallucinations. She is oriented × 3 and is of average intelligence. "I feel like I'm going crazy," Mrs. Gale stated. Her judgment appears impaired in relation to her niece. She stated she has not allowed her niece to attend school since the tornado, for fear of harm coming to her. She is capable of insight, as she knows not sending her niece to school will not necessarily keep her safe. She seemed very capable of showing empathy but seemed reluctant to talk much to this interviewer. "I don't like being here because I'm worried about what Dorothy is doing right now. I'm worried if she's okay."

2.   Using the assessment from Exercise 7.5, write an MSE for Dorothy Gale. Share it with a peer and ask for feedback. What were its strengths? How might it be improved?

Exercise 7.15: MMSE

1.   Locate a copy of the MMSE. You can order the official form at http://www4.parinc.com/Products/Product.aspx?ProductID=MMSE or find a copy elsewhere online.
2.   Conduct an MMSE on a peer.
3.   What did you find easy about using this tool? What was difficult?
4.   Think of a client problem for which using this tool during an assessment might be helpful. Discuss with your peer how this could be useful. In what ways might it not be useful?
5.   What have you learned about MMSEs related to your personal practice?

Exercise 7.16: Developmental History

1.   In your favorite search engine, type in "developmental history questions." Using a format you find, conduct a developmental history with a parent of a child under the age of 10 years. If you don't know anyone willing to participate, ask a peer for help in locating someone to interview.
2.   Write up your notes and share them with a peer. Ask for feedback on the document.
3.   Discuss what you found easy about asking these questions. What was difficult?
4.   Think of a client problem for which using this tool during an assessment might be helpful. Discuss with your peer how this could be useful. In what ways might it not be useful?
5.   What have you learned about developmental histories related to your personal practice?

Exercise 7.17: Exploring the DSM-5

The DSM-5 is a topic best covered in courses or seminars devoted to it. If you intend to work with client mental health issues, you will need to understand it.

This exercise provides an introduction to the DSM-5 but is not meant to be a comprehensive overview.

1. Using your favorite search engine, type in "DSM-5 and social work." Explore some of the sites that interest you. Make notes of some things that you learned.
2. Type in "DSM-5" for access to sites that are not specific to social work. Add to your list of interesting things that you learned.
3. Keep exploring until you are able to answer the following questions:
    a. In formal documentation, codes often appear with diagnoses. What do these codes mean? What is their significance?
    b. From a social work perspective, what are the pros and cons of using the DSM-5?
    c. What are some major changes with the DSM-5?
    d. When are updates to the DSM-5 expected?
    e. How do you believe the DSM-5 will be useful to you in your practice?

Exercise 7.18: Trauma Assessment

1. Go to http://www.ncswtraumaed.org/resources and click on "Child and Adolescent Trauma Measures: A Review."
2. Explore the numerous trauma measures located there.
3. Select one measure that you might use in your practice.
4. Critically analyze the measure you selected. What do you like about it? What do you think could be added to improve it?

Exercise 7.19: Suicide Assessment

1. With a peer, role-play a social worker assessing a client who is suicidal. During the role play, use the SAFE-T tool (found on pages 94–95 or at http://store.samhsa.gov/product/Suicide-Assessment-Five-Step-Evaluation-and-Triage-SAFE-T-/SMA09-4432).
2. Follow each of the five steps (identify risk factors, identify protective factors, conduct suicide inquiry, determine risk level/intervention, and document).
3. Process the role play and discuss how the five-step process worked for this client.
4. Share the documentation with the peer and ask for feedback. In what ways could there be improvements?

Exercise 7.20: Workplace Risk Assessment

Conduct a workplace risk assessment of an agency in which you have worked or are currently working. Write up your findings and share your assessment with either an agency supervisor if you are still affiliated with the agency or a peer. Obtain feedback on your report. Your assessment should include the following elements:

1. Describe the type of agency.
2. What members of the public have access to the agency? How do clients access the agency?
3. Which types of risk are more likely than others at the agency? For example, clients who are suicidal may be more likely to be found at a mental health center than at a community-based program.
4. What security measures are in place at the agency? What security measures are not in place?
5. Do employees know their role in the event of an emergency with a client?
6. What suggestions can be made to lower worker risk at the agency?

Exercise 7.21: Couple and Family Assessment

Using the model on pages 95–96, complete an assessment of your family of origin or a couple relationship of which you are a part. Share your completed assessment with a peer and ask for feedback. What were particular strengths of your report? In what ways could it be improved?

Exercise 7.22: Group Assessment

Select a group whose members are willing to let you observe a meeting, such as a local cancer support group or an Alcoholics Anonymous group. A work group that you are not typically part of would also work for this exercise. If a group is not available to you, watch the film *Twelve Angry Men*. Obtain permission to take informal notes that will help you answer these questions about the group:

*   What are the observable actions of the group?
*   What is the emotion or mood of the meeting?
*   How do members interact with one another?
*   Who influences other members?
*   Who are the formal and informal leaders?
*   Who moves the group forward?
*   What forces impede progress?
*   How are decisions made?
*   How invested are members in the group?
*   Is cultural sensitivity shown?
*   How is confrontation handled?

Share your informal notes with a peer and discuss the group process. What did you learn that will assist you in your future social work practice? How do you feel about the role of informal note taking in this context?

Exercise 7.23: Community Needs Assessment

Select a community with which you are familiar to complete a community needs assessment. It can be an actual community, such as a neighborhood struggling with a heroin epidemic, or a fictional community, such as one struggling with zombies or extraterrestrial visitors. If you cannot think of a community, read *The Hunger Games* or watch the movie and use District 12 as your community. Your assessment should include the following elements:

1. An overview of the existing problem(s) being focused upon
2. The goals, objectives, and methodology you would use in collecting and analyzing data
3. A review of existing policy and current programs available
4. The views of those directly affected by the issue
5. How other communities may have approached the problem
6. Unmet service needs
7. Suggested solutions and recommendations.

Share your assessment with a peer and obtain feedback. What did you learn that will assist you in your future social work practice?

Exercise 7.24: Intersectionality Exercise

Increasing sensitivity to the impact of difference on client systems should be a constant work in progress. Complete this exercise to help you on your journey and ask a peer to complete it also:

1. Listen to the TED Talk titled "The Mothers Who Found Forgiveness, Friendship" (9.54 minutes) at https://www.ted.com/talks/9_11_healing_the_mothers_who_found_forgiveness_friendship.
2. Write a progress note about each mother and her experience.
3. Share the notes with your peer and discuss how you incorporated the impact of culture and intersectionality into the note. In what way could you have included this information more fully?

Exercise 7.25: CFI

Ask a peer to role-play with you and offer to do the same for the peer. Select a problem that you would expect to see in your area of interest and ask the peer to portray that situation in a client who is being seen for the first time. Conduct a CFI, using the questions below.

1. What brings you here today?
2. How would you describe your problem to family, friends, or others in the community?
3. What troubles you most about your problem?

4. Why do you think this is happening to you?
5. What do others in your family, your friends, or others in your community think is causing your problem?
6. Are there any kinds of support that make your problem better, such as support from family, friends, and others?
7. Are there any kinds of stresses that make your problem worse?
8. For you, what are the most important aspects of your background or identity?
9. Are there any aspects of your background or identity that make a difference to your problem?
10. Are there any aspects of your background or identity that are causing other concerns or difficulties for you?
11. What have you done on your own to cope with your problem?
12. In the past, what kinds of treatment, help, advice, or healing have you sought for your problem?
13. Has anything prevented you from getting the help you need?
14. What kinds of help do you think would be most useful to you at this time for your problem?
15. Are there other kinds of help that your family, friends, or other people have suggested would be helpful for you now?
16. Have you been concerned about this and is there anything that we can do to provide you with the care you need?

Write up the CFI and ask for feedback. What was done well? What could be improved? What did you learn that will assist you in your future social work practice?

Exercise 7.26: ISP

With a peer, choose a film to watch that depicts an individual with a special need. Examples could be *Forrest Gump, Rainman, Of Mice and Men,* or *I Am Sam.* Complete an ISP for the character, using the list on page 101. Share the ISP with your peer and ask for feedback. What was done well? What could be improved? What did you learn that will assist you in your future social work practice?

Exercise 7.27: IEP

1. Go to your favorite search engine and type in "sample IEP."
2. Select a sample to critically analyze. What do you think was done well? What could be improved? Would you be proud to have your name at the bottom of it? Why or why not?
3. Go back to your search engine and select another sample to review. How does it compare with the first sample you reviewed? Which one was better, in your opinion? Why?
4. What did you learn that will assist you in your future social work practice?

Exercise 7.28: More on IEPs

If you believe you will be working closely with IEPs in your career, go to http:// sped.dpi.wi.gov/files/sped/pdf/iepguide.pdf for additional information on writing IEPs. Review the material and the case examples that begin on page 24 of the file. Answer the following questions:

1. What are the general steps involved in writing an IEP?
2. Which case example do you think is done best? Why?
3. What do you see as challenges to writing and updating IEPs?
4. What is the importance of client strengths in writing and updating IEPs?
5. What did you learn that will assist you in your future social work practice?

Exercise 7.29: Community Asset Mapping Exercise

Go to your favorite search engine and type in "community asset mapping workbook." Select a site that provides you with a workbook on how to complete an asset map. Select a community issue with which you are familiar and would like to see changed. If you are unable to do so, use a community from a recent movie or book that has exhibited a problem of some sort. Complete the worksheet for your selected community and share it with a peer. Ask for feedback. What did you learn about asset mapping? About yourself? In what ways might you use this in practice?

Exercise 7.30: Force Field Analysis Exercise

In your favorite search engine, type in "force field analysis examples" and select the "image" option. Select one example that looks interesting to you and review it. With a peer who has selected a different image, discuss the following items:

1. What made you select the image you did? What about it appealed to you?
2. In comparing the image you selected with that of your peer, discuss how the analyses differ. How are they similar? Would you find either one useful?
3. Select a community with which you both are familiar. It can be a real community where you reside, one that has recently been in the news, or a fictional one. Using one of the images as a model, conduct a force field analysis.
4. What did you learn? How would you use this technique in your practice? In what ways is it helpful? Not helpful?

ANSWER KEY

Exercise 7.7

Numbers 1, 4, 8, 9, and 10 are objectives. The rest are goals.

CHAPTER 8

Documenting Client Progress

Knowing how much—and how little—to document can be challenging for a social worker. "You cannot record all you observe, say, or hear, and so you must select" (Zuckerman, 2008, p. 21). Knowing what to select requires the ability to sift through a large amount of information and decide what material is necessary. "The practical challenge of clinical documentation is to record a maximum amount of information in a minimum amount of time" (Freedheim & Shapiro, 1999, p. 19).

This chapter covers the most common formats used when recording client progress; some are highly structured and others are not. Progress notes, contact logs, termination summaries, and follow-up notes can take many different forms, depending on the needs of the agency and the clients who are served. Experience in working with a variety of formats is provided in the exercises found at the end of the chapter.

PURPOSE OF PROGRESS NOTES

Progress notes provide the substance of a social work case record. Even historically, this has been true, as evidenced by Sheffield (1920): "This is the detailed story of the client's situation, the evidence that his need lies in this or that direction, and the account of the treatment given to meet his needs" (p. 75). In progress notes, the worker accurately details what occurred during service provision. Progress notes contain information about how the client is or is not progressing on established goals and objectives in the service plan. Also called "interim notes," their purpose is to demonstrate advances accomplished in the work.

Notes typically include details about sessions and telephone calls with the client and notations of contacts made regarding the client and his or her situation. Social workers have had little guidance in writing these notes, according to Kagle and Kopels (2008), who suggested that the following information should be included in progress notes (p. 74):

- New information about the client's needs
- The social worker's assessment of the status of the client's needs

- Steps taken toward completion of or movement away from the service plan
- Service activities
- Assessments of the purpose, goals, plan, process, and progress of service
- Changes in the purpose, goals, or service plan.

In addition, the client's viewpoints and choices should be noted (Kagle, 2002). The client's involvement in the decision-making process should be clearly stated in the written record.

FREQUENCY OF PROGRESS NOTES

The frequency with which progress notes are written varies from setting to setting and may depend on agency policy. Wilson (1980) suggested that the progress of the case should determine the frequency of writing notes: "More frequent entries are indicated during periods of intense activity in any given case. . . . If there are prolonged periods with no activity on a given case, brief notes should be made from time to time" (p. 110).

Kagle and Kopels (2008) said that in the ideal situation, "workers would update the record immediately after each service contact; however, in most agency settings, such an expectation would be unrealistic." (p. 76). A social worker's day usually involves multitasking to provide services for several clients quickly and without breaks. Given this reality, Kagle and Kopels developed these guidelines regarding how often one should document:

- Critical incidents should be documented within 24 hours.
- Significant changes in client needs should be documented as soon as possible, within three days at the latest.
- Indicators of progress toward service goals should be regularly noted following every third service contact.
- Contacts with other service providers regarding active cases should be recorded weekly.
- Progress notes should be updated regularly, following every third service contact or at least monthly.
- Notes should be updated before any planned social worker absence, case transfer, release of information, or case review. (Kagle & Kopels, 2008, p. 76)

GENERAL CONSIDERATIONS

Regardless of a progress note's format style or length, several considerations should be kept in mind when writing about a case.

All notes begin with the full date and the fact that the note is written by a social worker and end with a signature. If the signature is not legible, the name should be printed beneath it.

Note specific dates and times rather than relative times (Wilson, 1980). For example, instead of writing "the client will be in next week at the same time," it is better to write "the client's next appointment is June 3 at 9:00 a.m."

Be as succinct as possible while stating what is important. "Even if the material is the best ever done in the history of social work practice, who is going to have time to read it if it is twenty single-spaced typewritten pages?" (Wilson, 1980, p. 113). Quality is more important than quantity—whether the note contains required and pertinent information is more important than its length. Richmond (1925) wrote that "the most voluminous record is not always the most revealing, but the meager record in which significant actions and reactions are slurred over . . . is the worst of all" (p. 216).

Do not repeat information that has been stated elsewhere, unless it is important to a change that has occurred (Wilson, 1980).

Choose language responsibly. Provide precise, objective statements with descriptive examples rather than picturesque, subjective opinions (Sheffield, 1920; Wilson, 1980). For example, "the client had a difficult time fitting in the chair" is better than "the client is very fat and nearly broke the chair."

Avoid abbreviations that are not readily understood and symbols or jargon that may obscure the note's meaning (Wilson, 1980).

Write all notes in third person, using the phrase "this social worker" or "the worker" rather than "I" or "me."

In handwritten notes, a line should be drawn through any blank spaces that remain after the entry has been completed. This prevents anyone from adding to a note at a later time or tampering with the official record.

PROGRESS NOTE FORMATS

Case notes, which are often called "progress notes," have different formats in different agencies. Those unfamiliar with a case note format often have the most trouble knowing how much to write and what to include. This skill improves with practice, and practice exercises are included at the end of this chapter. The most common progress note formats are reviewed below.

Summary or Narrative Format

Probably the most common format, this is written in paragraphs. It does not repeat word-for-word what occurred but summarizes the content of the intervention. A typical summary note looks like this:

3/5/2015 Social Work Note

The client and this worker met today as scheduled. Her journal was reviewed and she reported having a "pretty good week, all things considered." She detailed continuing problems with her ability to focus on herself, but was pleased at being able to accomplish her goal for the week, which was to concentrate on ways of improving her relationship with her sister. "I feel good about our phone call," she reported, and discussed plans to meet her sister for lunch this weekend. Encouragement was provided to the client. This worker is impressed with the client's positive focus, but concerns were voiced about the client's possible reactions if the lunch does not go as hoped. This social worker reviewed options for continuing her involvement with a peer mentor, but no decisions were made. Plans are to meet again on 3/12 at 10:15 a.m. In the meantime, the client will continue her journaling and will make a decision related to the peer mentor. [Name], LSW

The reader of a good summary note should have a sense of what took place during the contact. Wilson (1980) recommended that the following information be included in a summary note: the contact's purpose, what occurred during the contact, any problem areas noted by the worker, an assessment of the situation, and plans for further intervention. Content will vary depending on the nature of the contact. For example, the following case note does not contain all of the above elements but is still considered complete:

3/5/2015 Social Work Note

This worker was contacted by the client's assigned peer mentor. The mentor strongly believes that it is important for her mentoring relationship with the client to continue. Although many improvements have been noted, there is still work to be done, she feels. This worker committed to sharing with the client the reasons that continuation is desirable. [Name], LSW

Structured Formats—Alphabet Soup

Some agencies prefer that case notes follow a formal structure. Structured notes can be easier to read. For example, if a member of a multidisciplinary team wishes to know what the social worker is planning to do next, he or she needs only to read that section of the note. There are several common structured formats, each designated by an acronym. The most common are SOAP, SOAPIE, SOAPG, SOAIGP, and DAP. PIG, GAAP, TIPP, SOAPIER, and CREW are also found in the literature. All are defined below.

Like summary notes, structured notes begin with the date and conclude with the writer's signature and credentials. The acronym is used in the note itself to label the different categories for which information is given. Not all categories need to be addressed in each note (Kagle & Kopels, 2008). For example, a note written in the SOAP format might contain entries only under O and P and still be considered complete.

SOAP. This format, most frequently used in medical settings, includes the following elements (Borcherding, 2000; Sheafor & Horejsi, 2012):

> **S—Subjective information:** This describes how the client feels or what he or she thinks about the situation. It is written from the client's

perspective and should include a statement that the client has made about his or her situation. Direct quotes are commonly found here.

O—Objective information: This describes facts that have been directly observed by professionals or indicated by testing or other data. This information can be verified and is based on the facts of the situation.

A—Assessment: This states the social worker's professional conclusions, drawn from the subjective and objective information.

P—Plan: This indicates what the worker and client will do next and when the next contact is scheduled.

The following example of an SOAP note describes the same contact that was described in the summary note above. Notice that the content of the two notes is very similar but organized in a different fashion.

3/5/2015 Social Work Note

S: The client reported having a "pretty good week, all things considered." She detailed continuing problems with her ability to focus on herself, but was pleased at being able to accomplish her goal for the week, which was to concentrate on ways of improving her relationship with her sister. "I feel good about our phone call," she reported.

O: The client and this worker met today as scheduled. Her journal was reviewed and plans were discussed to meet her sister for lunch this weekend. Encouragement was provided to the client. This social worker reviewed options for continuing her involvement with a peer mentor, but no decisions were made.

A: This worker is impressed with the client's positive focus, but concerns were voiced about possible client reactions if the lunch does not go as she hopes.

P: This worker and client will next meet on 3/12 at 10:15 a.m. In the meantime, the client will continue her journaling, meet with her sister, and make a decision about the peer mentor. [Name], LSW

Although the SOAP note is a common format, its critics have argued that it discredits client information by labeling it subjective and that it does not give room to describe goals and impressions (Kagle & Kopels, 2008). It has also been criticized as being biased in that the worker selects the problem to be addressed, marginalizing the client's viewpoint (Tebb, 1991). For these reasons, one occasionally finds variations of SOAP, keeping the four categories described above but adding, for example, goals (SOAPG) or interventions and evaluation (SOAPIE). SOAPIER adds revision of the intervention plan to SOAPIE.

SOAIGP. This suggested alternative to SOAP provides more detail to the report (Kagle & Kopels, 2008). SOAIGP includes the following elements:

S—Supplementary database information: This is provided by the client and significant other(s).

O—Observations: These are provided by the social worker, other agency staff, and other service providers.

A—Activities with and on behalf of the client: These may include summaries of client tasks, social worker tasks, and events or topics covered in helping sessions.

I—Impressions and assessment of the social worker: Tentative impressions and hypotheses may be stated here, from the perspective of the social worker.

G—Goals: In addition to goals that are being worked on, progress being made on goals and any necessary revisions to goals can be noted here.

P—Plans for the next actions by the worker and client: This is similar to the P section in the SOAP format. Additional plans for future actions may be noted as well. (Cournoyer, 2011; Kagle & Kopels, 2008)

Whereas some categories are expanded from the SOAP format, others remain similar. A key feature of SOAIGP is that it recognizes the importance of goals in the helping relationship. An example of an SOAIGP note follows:

3/5/2015 Social Work Note

S: The client and this worker met today as scheduled. Her journal was reviewed, and plans were discussed to meet her sister for lunch this weekend. The client reported having a "pretty good week, all things considered." She shared her completed journal for the week with this worker. She detailed continuing problems with her ability to focus on herself, but was pleased at being able to accomplish her goal for the week, which was to concentrate on ways of improving her relationship with her sister. "I feel good about our phone call," she reported.

O: The client was very animated today; she smiled and laughed appropriately with this worker.

A: The session was spent reviewing the journal and discussing the client's upcoming meeting with her sister. Several calls were made to locate more reliable transportation services, but because of budget cuts, none are available to the client at this time. This social worker reviewed options for continuing the client's involvement with a peer mentor, but no decisions were made.

I: Encouragement was provided to the client. This worker is impressed with the client's positive focus, but concerns were voiced about possible client reactions if the lunch does not go as she hopes.

G: The goal remains for the client to increase her self-esteem and learn better ways of coping with her mental health issues.

P: This worker and the client will next meet on 3/12 at 10:15 a.m. In the meantime, the client will continue her journaling, meet with her sister, and make a decision about the peer mentor. [Name], LSW

The SOAIGP format is more complicated than formats with fewer headings. Another challenge is that those familiar with SOAP may become confused about the differences between the two formats.

DAP. The shorter DAP format (Sheafor & Horejsi, 2012) collapses the SOAP format into three categories. D (data) combines information found in SOAP's subjective and objective categories, whereas the A (assessment) and P (plan) sections are the same as in a SOAP note. A sample DAP note follows.

3/5/2015 Social Work Note

D: The client and this worker met today as scheduled. Her journal was reviewed and plans were discussed to meet her sister for lunch this weekend. The client reported having a "pretty good week, all things considered." She detailed continuing problems with her ability to focus on herself, but was pleased at being able to accomplish her goal for the week, which was to concentrate on ways of improving her relationship with her sister. "I feel good about our phone call," she reported. Encouragement was provided to the client. This social worker reviewed options for continuing her involvement with a peer mentor, but no decisions were made.

A: This worker is impressed with the client's positive focus, but concerns were voiced about possible client reactions if the lunch does not go as she hopes.

P: This worker and the client will next meet on 3/12 at 10:15 a.m. In the meantime, the client will continue her journaling, meet with her sister, and make a decision about the peer mentor. [Name], LSW

According to Schmelter (2012), traditional SOAP and DAP notes are being replaced by the GIRPP format (goals, interventions, response, progress, plan). An example of a GIRPP note follows:

3/6/15 Social Work Note

G: Today's session focused on the goal of improving the client's socialization skills.

I: The social worker suggested ways to approach a colleague to have lunch, and the client participated in a behavioral rehearsal to practice this.

R: The client stated that she felt ready to approach her peer.

P: The client is making progress in her level of perceived readiness and for the first time seemed confident about extending herself to her peer.

P: The client will approach her peer tomorrow and will keep note of her reactions while this is occurring. The social worker will see the client next week to follow up and discuss next steps. [Name], LSW

Additional Structured Format Options. Three additional structured formats, which this writer has not seen used in practice, have been suggested in the social work literature: PIG, CREW, and GAAP.

PIG is somewhat similar to DAP. P stands for problem and, like D (data) in the DAP format, contains both objective and subjective information. I stands for intervention and G for goal (Sheafor & Horejsi, 2012). Although simpler than SOAP or SOAIGP, its focus on problems is seen as a drawback.

CREW was proposed as a more client-centered and self-determining alternative to the SOAP note (Tebb, 1991), intended to increase collaboration between the social worker and client. CREW stands for contributors (factors that contribute to the need for change), restraints (barriers to change), enablers (factors that encourage change), and ways (in which change can be fostered). Although it highlights the change process, it is not recommended for use because it has a limited focus and does not address accountability issues (Kagle & Kopels, 2008).

GAAP has been tentatively proposed by Cournoyer (2011) as a goal-focused format. The acronym stands for goals (and objectives reflected in the contract), activities (and interventions carried out by the social worker, the client, or others), assessment (and evaluation efforts supporting goal attainment), and plans (for additional work to be accomplished). Cournoyer called it "preliminary" and "experimental" (p. 418).

Other Formats for Progress Notes

Three other formats for recording a client's progress are substantively different from those already covered. Each is unique and may be found in a variety of settings. They are the problem-oriented record, the person-oriented record, and the problem-oriented checklist.

Problem-Oriented Record. The problem-oriented record is a common format found in multidisciplinary health and mental health settings (Kagle & Kopels, 2008; Wilson, 1980). Its origins in medicine mean that some adaptations are required for this format to be used in social work. Weed (1968) suggested that it be composed of four sections:

1. **Database:** This includes the client's primary complaint, history, symptoms, and social information.
2. **Problem list:** This is a numbered list of all problems defined during data collection. It acts as an index to the record. New problems can be added to the list and numbered. As a problem changes, the changes are noted.
3. **Initial plans:** These correspond to the numbered problems.
4. **Progress notes:** These are cross-referenced to correspond with the problem list and are written in the SOAP format (Zuckerman, 2008). Also included in this section may be flow charts that document overall status or progress made and a discharge summary listing each problem and describing how issues were addressed (Kagle & Kopels, 2008, pp. 131–132).

If this format is to be adapted for use by social workers, Kagle and Kopels (2008) suggested that the database be expanded to include more details, an MSE, and findings of psychological testing. The problem list, they noted, should also include mental health diagnoses where appropriate and descriptions of problems with daily living.

Detractors have criticized this format's focus on problems rather than strengths. It is also not considered client centered (Kagle & Kopels, 2008; Wilson, 1980).

Person-Oriented Record. Given concerns that the problem-oriented record is not well suited for social work, the person-oriented approach was developed (Hartman & Wickey, 1978). Although it is based on the problem-oriented record, it emphasizes the treatment plan. It lists problems and strengths, along with goals to resolve the problems and plans for achieving the goals. The client, social worker, and team (if appropriate) together identify problems and strengths and set time frames for goal completion. Client input is sought when setting goals.

Problem-Oriented Checklist. Some agencies, in an attempt to help streamline documentation requirements, have developed problem-oriented checklists featuring a list of common issues that clients in that particular setting experience. They allow the social worker to date, check off, and sign a form rather than providing a handwritten narrative.

This method of recording is not new. As early as 1925, Richmond wrote in the journal *Family* about the problems associated with this type of documentation. She argued that narrative notes were preferable to checklists:

> Take some of the cases quite fully described in *What Is Social Case Work?* . . . What social worker could have found the way out of these difficult situations with the aid of a series of check marks? Or how could these marks have made the sequence of events clear to any one else? (Richmond, 1925, pp. 215–216)

Despite these concerns, checklists are found in some agencies, and they do substitute in some settings for routine note taking.

CONTACT LOGS

Many agencies require staff to record their activities on each client's case on a contact log. This can also be called a "tracking form," a "summary log," or an "action log," among other names. The purpose of this log is to provide a quick summary of what has occurred with a case. It is sometimes used for ensuring the quality of services or determining the amount of time spent on a case. In addition, it can enable a supervisor to quickly review what has occurred and in what time frame.

This sheet typically consists of a graph that may have codes associated with it. The example below uses simple coding to denote a variety of service activities. In this example, for every client contact, one line is completed on the tracking

Case Action Tracking Sheet

Client's name:		
Date opened:		
Date closed:		

Service code		Progress code
C = Client contact F = Family/significant other contact G = Group meeting A = Advocacy	R = Other agency contact S = Supervision O = Other	N = None F = Fair G = Good E = Excellent

Date	Service	Progress	Signature

form, and the social worker's signature is required for each entry. This method provides a means of quickly reviewing the status of an open case, and it can assist a worker in writing his or her case notes. Although the example given is rather basic, some coding schemes are a great deal more complex (Wilson, 1980). Their purpose, however, remains the same: to track in standardized fashion the social worker's activities related to a client's case.

An agency may maintain this data only for internal use, or it may be part of a computerized database that assesses trends and tracks cases across settings or jurisdictions.

PERIODIC SERVICE REVIEWS

Case files are formally reviewed at different intervals, depending on the type of agency and its requirements. For example, the file of an adolescent client receiving inpatient psychiatric services may be reviewed every 30 days to determine if progress is being made and services should continue, whereas an outpatient client's file may be reviewed every six months for the same purpose. Reviews may be required by agency policy, public policy, the social worker, or a supervisor seeking insight into a problematic situation (Kagle & Kopels, 2008). In addition to the social worker, supervisor, or team working with the client, others may be involved in the review. Practitioners, administrators, other involved providers, the client, and the client's family or friends may participate. It has been suggested that periodic review include the following (Kagle & Kopels, 2008, p. 84):

- The date, names of review participants, and subjects addressed
- A review of service activities and movement
- Recommendations for changes in the assessment of the client's needs
- The level of consensus among participants
- Any other recommendations or plans.

Periodic summaries are considered part of the client's official record and are maintained with the file. Wilson (1980) suggested the following guidelines be kept in mind when writing periodic summaries:

- Review existing entries to avoid unnecessary repetition and to determine what needs to be said that has not been said, what has changed, and what has been recorded for all goals and plans.
- Clearly state sources of information, making it obvious to the reader who the main contacts have been.
- Make sure important case details are clearly expressed. If any information is not provided, explain why.

The following example of a summary completed three months after services were initiated is written in the same style as a narrative note and is clearly labeled as a periodic review note.

2/12/2015 Quarterly Summary

The client was referred for services to this program three months ago by her physician. The client voluntarily entered the program, as she stated she realized that she was going to "end up dead" unless she got help for her substance abuse. In that time, an assessment was completed and the client began a comprehensive treatment program. Goals included functioning independently, living a drug- and alcohol-free life, seeking and gaining employment, and reuniting with her three-year-old child.

The client has high blood pressure and is obese but has no other health problems. This social worker has met with the client three times weekly for individual sessions and once weekly with the client and her mother, who is presently caring for the client's daughter. In addition, this worker has observed the client in a weekly group session for which the worker is a cofacilitator.

The client has made good progress on her goals, in that she has remained free of substance abuse, updated her résumé with a job coach, applied for admission to community college in the fall, and successfully had three supervised visits with her child. Appropriate group social skills have been difficult for the client, as she exhibits impatience with her peers, which she realizes comes across as accusatory and blaming. An added goal is to reduce her weight by 50 pounds, in an attempt to improve her self-image.

This worker has found the client to be motivated but somewhat unrealistic about her ability to parent an active three-year-old child. She admits to not having the energy to deal with her daughter in addition to working on her other issues. Her relationship with her mother has been aggravated by disagreement over parenting styles. This is also related to her desire to lose weight. The plan at this time is to continue the program, with the addition of goals as noted above. No discharge date has been set at this point. [Name], LSW

TERMINATION SUMMARIES

Also called "closing summaries," these notes are completed at the time the case is closed. A well-written termination summary provides an overview of the services provided and activities undertaken. It should serve as a comprehensive overview for future social workers if the case needs to be reopened or for external agencies that request it (Wilson, 1980). Wilson (1980) referred to it as "the single most important document in a case record once it has been closed" (p. 120).

Kagle and Kopels (2008) suggested that a termination summary should include a brief description and analysis of the client's situation from the time of case opening to closure, reasons for terminating services, a review of the purpose of intervention and the goals and activities undertaken, an analysis of the outcomes of services provided, any referrals or plans for further intervention, and follow-up plans if indicated. Wilson (1980) added that a brief description of any unresolved issues is also warranted. Beginning and ending dates of service and the reason(s) contact was initiated have also been suggested for inclusion. Cournoyer (2011) has suggested organizing the closing summary by using the following headings: process and issues, evaluation, continuing goals, current assessment, and ending process (pp. 431–432).

The document must be signed, clearly labeled, and dated by the social worker writing it. An example of a termination summary follows.

5/11/2015 Termination Summary

This 42-year-old client has been seen by this worker since 2/22/2015. She was referred by her physician for stress management. A single parent, she is the primary caregiver for her 15-year-old daughter and her 70-year-old mother and also works full-time. An assessment revealed that her mother has been recently diagnosed with Alzheimer's disease and requires an increasing amount of attention. She also expressed worry about her daughter, who is now six months pregnant.

Mutual goals for services included getting educated about her mother's medical situation, working through her feelings regarding her daughter's pregnancy, and managing her responsibilities in a way that leaves room for self-care. Weekly intervention included active listening, information and referral regarding the daughter's pregnancy options, and assistance with exploring assisted-living settings for her mother.

Last month, the client's mother was successfully moved into a unit that is appropriate for her care, and she seems to be adjusting well. The client's daughter is planning on keeping her child, and the client has come to terms with that decision. The client is now able to demonstrate several techniques that will assist her in managing her stress and appears more focused on healthy living habits than she had been. The client was assured that the case could be reopened if necessary in the future. It is this worker's opinion that although issues remain for the client, she now has better ways of coping. [Name], LSW

FOLLOW-UP NOTES

Depending on the agency setting, a social worker may be required to follow up on a client after he or she has formally terminated active services (Kagle, 1984a). Follow-up may occur after an agency-designated period of time or after an important event in the client's life that was a central focus of services. For example, a hospice social worker may routinely follow up with family members of a deceased patient one month, three months, and one year from the date of the loved one's death. In such cases, a note should be written detailing the date of the contact, with whom contact was made, how the former client or contact person presented, and any concerns that were noted or additional referrals that were made. Follow-up notes are typically written in a narrative format and, like any progress note, contain a label, a full date, and a complete signature. An example follows.

1/4/2015 Follow-up Note

This worker contacted the former client by phone to check on continuing progress. The client indicated he was well and "feeling better about life every day." Problems with transportation to Alcoholics Anonymous meetings were noted, and suggestions were made for access of the regional bus system. The client was encouraged to recontact the agency if his needs changed. [Name], LSW

RECORDS OF GROUP SESSIONS

Documenting what transpires in a group session often poses a challenge for social workers. As with any type of social work service, relying on memories of what occurred in a group session is not considered acceptable (Doel, 2006). Although agency policies vary, it is generally not feasible to record a note in each participant's individual case file after every group meeting (Wilson, 1980). What is typically acceptable is keeping a separate record for each group and adding notes to the individual files at intervals or when something that is unusual or affects a client in an atypical way occurs at a group event. For example, a group session may be routine for most members, but one individual may experience a breakthrough in treatment. The social worker would document what occurred in both the group folder and that client's individual file.

The group file is considered a legal document, as is an individual file. A group file typically includes a face sheet that states the group's purpose; names of initial members; meeting logistics, such as frequency, location, and time of meetings; first and last meeting dates; and techniques the group facilitator(s) may use (Wilson, 1980). For each group meeting, a session summary sheet should be completed. Doel (2006) referred to this summary as a snapshot that "builds into an album of the group's progress" (p. 158). Kagle and Kopels (2008) suggested that this sheet should contain the date, facilitator name(s), session number and length, and names of those present. A summary of what happened in the session, interventions used, specific problems or issues that arose, and plans for future group activity are also included.

Kagle and Kopels (2008) further suggested that a diagram of the group's interactions may be helpful. A drawing of the group's seating chart and a key that depicts the types of communication among members can be easily sketched. Doel (2006) added that it may be helpful for the group facilitators to note the general atmosphere of the session, the main contributions of each facilitator, and what each facilitator learned from the session. This self-reflection can be an important component of a social worker's personal growth as a group facilitator.

Wilson (1980) suggested that a termination summary containing an overview of main topics discussed, goals accomplished, progress made, and reasons for the group's termination be completed at the time of the group's closure.

The group summary format can also be used when documenting family sessions.

Focus Group Reports

A focus group is a commonly used tool in group work or in community organization settings, useful when discussing or evaluating a specific issue. "Such groups are often established to acquire information and generate ideas that would not be as accessible through individual interviews" (Barker, 2014, p. 164). Although a great deal of information is typically obtained in a focus group, the report need not be lengthy. The University of Idaho Park Studies Unit's (2009) format for writing a focus group report shown below highlights the importance of including reasons why the focus group was convened, how evaluation occurred, and what was discovered.

WHY did we evaluate?
1. Cover page: title, date, names of people involved in the study
2. Executive summary: a brief summary of findings
3. Introduction: a short description of why the focus group was conducted. This can be thought of as guiding specific questions about what the group or its conveners hoped to learn. Examples are "Are

clients satisfied with services?" or "Does the community need a different approach to ensure resident safety?"

HOW did we evaluate?
4. Description of methods: a description of how the study was conducted, including the number of focus groups held, date and time held, number of participants, recruitment procedures, types of participants, where the groups were held, and special circumstances that may have affected the groups.

WHAT did we find out?
5. Results: For each key question, list the key points, a summary, and a few representative comments from participants.
6. Conclusion and interpretation: a description of how the results of the study help answer questions about the guiding questions. An interpretation of what the findings mean and what should happen next can be helpful to include.

Community Organizing Reports

It is just as important to record progress made in community organizing efforts as it is to document other types of social work services in writing. Gold and Simon (2002) explained, however, that the work of community organizers is often invisible and takes place behind the scenes. With so many demands on their time, organizers often lack the ability to systematically record their own work process. This is not acceptable practice, just as it is not acceptable practice to fail to record services delivered to individual clients. Imagine what would be helpful for the next social worker involved in the community organizing project to know, if all he or she had were records on which to rely. It may also be helpful to ask, "What would I want to know about if I were newly assigned to this project?"

Keeping track of activities related to the organizing or advocacy should be done in an organized, coherent fashion, whether the work is being conducted online or in person. A community organizing report should be as clear as a client's case file. Notes about assessment, progress, actions taken, publicity, and meetings are all important. Starting from scratch with macro-level efforts may be unnecessary and duplicative, if good records exist.

Minimally, records should contain an overview of the project; an assessment of the project, issue, or community; pertinent research regarding the topic; notes from organizational meetings; records of contacts with key leaders or community groups; notes of strategy sessions; date-stamped publicity efforts; copies of correspondence used to communicate with constituents; any diagrams or visual aids used to illustrate the issue; plans for future action; and any other notes that would be helpful in understanding the situation. Regarding diagrams, computer programs are available to assist with mapping community relationships. An online search for "mapping software community relationships" or "power mapping" will return links to free or inexpensive software that can be used to create visual diagrams.

SUMMARY AND EXERCISES

A wide range of styles and formats exist to document clients' progress. It is important to be familiar with the most common formats and to understand the various acronyms used to document progress notes. The note format may vary, but the content of a high-quality note remains essentially the same. Practice and experience will help the social worker to develop the skill of writing progress notes.

The following exercises provide practice with a variety of reporting formats. As in other chapters, you will get the best results if you work with a peer, comparing your work and offering each other feedback.

Exercise 8.1: Avoiding Excessive Detail

Critically analyze each note below, then rewrite as necessary. Use the comments after note 1 as an example.

Note 1

The client left a message over the weekend sometime, asking me to call him as soon as I could. He knows very well that I don't work on weekends, yet he wanted me to call him. So this morning I picked up the phone but there was no answer and his answering machine didn't pick up either. Not that I would leave a message but still. I'm wondering if he's okay, given how desperate he sounded in his message. I have an appointment with him tomorrow but I'll try calling again later after my group session is over.

Critical Analysis: Too much detail, irrelevant information, not written from third-person perspective, no clear plan.

Revision: 6/4/2015. The client left a message on this worker's voice mail on 6/2/2015. Upon returning from the weekend, this worker called the client back, but there was no answer. The plan is to try again later today. The client's next appointment is scheduled for 6/5/2015.

Note 2

The client's daughter contacted me to say that she thought her mom wasn't adjusting very well to the nursing home. She said her mom's very confused and has started wandering, which she didn't do before in her assisted-living facility. The daughter also said that her sister isn't happy with the situation and is threatening to remove mom from our facility. I indicated that it had only been two days and that it was pretty normal that there would be a period of adjustment for everyone. I also asked what the deal was with the sister, who isn't really all that involved, according to my case notes. The care here is better than good, but I didn't want to seem defensive with the daughter. I told her I'd look into how her mom was doing and get back with her as soon as I could, which won't be until tomorrow probably.

Note 3

The group got started late and it was a bad situation, because everyone was blaming the staff for holding things up. It wasn't the staff's fault and I knew it but couldn't share the real reason because of client confidentiality. Finally, everyone got off of that and onto today's topic, which was how family visitations are going for everyone. It's always amazing how much everyone knows in such a confidential setting! Anyway, it's not going well for C, mostly because of her inability to see that her reactions escalate every time her dad shows up. The group members pointed this out to her, which was very gratifying to see, and C reacted angrily. She would have left but didn't want to lose her privileges like she did last time.

Exercise 8.2: Elements of Structured Notes

For each of the following statements, determine under which section of a SOAP note it most logically belongs. Answers can be found at the end of the chapter.

1. The client is angry at herself for having missed her last appointment.
2. This worker is impressed that the client has been able to remain motivated despite her chaotic week.
3. The next appointment has been set for 3/16/2015.
4. The client stated, "I feel numb," when asked about her reaction to her dog's accidental death.
5. The client and significant other attended the first meeting with the family strengths support group last week.
6. The plans that were made last week were not followed up on because the client's car broke down.
7. This social worker researched housing options for the client but, because of his income restrictions, was not successful in locating any.
8. "What do I care, anyway?" the client responded when asked about her friend's comments.
9. Following the client's discharge, arrangements will be made for home health care services.
10. This worker believes that termination is appropriate at this time.

Read the following statements and determine under which section of an SOAIGP note each most logically belongs. Answers may be found at the end of the chapter.

11. The secretary noted that the client arrived for her appointment in tears.
12. The client's objective of applying for program assistance, as a means of achieving some independence, has been met.
13. This social worker is hesitant to believe that the client has turned a corner, despite her insistence that she has.

14. Educational materials were collected and provided to the client by this worker.
15. The client's grandmother indicated that the client failed to meet her previously agreed-upon curfew hours five times last week.
16. The client hopes to tell her parents about her pregnancy tomorrow morning and will invite them to meet with her and this worker in the afternoon.
17. The client stated, "I know I'm dying, but I want to enjoy the time I have left."
18. The behavioral rehearsal technique was used to demonstrate how the conversation with her brother might go.
19. The client seemed to respond very positively to the relaxation techniques.
20. This social worker shared a list of community resources with the client.

Exercise 8.3: Using Different Note Formats

Organize the following notes about a session into a summary note, a SOAP note, and an SOAIGP note.

> The session with the couple occurred today. Next appointment is in one week at 3:30 p.m. They wish to explore pros and cons of adoption. She wants a baby and he wants her to be happy. They can afford it financially. He would adopt an older child, but she wants a newborn. Encouraged her to consider older child. Artificial insemination has not been successful. They've been together for six years. Her family is supportive but he is estranged from his family. History of substance abuse in his family. He would care for the child, as he doesn't work. She works full-time at a well-paying job. He lost his job in the latest downsizing at the local factory. Encouraged them to write down questions that come up between sessions. Emotionally they both seem stable and devoted to each other. Gave them papers to fill out that will start the process. Explained details of adopting through this agency and what to expect. Answered a lot of questions.

Which format do you prefer? Which style was easiest to write? Most difficult? Why?

Exercise 8.4: Rewriting a Poorly Written Summary Note

Review the following poorly written summary note about a session. Rewrite the note into an improved summary note, a SOAP note, and an SOAIGP note.

> 5/10/2015. I met with the client after she had canceled her last two appts. I let her know that this is a problem. She was apologetic and said she would try harder to get up in the mornings. I explained that if it were important enough to her, she would get up. How will she ever be able to

get her son back? I offered her a later appointment, but am unsure if that was a good idea. She is unmotivated and obesely overweight, weighing at least 350 lbs. Her lack of motivation results in not being able to get up in the morning, not caring if she made our appointment. To get down to business, she said she wants to get her child back from us and is willing to do what it takes to be "a better parent." I asked her what that meant to her and she said "you know, taking better care of my son." She shows very little insight. I laid out for her what would happen when we next went to court, and how I would be required to report that she hasn't made very much progress on her goals: She hasn't been to parenting classes, she missed her appts with me, she was late for her one visitation with her son. My professional assessment is that he's better off in foster care right now, despite the fact that the goal is to preserve her family. I gave her a list of appointments that she HAS to make or else. She verbalized understanding. Our next appt is set for 5/13/2015, which will give me time to look into a few things for her.

Exercise 8.5: Rewriting a Note with Too Much Detail

Review the following note and answer the questions at the end.

6/30/2015. The client arrived at 9:02 a.m. and entered my office. He took a seat in the chair facing my desk. He looked tired and had big circles around his eyes. His eyes were puffy and red. I asked him how he was doing and he shook his head, unable to speak for a few seconds. I gave him a minute to pull himself together because he looked pretty embarrassed about tearing up. He finally said, "I can't believe she's left me." I didn't push him but let him take his time in telling me what had happened. Apparently his wife of 10 years packed up the day before, took the two kids and the dog, and left. He says he didn't see it coming. So I explained to him that we needed to do an assessment and I was going to be asking him a lot of questions, to better understand his situation and how to help. He was okay with that. So I asked him to start by telling me about himself, just to get him to open up a bit. He did open up, too, and I was impressed that he was able to do so, given how upset he was. I learned a lot about his family and his marriage, which he considered a good one up until the past six months or so. He seems angry with himself for not being a better husband, but he is not angry with his wife. He had only good things to say about her and about their relationship. I'll put all of this in my assessment report so it will be easier and more organized to follow. I assessed his supports and he seems to be somewhat of a loner. He agreed to return in three days to complete the assessment and start to set goals for our work together.

What do you like about this note? What could be improved? Rewrite this note using the summary format. Then rewrite using the SOAP format.

Exercise 8.6: More Practice with Note Formats (I)

Review the note you wrote for exercise 3.3 in chapter 3, in which you summarized a note about your day. Rewrite it as a summary note on the basis of what you have learned since then.

Next, write the same note as a structured note. How are the two notes different? Which format do you prefer? What have you learned from this exercise?

Exercise 8.7: More Practice with Note Formats (II)

Review the note you wrote about a television interview for exercise 3.4 in chapter 3. Rewrite it in summary format on the basis of what you have learned since then.

Now, write the same note as an SOAIGP structured note. How are the two notes different? Which format do you prefer? What have you learned from this exercise?

Exercise 8.8: Practice with a YouTube Interview

A number of social work interviews have been posted to the Web site http://www.youtube.com. Use search words "social work interview." Choose one and watch it.

Write a summary note describing what you saw, using today's date. Next, write it as an SOAP note. How are the two notes different? Which format do you prefer? What have you learned from this exercise?

Exercise 8.9: Practice with GIRPP

Write a GIRPP note for the following scenario:

> A new client is referred to you by a pastor from a nearby church. The pastor is concerned about the client's homelessness. The client says she is not homeless, only between residences right now. She was a victim of domestic violence but has no other place to go right now, until a friend moves into a new apartment where there will be room for her, too. She hopes this will be within the month. In the meantime, the client is living in her car, which she parks in the church parking lot. She is satisfied with this arrangement but understands some members of the congregation are unhappy. She suggests that she can move her car to another location when church services are scheduled and agrees to visit a nearby shelter that may be able to assist her. You offer to set up an appointment at the shelter for her visit and provide her with a small food voucher. She agrees to check in with you tomorrow.

Compare your note with that of a peer who has also done this exercise. What have you learned? Do you prefer GIRPP over the other types of notes? Why or why not?

Exercise 8.10: Problem-Oriented Checklist

A client comes to see you at the agency in which you are employed. The client, Snow White, has been caring for seven difficult men. She asks for help in thinking through her life goals and in dealing with her current living situation. You conduct an assessment. Your agency also requires a problem-oriented checklist. Complete the following checklist. What do you think of this style of documenting a session with a client?

Problem-Oriented Checklist

Client's name:		Case number:	
Today's date:		Date case opened:	

Referral source:		
❏ self	❏ other agency	❏ medical personnel
❏ family member	❏ court or legal entity	❏ clergy person
❏ friend	❏ school	❏ other:

Services provided this session (check all that apply):	
❏ information and referral	❏ referral to internal services
❏ assessment	❏ referral to other agencies
❏ individual counseling	❏ suggestion for medical evaluation
❏ couples counseling	❏ housing resources shared
❏ family counseling	❏ safety assessment completed
❏ financial planning	❏ client empowerment
❏ crisis intervention	❏ educational assistance
❏ advocacy	❏ other:

Services planned for future sessions (check all that apply):	
❏ information and referral	❏ referral to internal services
❏ assessment	❏ referral to other agencies
❏ individual counseling	❏ suggestion for medical evaluation
❏ couples counseling	❏ sharing housing resources
❏ family counseling	❏ completing safety assessment
❏ financial planning	❏ client empowerment
❏ crisis intervention	❏ educational assistance
❏ advocacy	❏ other:

Exercise 8.11: Contact Log

Read the case notes below and use the information to complete a case action tracking sheet.

> 4/12/2015. The client appeared very anxious this morning as she presented herself for the first appointment with this worker. She described her living situation as "very chaotic." She lives with seven small men and performs all of their household chores. She appears visibly frightened of her stepmother, who does not know where she is living. Assessment information was gathered and agency policy was explained. The client verbalized understanding. The next appointment was set for 4/15 at 10:30 a.m., and goals and plans will be discussed in detail then. [Name], LSW

> 4/15/2015. The client seemed much calmer today and indicated that she is feeling better. She has set up a schedule of housework and has requested assistance with it from her housemates. A safety plan was discussed in detail because of the continuing fear she exhibits related to her stepmother. Her housemates are reportedly very protective of her and understand her fears. The next appointment is scheduled for 4/20 at 10:30 a.m. [Name], LSW

> 4/20/2015. The client and this worker met for 15 minutes, as the client stated she could not stay longer. "I'm too anxious today to sit and talk. I have to keep moving." This worker expressed concern for her safety and suggested a medical referral. The client refused but agreed to return on 4/21 at 2:15 p.m. [Name], LSW

> 4/21/2015. The client did not show for her appointment. Telephone calls were unsuccessful in reaching her. This worker discussed her concerns with her supervisor. During the meeting with the supervisor, the client called the worker. The client indicated that she cannot sleep, eat, or function because of her overwhelming fears. She admitted to thoughts of "ending it all." She agreed to come to the agency, where she was accompanied by this worker for psychiatric inpatient assessment. She was admitted to the treatment unit and is under suicidal precautions. [Name], LSW

Exercise 8.12: Periodic Evaluation

Read the following 30-day evaluation summary completed by an inpatient psychiatric social worker.

5/21/2015. 30-Day Evaluation—Snow White

The client was admitted to the inpatient program on 4/21/2015 for suicidal ideation. She was referred for treatment by her outpatient social worker, who was pretty concerned about her and has been to see her a few times since she's been here and who will continue to see her after she's discharged from our program, although no discharge date has been set yet. She voluntarily entered our program and has been an active participant in her treatment. She has had no family contact and persists in expressing a dread of her step-mother, with whom she had previously lived and who she professes "hates me." She has had a few visitors, all of whom claim to be her housemates. She apparently was their housekeeper, but they appear to genuinely be concerned about her welfare. She reports long-standing abuse by stepmom, but there are no police records to support this claim, so we are left to wonder if this is part of her psychosis. She also consistently expresses a fear of mirrors, for reasons that also seem to be related to her stepmother. We can't get a clear explanation of why this is, so I'm not sure this is really all that important. She has been engaged in intensive one-on-one treatment, as well as group intervention. She no longer expresses a desire to kill herself as she did when she first arrived. She is currently on medication to assist with her depression, although she has been reluctant to take it on a regular basis. For being such a bright, pretty girl, she is certainly still a mystery to us in several ways. Plans are for her to continue treatment and work on her goals, which include get-ting out of her housekeeping job and getting enrolled in school. Like I said, no discharge date has been set yet, although I suspect it's a few weeks off yet. I'd like to meet up with the stepmom, but I'm not sure the client will allow that.

Critically analyze this summary. What do you like about it? How could it be improved?

Rewrite the summary, using what you know about proper recording.

Exercise 8.13: Family Session Record

Using the following information, write a summary note of the family session that took place today.

1. Mom and Dad are not making eye contact.
2. 13-year-old son J is physically turned away from both parents.
3. 10-year-old son E is sitting between parents and brother J and attempting to make everyone talk to each other.
4. J is angry and refuses to talk to anyone.
5. Mom keeps repeating that she only wants to enjoy her family again.
6. Dad blames J for causing constant turmoil; J does not respond.
7. Mom agrees with dad that J's refusal to attend school is problematic.
8. J has not attended school in the past two weeks; he leaves in the morn-ing but never appears at school. Parents were notified by school that J was not present.
9. Options to ensure that J attends school are discussed.
10. J reacts by closing his eyes and not communicating with anyone.
11. J refuses to discuss why he won't go to school or what he does during the day.
12. Dad storms out of meeting in frustration, saying, "This is going nowhere."

After you have written the summary note, critique it. What do you like about it? How can it be improved?

Exercise 8.14: Group Session Record

Imagine you are facilitating the adult breast cancer support group session described below.

> This is the group's 21st meeting. Five participants are part of the group: Aleshia, Betty, Christine, Dena, and Elena. Aleshia is currently undergoing treatment and is not in attendance at this meeting. This session, group members had planned to talk about their relationships with their parents, all of whom are living and assisting them in some way. The topic, however, is abandoned as fears are expressed about Aleshia and her cancer recurrence. She is the first member of the group to experience this, and group members are feeling like this possibility has become very real for them. They are worried about Aleshia and scared for themselves, too.

Using this information, complete as much as possible on the group recording sheet. Feel free to add additional information if it would help. When you are finished, share your work with a peer and ask for constructive feedback on your work's strengths and ways it could be improved.

Group Recording Sheet

Group Summary	Date:	Session number:	Session length:
Facilitator(s):			
Present:			
Not present:			
What happened during the session?			
What interventions were used?			
What new issues arose?			
What plans for the future were made?			

Exercise 8.15: Closing Summary (I)

Write a closing summary based on the following information.

1. The client is happy to have reached most of his goals; case closed today.
2. The client is a 32-year-old gay man, recently separated from his partner of 12 years. He works as a nurse at the local hospital.

3. Depression resulted after his partner left him; he worried about never being loved again and started drinking to the point of passing out.
4. Goals: manage depression, put closure on relationship, make plans to move forward.
5. Services provided: one-on-one counseling, referral to MD for medication assessment, support group attendance, Alcoholics Anonymous referral.
6. Issue remains with drinking: has not committed to AA fully. Says is motivated to keep trying, though.
7. Strengths: enjoys work, strong friend and family support network, depression controlled.
8. Concerns: drinking.

Exercise 8.16: Closing Summary (II)

Watch a movie in which a client works with a helping professional—for example, *Good Will Hunting, Ordinary People, Precious,* or *The Fourth Kind*. Then write a closing summary for the client depicted in the movie.

What are the areas of strength for this summary? In what areas could there be improvement?

Exercise 8.17: Follow-Up Notes

Write a follow-up note for each of the following contacts, which were made after a case was closed.

1. A client stopped in to see you on his way to work, which is located next door to your office. He indicated that he is doing fine since his discharge from the agency three weeks ago, is involved in his support group, has started dating an acquaintance, and has made plans to move out of his parents' basement and into his own apartment. You congratulate him on the progress he had made.
2. Four attempts to reach a client have been unsuccessful. You don't want to leave a message on voice mail, but you are concerned for her well-being following crisis intervention services you provided after she lost her home to flooding.
3. A former client responds tearfully when contacted by phone for follow-up. He apologizes for being emotional and says he is feeling overwhelmed because of the recent death of his pet parrot. He lost his wife six months before to cancer and had been doing well. He agrees to a home visit tomorrow.
4. A patient was released from the psychiatric unit after a serious suicide attempt. Three days after discharge, you follow up to find out that he canceled his aftercare appointment with the community-based social worker and did not fill his medication prescription. He agrees to meet with the community social worker if he can be fit in. You call and are able to get him an appointment this afternoon. He promises that he will keep the appointment.

Exercise 8.18: Focus Group Reports

In your favorite search engine, type in "focus group report sample." With a peer, select a sample report on a topic that interests you. Answer the following questions individually, then compare your responses:

1. What are the strengths of this report? How might it be improved?
2. Is the length of the report acceptable? Why or why not?
3. Would you be pleased to sign your name as the author of this report? Why or why not?
4. What are the next steps that should be taken with this report? If you were the administrator receiving this report, what action would you take next?
5. What additional information is still needed for you to feel comfortable taking these next steps?
6. What did you learn from this exercise that will inform your future social work practice?

Exercise 8.19: Community Organizing Progress Notes

Go to http://www.youtube.com and type in "American freedom stories: Montgomery bus boycott" in the search bar. Watch the under-four-minute video about the successful 382-day boycott of the bus service in Montgomery, Alabama, by nearly 50,000 local blacks in 1955 and 1956. Answer the following questions:

1. Community organizers clearly worked together to make the boycott a success. If you were in charge of organizing volunteers to provide alternate transportation to those boycotting the bus system, what community strategies would be important to use?
2. Which documents would be most important to maintain in a file on organizing this boycott? Which documents would be less important? Why?
3. Imagine you were asked to organize a similar boycott in another city. What records would you ask for to help you in your organization efforts?
4. Discuss your responses with a peer. What did you learn about community organizing documents?

Exercise 8.20: Exploring Ways to Diagram Community Relationships

1. In your favorite search engine, type in "mapping software community relationships." Explore some of the sites highlighted there.
2. Explore "power map" in your search engine and answer the following questions:
   a. How can diagraming community relationships be helpful?
   b. In addition to using software, how can community relationships be diagramed?
   c. What Web-based mapping software did you find that was free or that featured free trials?

    d. What are the advantages and disadvantages of using software for this purpose?

    e. How do diagrams help in your documentation of community assessment activities?

    f. How can you document or preserve diagraming that is not software based (for example, if sticky notes cover a conference room wall from a community meeting where relationships are mapped)?

3. Compare your findings with those of a peer who also completed this exercise. What did you learn that can help your future practice?

ANSWER KEY

Exercise 8.2

1 = S; 2 = A; 3 = P; 4 = S; 5 = O; 6 = O; 7 = O; 8 = S; 9 = P; 10 = A; 11 = O; 12 = G; 13 = I; 14 = A; 15 = S; 16 = P; 17 = S; 18 = A; 19 = I; 20 = A.

CHAPTER **9**

Communication with and about Clients

"Documentation can be a daunting task," according to Kane et al. (2002, p. 206). Social workers are often called on to communicate complex information about their clients, once informed consent has been obtained. Such information is shared in a variety of formats with a range of purposes. It is important to remember that "there is magic in the written word" (Houghkirk, 1977, p. 29). How information is communicated to clients and the manner in which it is approached often matters from a therapeutic standpoint. Increasingly, technology is being used to communicate client information. This chapter reviews the most common of these formats and looks at ways to manage communications received from clients.

LETTERS

Communication often occurs via formal letters. Social workers send letters to clients, community agencies, referral sources, and other interested people for a wide variety of reasons (Wilson, 1980). These become an important part of the case file. As with any other part of the official record, attention should be paid to their format and structure. Letters should contain an introduction, a body, and a conclusion. A helpful way to organize a letter is suggested by Young (2014). In the introduction, connect with the reader as one person to another. In the body, explain to the reader details and facts. In the closing, state the action being requested.

Before writing a letter about or on behalf of a client, consider the following questions:

- What is the letter's purpose? What information does the recipient need the letter to provide? Is this consistent with what the client has consented to be released?

- Who is the audience? Is it the social worker at the agency to which the client is being referred or a team of professionals at a physician's office? Who will have access to the letter once it is mailed?
- If a postcard is being considered, is there assurance that it will not embarrass the client if someone else should read it? For confidentiality reasons, postcards are rarely used (Sheafor & Horejsi, 2012; Wilson, 1980).

When writing a letter, keep the following information in mind:

- Ordinarily, letters are typed on agency letterhead (Sheafor & Horejsi, 2012). The most common paper size used is the standard 8½ × 11 inches.
- Letters should always be dated, using the full date. For example, use November 23, 2015, not 11/23/15 ("Letter Writing Tips," n.d.).
- The letter should begin six lines down from the top of the page, to leave room for the letterhead (Ward & Mama, 2010).
- First names are typically used only to address a child or someone with whom there is a close relationship (Sheafor & Horejsi, 2012). Instead, titles or honorifics such as "Ms.," "Mrs.," "Mr.," "Dr.," "Rev.," and (for judges) "The Honorable" are used.
- If the letter is longer than one page, use a blank second sheet of paper rather the reverse side of the first page ("Letter Writing Tips," n.d.). Letterhead is used only for the first page of a letter (Ward & Mama, 2010).
- Professional letters should remain positive and polite, even if a complaint is involved (Glicken, 2008; "How to Write a Business Letter," n.d.). The social worker should avoid threatening language and opinions not based in fact.
- A letter's content should be focused and to the point. Information that does not relate to the main purpose of the letter should be deleted.
- Unlike in most forms of client documentation, the first- and second-person points of view (I, you, my, your) are acceptable in letters.
- Letters lodging a complaint or advocating on behalf of a client should include all relevant facts and state clearly what action is desired to resolve the matter ("How to Write a Complaint Letter," n.d.). If possible, limit the letter to one problem that requires immediate attention rather than detailing several issues (Glicken, 2008).

Structure of a Formal Letter

Most formal letters follow a common outline ("Letter Writing Tips," n.d.). Using the correct format will help the social worker craft a professional appearance (Ward & Mama, 2010). The following format can be adapted for special situations, but it is generally used in social work settings:

- Six blank lines—to allow space for agency letterhead
- Return address—one line for the full name of the social worker sending the letter and two lines for the full mailing address
- One blank line
- Date—month, day, year

- One blank line
- Recipient name and address—one line for the recipient's full name and position, one line for the agency name, and two lines for the mailing address
- One blank line
- Salutation—usually "Dear Ms./Mrs./Mr." followed by the last name and a colon (when recipient's name is not known, use "To Whom It May Concern")
- One blank line
- Body of letter—single-spaced paragraphs with an extra line between paragraphs and after the last paragraph
- Closing—typically "Sincerely," "Sincerely yours," or "Thank you"
- Three blank lines (space for the signature—sign in full using black ink)
- Name—full name and title, typed
- One blank line
- Any additional notation—for example, "Enclosure" with the number of enclosures.

Although this format is a good starting point, agency policy may require a different format. Review copies of letters written by other agency staff to obtain a sense of how correspondence is formatted in that particular setting.

A sample letter adhering to this format follows:

Nancy Sidell, LSW
17 Cherry Tree Lane
Hollidaytown, PA 12345

April 12, 2015

Sally Jo Stein, Caseworker
XYZ Agency
3712 Cherry Tree Lane
Tree City, PA 56789

Dear Ms. Stein:

I am writing to you regarding my client, Michael J. Ramirez. This is to verify that he has completed emergency services with me and is being referred to you for ongoing counseling. I am enclosing a signed release form from Mr. Ramirez and a copy of his assessment and termination summary.

Thank you in advance for your work with Mr. Ramirez.

Sincerely,

Nancy Sidell, LSW

Enclosures (2)

After writing the letter, review it carefully using the following steps:

1. Proofread it, checking for spelling errors and grammatical mistakes, including incomplete sentences. "Typos, poor grammar, and sloppy formatting reflect poorly on you, your agency, and the profession" (Ward & Mama, 2010, p. 84).
2. Make sure the language is clear. Avoid jargon and abbreviations that can be easily misunderstood.
3. If the letter involves a complaint or argument, wait a day and reread it. As Sheafor and Horejsi (2012) pointed out, this may prevent later regrets.

Sign the letter in black ink, make a copy for the file, and mail the original to the recipient.

Addressing the Envelope

Care should be taken when addressing an envelope. Something as simple as identifying an agency on the outside return address can lead to a breach of confidentiality (Wilson, 1980)—for example, if a letter is sent to a client's home, a family member can tell that the client has been in contact with the organization. The following guidelines should be followed when addressing an envelope ("Addressing an Envelope," n.d.):

*   Check on agency policy regarding using return addresses on envelopes.
*   Place the sender's name and return address in the upper left corner, unless agency policy dictates otherwise.
*   Place the postage stamp in the upper right corner.
*   Write the recipient's name and address clearly in black ink in the center of the envelope. Address the envelope before you stuff and seal it; this will produce a flatter surface on which to write legibly.

Sample Stamped Envelope

```
┌──────────────────────────────────────────────────────────────┐
│ Sender's name                                                  │
│ Return address line 1                               Stamp      │
│ Return address line 2                                          │
│                                                                │
│                                                                │
│                   Recipient's name                             │
│                   Recipient address line 1                     │
│                   Recipient address line 2                     │
│                                                                │
│                                                                │
└──────────────────────────────────────────────────────────────┘
```

- If the letter is being mailed to another country, add the country name on the last line of the recipient's address and the country the letter is being mailed from on the last line of the sender's address.

PHOTOS IN RECORDS

Photographs have been used to document injuries and suspected instances of abuse and neglect for as long as the technology has been available. When photos are taken, they become part of the client's case file. Informed consent should be obtained before taking photographs, except in the case of suspected child abuse in jurisdictions that do not require the consent of a parent or guardian for photography in such scenarios. It is recommended that two sets of instant photos (like Polaroids) be taken, one for the permanent record and one to be placed in a sealed envelope and labeled for law enforcement or reporting purposes (Stanford School of Medicine, 2014). Each photo should include the following identifying information: name of the person in the photo, date of birth, date and time taken, case file or medical record identifier, and the signatures of the photographer and a witness. In the case of domestic violence, the signature of the client or patient may also be included.

Photos are additionally being used in alternative ways today, unrelated to providing evidence of possible abuse or neglect. Children's Hospital Colorado conducted a quality improvement program that examined whether including a patient photograph on a verification screen in the electronic medical record (EMR) could reduce provider errors caused when incorrect orders were placed. The program was launched in reaction to the dozen medical errors made in 2009 at the hospital, which were caused by incorrect orders being placed in patients' EMRs. The program showed that when the EMR contained the patient's photo, misplaced or mistaken orders were virtually eliminated (Latner, 2012). Given the success in Colorado, Stanford Hospital and Clinics began a patient photo project, asking every patient admitted to the Emergency Department to sign an informed consent form so a photo could be taken. The photo is then uploaded to the patient's EMR and visible to all practitioners. Besides reducing medical errors, other possible outcomes include better tracking of patients during large disasters and reductions in insurance fraud (Hammerstrom, 2014). The ability to take digital photos has become easy and widespread, and it is anticipated that additional uses for visual identification in permanent service records will be found.

E-MAIL MESSAGES

Sharing client information via e-mail is considered risky for several reasons. First, one is never sure where an e-mail will end up or who will have access to it. For example, many spouses share e-mail accounts. Sending sensitive information in this manner can result in major breaches of confidentiality. Agency computer specialists may read e-mails that are sent from the office, posing another confidentiality issue. E-mail messages are not as private as is often believed. E-mail correspondence may be reviewed by the courts and can be considered part of the official record. Computers can also fail, leaving no record of e-mail correspondence that has not been backed up onto a network or cloud. For these reasons, caution is urged when communicating about clients by e-mail.

Despite these difficult issues, however, e-mail can be an efficient means of sharing information, for example, with referral agencies. It can provide a way to transmit information quickly, to provide support to peers and clients, and (at an advanced level) for client counseling and advice giving (Sheafor & Horejsi, 2012). The following considerations should be kept in mind when using e-mail ("Business Email Writing," n.d.):

- Know who may have access to the e-mail before it is sent.
- Be aware of agency policies regarding e-mail use for social work tasks.
- Avoid using a personal account for professional correspondence, which blurs boundary lines and can present an unprofessional appearance.
- Humorous or idiosyncratic e-mail addresses are acceptable when communicating with friends but should not be used for professional correspondence.
- A heading that includes the return address, recipient's address, and date is unnecessary.
- Use a descriptive subject line that explains the purpose of the e-mail. "Appointment requested" would be a better subject line than "help."
- Update the subject line on replies to earlier e-mails to reflect new information (Young, 2014).
- Use simple formatting; keep all lines flush with the left margin.
- Proper spelling and grammar and complete sentences should be used, and jargon and abbreviations should be limited, the same as in a hard-copy letter.
- Use a simple closing such as "Best regards" or "Take care" (Young, 2014).
- Keep the message to about one screen in length.
- Ask for a reply, verifying that the e-mail was received.
- Keep copies of all e-mail correspondence in the case file.

E-mail etiquette is also important to keep in mind ("Business and Workplace Email Etiquette," n.d.):

- Use normal capitalization. Using all capital letters or all lowercase letters is considered unprofessional. Write as if composing a printed letter.
- Skip a line when starting a new paragraph instead of using tabs, which can be read differently by different e-mail programs.
- Avoid excessive use of exclamation points and other punctuation marks, such as ellipses and question marks.
- Avoid emoticons such as ☺ and informal abbreviations such as IMHO and TTYL.

- Keep the message as concise as possible.
- Always use a signature line.
- Spell-check and proofread before sending.
- Reply to received messages promptly.

Using E-Mail with Clients

E-mail can be helpful when working with clients, if managed correctly. Zuckerman (2008) cited several safe uses for e-mail with clients, including sending intake and informational material, scheduling and confirming appointments, answering simple questions, and responding to potential clients' questions about one's area of specialization. He also cited some clinical examples of e-mail usage that may be of value, such as setting boundaries with a client who makes frequent unnecessary telephone calls. Placing limits by asking the client to e-mail instead may be therapeutic. However, caution is urged in all use of e-mail with clients, which should be considered an adjunct to services already being provided (Drude & Lichstein, 2005). The following steps can help establish boundaries and procedures regarding e-mail communication with clients:

- During the first session, explain to the client how technology will be used and obtain informed consent regarding it (NASW & ASWB, 2005). Issues such as the frequency and length of e-mails and efforts to secure shared information should be discussed.
- Explain to the client the risks and benefits involved with e-mail, and obtain a signed informed consent regarding e-mail use.
- Discuss ending e-mail communication if necessary. "The social worker must always reserve the right to retract an agreement to communicate via email and insist on face to face contact if [email is] counterproductive to the client's best interests" (Mattison, 2012, p. 256).
- Print out all e-mail exchanges for the hard-copy case file, or save them in the electronic case file.
- Discuss confidentiality issues on the client's end and who may have access to his or her e-mail. Limitations and possible threats to confidentiality should be clearly explained (Mattison, 2012).
- Consider a password system that verifies the client's identity as the sender. Code words or electronic signatures may also be helpful.
- Consider an encryption program for additional privacy.

DOCUMENTING ONLINE OR E-THERAPY

Online counseling, e-therapy, or distance therapy involves a mental health counselor or therapist providing professional services over the Internet. It can occur once or over a long period of time. It can be delivered via e-mail, real-time chat, Internet phone (voice over Internet Protocol), or interactive audiovisual technology (IAVT) such as Skype. Modern telemedicine has been delivered in some forms since the

1960s, although its growth has expanded rapidly with technological advances such as Skype, particularly in rural and underserved areas (World Health Organization, 2010). Today, over 100 mental-health-specific online venues and over 40 practice networks are available, thanks to advances in video computing and encryption technology (Behavioral Health Innovation, 2014).

Despite the tremendous growth of these services, several issues have not been resolved regarding social work and distance therapy provision via the Internet. Zur (2012) identified some that must be considered: confidentiality of client communications, HIPAA compliance issues, informed consent, and competency and scope of practice concerns. Licensing issues across state lines is another thorny problem. DeAngelis (2012) noted that there is "little consistent guidance across states" (p. 52) on electronic communication use. The need to be licensed in the jurisdiction in which the client is located is a barrier that currently exists for social workers wishing to pursue online therapy. Although NASW (2012) acknowledged the wide use of telemental health services in general and Skype in particular, the organization remains concerned about ways in which client confidentiality can be assured. If these issues are resolved and services are provided online, they should be documented in a manner similar to the way records of other kinds of client interactions are kept (Zur, 2012).

TRANSMITTING RECORDS ELECTRONICALLY

Innovations in technology have allowed social workers to transfer confidential client information with great speed and efficiency. For example, transmitting client data in an e-mail attachment or by fax is acceptable in some situations—for example, in emergencies when time is critical.

Converting files to PDF (portable document format) is becoming increasingly commonplace, and e-mailing PDF files is preferred over sending faxes in some settings because it is more cost-effective. It can also be an effective way to send a document containing a signature (Young, 2014). With the ease and efficiency these advances make possible, however, come risks that must be addressed. Care should be taken when electronically transferring data to minimize the risk of confidentiality breaches. Protecting client privacy is the social worker's responsibility (NASW & ASWB, 2005). The following points should be considered when sending any electronic transmission:

- Password protect any confidential client documents sent as attachments. Most word processing programs have this capability.
- Do not send e-mail attachments or faxes unless the recipient is expecting them. "Social workers should notify the recipient by telephone that a fax is being sent and obtain the recipient's agreement to go to the fax machine immediately to await the document's arrival" (Reamer, 2001, pp. 11–12).
- If sending a fax, include a cover sheet—typically a typed sheet of paper that contains the date; the recipient's name and fax number; the sender's

name, agency, and fax and telephone numbers; and the total number of pages in the fax (including the cover sheet). A cover sheet usually also contains space for a comment or message ("Fax Cover Sheet Info," n.d.). Social workers would be wise to include a notation that if the receiver is not the intended recipient, he or she should contact the sender immediately. A template can be easily developed using a word processing program or downloaded without cost from the Internet.

- Always confirm that the attachment was received and can be read. Fax machines run out of paper and toner, and printing can be illegible ("Fax Cover Sheet," n.d.).
- Recognize that confidentiality breaches can occur. Electronically submitted information can be received by the wrong person or viewed by people with no right to access it. "You, the professional, are the only one who will be held responsible for violations" (Zuckerman, 2008, p. 431).

TEXT MESSAGING AND IAVT

Setting or changing client appointment times, communicating easily with a self-help group, and touching base with a client between sessions are all uses for text messaging or IAVT such as Skype. Reamer (2011) suggested that clients can be easily exposed to confidentiality and privacy breaches through this use of technology. He urged agencies to develop policies about appropriate uses of this technology to ensure that boundaries are clear and well established. Clients should understand that these communications could lack security. Any electronic text messages should become part of the client's case file.

Rules governing the use of text messaging or IAVT technology should also be clearly delineated in agency policy. Although its limited use may be very appropriate at times for clients, clients need to understand its limitations and its lack of security and privacy (NASW, 2012). Documentation of their informed consent must be obtained.

SOCIAL MEDIA DOCUMENTATION

The definition of *social media* has broadened and likely will continue to expand. Wikipedia ("Social Media," 2014) suggested that the term includes collaborative projects (such as Wikipedia), blogs and microblogs (such as Twitter), social news networking sites, content communities (such as YouTube), social networking sites (the largest is Facebook), virtual game worlds (such as World of Warcraft), and virtual social worlds (such as Second Life).

Reamer's (2011) recommendation that agencies develop policies on how technology will be used by staff and clients extends to social media usage. Staff and clients should be clear on how social media will be used so that boundaries are understood by all parties. Informed consent is again critical when using social media, and documentation of its use is essential.

CLOUD SERVER USE

Cloud computing is the term used for storing and accessing data and programs over the Internet rather than on one's computer hard drive (Griffith, 2013). If one has an online connection, cloud computing can occur anywhere. Common examples of cloud storage services include iCloud, Dropbox, and SugarSync, although there are many others. Social work agencies are increasingly using cloud servers to store and manage data. They often use the cloud to store their electronic records or to access those records from mobile locations. Sensitive client information is stored on the cloud servers, making the issue of confidentiality breaches an important one. The privacy of personal information is potentially at risk when client information is uploaded to a cloud server, according to a World Privacy Forum report (Gellman, 2009).

Tips provided in the report for businesses are applicable to social service providers. First, policies should be in place specifying how and when cloud computing may be used and data can be stored there. Second, cloud computing should not be used for any information one would not wish to share with a competitor or with the government. Next, read the terms of service before using. "Many users are likely not aware of the details set out in the terms of service for cloud providers or of the consequences of sharing information with a cloud provider" (Gellman, 2009, p. 6). Last, consult with technical, security, or other advisors about cloud use.

Questions to ask about professional technology use were posed by Reardon (2011):

- Why do I want to use a particular piece of technology in practice?
- What is my professional organization's stance about the use of this technology?
- What best practices exist surrounding this technology in practice?
- Does my agency have a policy about this technology? How does it ensure client confidentiality and privacy?
- How available is my personal information to my clients? Could they access my Facebook account? What negative ramifications could there be?
- If I use blogs, Facebook, or Twitter professionally, is all content topic focused rather than client focused?
- Do I think before I post anything?

DOCUMENTING TELEPHONE COMMUNICATIONS

Sheafor and Horejsi (2012) noted that the telephone is commonly used in social work practice but that a telephone call leaves no record of its purpose or what it has accomplished. It may be important to document a telephone call, if it is of a critical nature or involves an important aspect of a case. For example, a call to a referral agency to determine the client's eligibility may require a notation, as would a frantic call from a client experiencing extreme stress. Important telephone contacts are typically recorded in progress notes, although some agencies require that all telephone contacts on a particular case be logged on a form designed for that purpose. An example of a phone log entry follows.

> 10/22/2015. The client left several messages this morning. When her calls were returned, she indicated that she had not been able to stop crying since getting up this morning. This worker listened to her concerns, and an appointment was set for this afternoon. In the meantime, she is with her best friend, who will stay with her until her appointment. [Name], LSW

DOCUMENTS PRODUCED BY CLIENTS

Clients sometimes generate data for inclusion in the case record. Although not written or initiated by the social worker, these documents can become an important component of the record. Some of the more common client-generated documents are discussed in the next sections.

Assessment Data

A social worker may ask a client to complete a checklist that can help assess the situation from an emotional or behavioral standpoint (Zuckerman, 2008). In addition, pretests may be completed and compared with posttests to demonstrate service outcomes or changes in client functioning. These completed forms are typically maintained in the case file.

Diaries, Journals, and Logs

As early as 1928, social workers determined that asking clients to write their own version of life events could be helpful (Swift, 1928). With the "rare client . . . capable of analyzing objectively his own situation," Swift (1928, p. 537) said, reviewing such notes could assist in better client understanding. Today, asking a client to keep a journal, diary, or log is common and useful in a variety of treatment situations (Kagle & Kopels, 2008). Journals should be used only when they provide meaning and contribute to the goals being addressed.

Who will maintain client-generated data should be discussed openly. "Practitioners should be aware that the role of recordkeeper carries power with it" (Kagle & Kopels, 2008, p. 188). Most commonly, clients maintain their own journals and diaries, although information from them may appear in the social worker's case notes. Logs are more commonly maintained by social workers. The client must be made aware that these may become accessible to others within or outside the agency setting.

Case Notes

In 1991, Albeck and Goldman described a process called *codocumentation*, in which a client and therapist jointly wrote a progress note after each session. By reading one another's viewpoints, insight is gained and the process of therapy enhanced. Similarly, Wilczynski (1981) described *client recording* as a clinical tool that involves the client writing a brief summary of what he or she believes is important. These summaries were collected from clients and added by the worker to the case file as an adjunct to the clinician's summaries.

The concept of collaborative documentation, sometimes called "concurrent documentation," builds on these earlier efforts and is gaining ground as a way to record client interaction and progress. By engaging in this process, social workers and clients jointly document progress (Schmelter, 2012). It is viewed as a way to save clinician time in documentation activities following sessions, to more fully empower and engage the client, and to focus on and improve client compliance with treatment goals. The client and the social worker discuss what should be recorded as the social worker makes entries into the documentation system. The client sees what is being recorded and has input in real time. For example, at the end of a session, the social worker might say, "Let's review and write down the important parts of our session today" (Schmelter, 2012, p. 13). Assessments and service plans are also jointly constructed in this manner. By processing with the client, social workers achieve a higher degree of transparency.

Other Supplemental Material

Zuckerman (2008, p. 369) described asking some clients to maintain a notebook called *The Book of My [or Our] Therapy.* It can hold handouts, notes taken, questions raised, information found online, or artwork pertaining to the work being done. Such a notebook is maintained by the client. Supplemental material can also include therapeutic art sessions or scrapbooking material. Where these items will be maintained and by whom should be negotiated in advance with the client.

SUMMARY AND EXERCISES

Social workers use many methods to communicate with and about their clients. Communication produced by clients may become part of the case file for which the social worker is responsible. Undoubtedly, given ongoing technological advances, additional ways to communicate will present themselves to future social workers. It is important to keep issues of confidentiality in mind, no matter what technology is used.

The following exercises will be most beneficial if you work through them with a peer, sharing results and giving each other feedback.

Exercise 9.1: Letter on Behalf of a Client

Critically analyze the format and content of the following letter. Would you be comfortable signing this? Why or why not? When you have finished critiquing it, rewrite it to improve it.

May 4, 2015:
[Name], Administrator
ABC Agency

Dear [Name]:

I am writing to you to lodge a complaint on behalf of my client. What were yiou thinking when you denied her services? She's feeling like this is a real slap in the face, and I have to agree with her. You're asking for discrimination charges against you, because I don't see that denying her was done fairly or accurately. Give mea call, will ya? If I don't hear from you within the week, I'm sure you'll be hearing from her attorney.

Thanks for reconsidering her application.

Sincerely,

[Name]
XYZ Agency

Exercise 9.2: Appropriate Content to Include in a Letter

Consider each statement below. Would it be appropriate to include in a letter written by a social worker about a client? Why? If necessary, rewrite the item to reflect a more appropriate statement.

1. I am writing to you to see if you can do me a huge favor.
2. I don't want to give you my group members' names but need you to find out what you can about their situation.
3. Please consider the attached information to be confidential.
4. Once this problem has been resolved, let's get together for drinks some night.
5. My client has signed appropriate consent forms for me to release this information.
6. Thank you for taking on what will be a challenging case for you and your agency.
7. Can you get back with me about this matter at your earliest convenience?
8. I am following up with you about a matter of which we spoke yesterday.
9. I owe you one!
10. I'm sure you'll enjoy working with this family as much as I have.

Exercise 9.3: Advocacy Letter (I)

Think of a local issue that concerns you as a private individual. You may be concerned about traffic issues in your neighborhood or feel that your local school board is not responding effectively to budget cuts. Determine the appropriate authority to whom to direct a letter on the issue. Compose a professional letter to that person that indicates your concerns and asks for help in resolving the matter to your satisfaction.

Get feedback from a peer, rewrite the letter if necessary, and send it to the appropriate authority.

Exercise 9.4: Advocacy Letter (II)

Read the list of facts below and compose a professional letter to a local agency asking for assistance in resolving the matter.

1. Eight clients attend a senior center at which you are employed.
2. They approach you, upset that the town has changed the local bus routes in a way that makes it impossible for them and others to arrive for lunch on time.
3. They spoke with the bus driver, who referred them to the supervisor of the transportation authority.
4. The supervisor dismissed their concerns and told them to eat someplace else.
5. They ask that you write a letter on their behalf to the administrator of the transportation authority.
6. You agree to assist in educating the authority about the importance of the meal to the seniors involved.

Exercise 9.5: Appropriate E-Mail Statements

Read each statement below. Is the content and means of expression appropriate for inclusion in a professional e-mail? Why or why not? If necessary, rewrite the item to reflect a more appropriate statement.

1. Hey! Just checking in with you about your appointment time.
2. IMHO i dont think we need to get this worked up, do u?
3. Please find the attached signed consent form that we discussed earlier today.
4. Can you verify that you've received the information I mailed to you last week?
5. I'm e-mailing to verify that your appointment with Dr. Cruz is set for next Wednesday at 9:20 a.m.
6. Thanks for adding this client to your group, I appreciate it.
7. Please let your staff know that tonight's community meeting has been canceled due to the weather.
8. I'm searching for a nursing home bed for a patient who will need short-term physical therapy for approximately six weeks. Do you have an opening?
9. Don't be put off by how she presents herself; she's really very motivated.
10. Not sure how my supervisor will feel about it. LOL

Exercise 9.6: Case Notes on Telephone Calls

For each scenario, decide if the contact needs to be documented. If so, write a case note for it.

1. You have contacted five local agencies, looking for funding for food and rental expenses for a client. The last one, Good Samaritan Services, agrees to consider your client if he completes and returns their application form by noon tomorrow. (If this needs to be documented, write a narrative note.)
2. You receive a telephone call from a client whose daughter was killed six months ago while serving overseas in the military. Your client is angry about an Internet article that suggests that her daughter was at fault somehow. You calm her enough to find out how to locate the article. You offer to meet her later in the day before her support group meeting. She agrees. (If this needs to be documented, write a SOAP note.)
3. The local hospice calls to tell you that they have scheduled an education session for the community in two weeks. They are e-mailing flyers to you for posting and distribution. (If this needs to be documented, write a narrative note.)
4. A former client calls to ask for an appointment. He has just learned that his father committed suicide, and he is distraught. You have no openings today but make an appointment for him to meet with a colleague later this morning. (If this needs to be documented, write a narrative note.)

Exercise 9.7: Telephone or Text Log

Keep a log of the next 20 telephone or text contacts you make and receive. Use the log sheet below, which is similar to one that might be used in an agency setting.

Agency Telephone Log

Social worker:			
Date:			
Time	Caller	Purpose of Call	Follow-Up Needed

When you have finished, consider the following questions:

1. What purpose would such a log serve in an agency?
2. Where might an agency maintain such a log?
3. Would a log specific to a client, maintained in the case file, be useful? Why or why not?

Exercise 9.8: Electronic Transmissions

Some of the skills necessary for the exercises below may be new to you. The exact steps are often different from one computer or software program to the next. When necessary, find specific instructions in the help function of the software program or get help from a colleague. Administrative and technical support staff can often be very helpful in this regard.

Password Protect a Document.

1. Using your word processing program, create a new document with a few lines of text.
2. Password protect the document. Make a note of the password.
3. Save and close the document.
4. Open your e-mail account and send the document to yourself as an attachment.
5. Delete the original document or move it to a separate folder.
6. Open the e-mail you sent to yourself and download the attachment.
7. Open the document using the password you just set up.

What are the advantages of a password-protected document? Disadvantages?

Encrypt E-Mail.

1. Determine how to encrypt an e-mail. In Outlook, for example, you can go to Options–Account–Settings to learn how to do this (the menu items may vary slightly depending on the version of Outlook you have installed).
2. Set up a digital signature that verifies you as the e-mail sender.
3. Send an encrypted e-mail to yourself and open it.

What are the advantages of encrypted e-mail? Disadvantages?

Send a PDF Document.

1. Open a document created in your word processing program, or create a new one.
2. Save it as a PDF file.
3. Send it to yourself and open it.

What are the advantages of PDF files? Disadvantages?

Send a Fax from Your Computer.

1. Determine if your computer has the ability to send a fax.
2. If so, fax yourself a document that you have created.

What are the advantages of sending a fax via the computer? Disadvantages?

Research Agency Use of Technology in Documentation.

1. Contact an agency to determine if it has policies and procedures governing social work staff use of electronic documents.
2. Contact a social worker to determine how he or she uses technology at work.

What policies do you believe agencies should have in place regarding the use of electronic technology in documentation?

What have you learned from completing this exercise? Were there any surprises?

Exercise 9.9: Photo Usage

Photos are increasingly being used for documentation and verification purposes. Consider the following scenarios and compare your responses with those of a peer.

1. You are a client at a mental health agency and are asked to sign a consent form to have your photo taken by your social worker. The social worker explains that this is agency policy and may be helpful in identifying you at some point in the future. Would you give permission to have your photo taken? Why or why not?
2. Your mother is asked to sign a consent form to have her picture taken when being admitted for minor surgery. It is explained that this is necessary to help prevent medication and treatment errors. Your mother is unsure about signing the consent form and asks you to make the decision. What is your response? Why did you respond as you did?
3. You volunteer at a community agency following a major disaster in your area. You are assigned the task of asking victims in a triage setting to allow their photos to be taken to help ensure identification during the confusion following the disaster. No consent form is available because there is no electricity to power copy machines. What is your response? Why did you respond as you did?
4. You are given a box full of photos taken at your agency over the past five years. The photos were accidentally separated from the case files. Each photo is identified by a date and case number, which you are asked to match with its case file. The supervisor explains that the goal is to add the

photos to the files. What is your response to this request? Why did you respond as you did?

5. Agency policy is that group members' photos be taken at the first group session so group facilitators can learn group members' names before the next session. As a new group facilitator, you are told to explain the procedure, obtain consent, and take the photos. The first group member you approach refuses to participate and encourages others to not participate either. What is your response? Why did you respond as you did? How will you document this incident?

When comparing your responses with those of a peer, what did you learn? What might be helpful to you in your future social work practice?

Exercise 9.10: Online Counseling

Using your favorite search engine, type in "large e-therapy clinics." From a list of clinics, choose one that looks interesting to explore. Ask a peer to explore another. Answer the following questions about the site you selected:

1. How many therapists are involved in the site? What are their credentials?
2. What areas of specialization are marketed on the site?
3. What is the cost of the services if you were a client? How do clients select a provider? Are informed consent procedures discussed?
4. What is required to join the e-clinic as a provider?
5. How are services delivered (for example, through online chats, Skype, another method)?
6. What security measures are in place to protect client confidentiality?
7. Are any forms of documentation discussed on the site?
8. What are the risks and benefits of being a provider associated with this site?

Compare your findings with those of your peer. What did you learn? Were there any surprises?

Exercise 9.11: Skyping with Clients

With a peer and while using Skype technology, role-play a new client situation of interest to you in your career. Document the session. Using the same situation, role-play in person with the same peer, imagining this to be a second session with the same client. Document the second session. Answer the following questions:

1. What did you like about the Skype role play versus the in-person role play? What were problems?
2. What were differences, if any, in your documentation between the Skype session and the in-person role play?

3. Which method do you prefer? Why?
4. What issues do you believe would be problematic if you were to see a new client on Skype for an initial session?
5. What did you learn from this exercise that could help you in your future professional career?

Exercise 9.12: Exploring Cloud Servers

Select a cloud server and explore its site. Ask a peer to select another cloud server to explore. Answer the following questions:

1. What are the cloud server's terms of service?
2. How might you envision using this service to store client records? What problems would you encounter?
3. What provisions, if any, does the server make for the security of client information?
4. What are the benefits and risks of using this cloud server for social work purposes?

Compare your responses with your peer's. What did you learn that could help you in your future professional career?

Exercise 9.13: Collaborative Documentation

With a peer, discuss the following situations related to collaborative documentation.

1. A client says he does not wish to participate in collaborative documentation with you but would rather you document after he leaves your office. How would you respond?
2. A client argues that she does not want you to note in the case file that she has been depressed, despite the fact that the session was spent developing ways in which she can better manage her ongoing level of sadness. How would you respond?
3. A client asks if she can input a case note about your session into the computer system you are using. Agency policy requires that the social worker, not the client, must input the collaborative notes. How would you respond?
4. Discuss a client you have seen in the past who would not be appropriate for collaborative documentation. Why do you think this? What other kinds of clients would have a difficult time with collaborative documentation?

Exercise 9.14: Role Play of Collaborative Documentation

With a peer, role-play a client being seen by a social worker for a specific problem. After you have assessed the client situation, explain that you want to summarize and collaboratively document the session. After you have completed the role play, answer the following questions:

1. How difficult was collaborative documentation in this role play?
2. What worked well?

Switch roles and repeat the role play, using a different scenario.

3. What did you learn about the process of collaborative documentation?

PART III

Beyond the Basics

This section moves past the basics of documentation and features ways in which documentation is evaluated and constantly improved. Social workers are used to giving and receiving feedback about their work with clients and recognize it as a valuable way of improving service delivery. They also give and receive feedback about their documentation, which has not been a highly valued professional activity. Chapter 10 addresses documentation feedback and provides suggestions on incorporating self-review, peer review, and supervisory review into one's ongoing professional development. Chapter 11 focuses on issues related to supervision and documentation. For a supervisor, documentation can be an important tool as supervisees are mentored in their career paths. Chapter 12 provides a look toward the future of documentation and predicts what can reasonably be expected in the area of recording social work services.

CHAPTER 10

Getting and Giving Feedback

Feedback regarding documentation is as important to give and receive as feedback on other aspects of social work practice. "It is not possible to develop practice skills in working with clients or supervision of staff without some ongoing means of examining the details of one's practice efforts" (Shulman, 1993, p. 311).

Many services provided by a social worker are intangible and difficult to quantify. Records kept by a worker are often the only concrete means by which service quality can be reasonably assessed. Therefore, it is important to become adept at evaluating the quality of one's recording. A file's quality hinges largely on the critical thinking skills and practice abilities of the worker. "Ultimately, the quality of social work records can be no better than the practice they document. . . . Good practice is a prerequisite of good recording, but good practitioners do not always prepare good records" (Kagle & Kopels, 2008, p. 175). The challenge for the social worker is to mirror good practice skills with equally sound documentation skills.

What does high-quality recording look like? Is it easy to recognize? What elements do agencies and accrediting bodies look for when reviewing documentation? Although the answers to these questions vary tremendously, some elements are consistent. It is possible to recognize elements of good documentation and to learn from feedback on recording practices.

Documentation can be assessed from two perspectives: format and content. Format (such as whether the document follows agency policies on timeliness and legibility) is often easier to assess than content (whether what the record says is appropriate). Both are important aspects of high-quality documentation.

Working through this book is a good way to start to improve documentation skills, but one must work constantly to truly achieve this goal. A combination of self-review, peer review, and supervisory review can hone documentation skills. Each strategy will be covered in this chapter.

SELF-REVIEW

Self-review involves objectively reviewing one's own documentation to determine if key standards have been met. During self-review, one reflects objectively and considers ways to improve. One does not modify the record or fix any problems that may be found while conducting a self-review. It is a learning tool that should be practiced on closed case files. It requires one to step back for a moment and try to forget who wrote the document. The following steps are recommended for self-review:

1. Schedule regular self-reviews—for example, by reviewing three to five recently closed cases at the end of each month. Make a habit of doing this on a regular basis until the process becomes routine. This can make it easier to carve out the necessary time.
2. Consider asking agency administrators to allow self-review activities to occur on an agencywide basis. When the process is institutionalized, weight is added to the importance and legitimacy of good record-keeping practices.
3. Produce a worksheet to use during the self-review process. It should be brief and easy to complete and cover both format and content. A sample worksheet, which can be modified as needed, follows. The worksheet can provide a structure for self-review and can help identify patterns and trends in documentation.
4. Although self-review worksheets are designed for the social worker's use only and are not part of the client's official record, they may be useful in guiding discussions during supervision. For example, self-review may reveal a documentation issue that a supervisor could help resolve.

Blank Self-Review Worksheet

	Yes	No	N/A	Comments
Format				
1. All entries dated and signed?				
2. All entries legible?				
3. Agency forms used?				
4. Agency note structure followed?				
5. Frequency of notes acceptable?				
6. Assessment timely?				
7. Closing summary done?				
Content				
1. Reason for referral stated?				
2. Client feelings noted?				
3. Confidentiality, informed consent noted?				

(continued)

Blank Self-Review Worksheet (*continued*)

	Yes	No	N/A	Comments
4. Clear plans established?				
5. Goals measurable and noted?				
6. Service provisions clearly indicated?				
7. Comprehensive assessment noted?				
8. Client strengths noted?				
9. Referrals noted?				
10. Closing summary clear?				
11. Date of best note:	Why was this best?			
12. Date of worst note:	Why was this worst?			
13. How could this record be improved?				

PEER REVIEW

Many of the exercises in this book are based on a model in which feedback is obtained from a peer about recording activities. Agencies often participate in similar but more formalized peer review activities.

The term *peer review* has a dual meaning in social work. It can refer to the process used by professional journals in which anonymous peers read and comment on manuscripts that are under consideration for publication (Szuchman & Thomlison, 2008). Or, more relevant in this context, it can be defined as "a formal periodic process in which professional standards of intervention have been spelled out and practices are monitored by colleagues" (Barker, 2014, p. 316).

Peer review of social work documentation helps promote uniformity and consistency of service delivery and assists the agency in identifying staff members' strengths and areas needing work. In addition, social workers are exposed to the recording styles and skills of peers, enabling them to improve their own documentation by reviewing that of others (Moreland & Racke, 1991).

Many agencies are required by their funding sources or governing boards to have a peer review process in place. The case file is commonly used as the basis for evaluating the quality and quantity of services in such a review (Kagle, 1984b). Each agency manages its review program to meet its unique needs, but there are some commonalities in the practice of peer review:

- In most cases, a peer review committee oversees the process, assigns cases to be reviewed, and assesses results for overall patterns and trends (Moreland & Racke, 1991). Peer review works best when all workers in an agency participate in it.
- It is considered a confidential activity, and formal reports do not contain the names of individual workers or cases. Instead, raw data and numerical frequencies are reported, indicating the degree of compliance with established indicators.

- Forms similar to the model self-review worksheet described and shown earlier (see page 172) are used to assess format and content of case file documentation. Like with self-review, these sheets are not considered part of the official client record and are not maintained there.
- The most difficult task is often choosing criteria for assessment: "One of the major problems in evaluating social services is deciding what to measure" (Coulton, 1982, p. 397). There should be some agreement on the indicators that will be used, as well as clarity in how they will be interpreted. This is typically accomplished by a small committee that makes recommendations and seeks feedback from all involved in the process.

Although having case files scrutinized under peer review can cause anxiety for any social worker, the process can be very helpful. Below are a few suggestions for ways to best use the peer review process:

- Remember that it is a confidential activity. Specific findings should not be discussed with anyone, including the author of the file under review, except the peer review committee (it is the role of the committee to discuss the findings with the author). Discretion should be used during these discussions.
- A peer's documentation should be evaluated in a professional manner. Peer review activities, a form of evaluation, should be undertaken "in a fair and considerate manner and on the basis of clearly stated criteria," according to the NASW *Code of Ethics* (2008, p. 19). The code also states that "social workers should avoid unwarranted negative criticism of colleagues in communications . . . with other professionals" (p. 15).
- Learn as much as possible from the work of peers. Remember that the review not only involves assessing peers but also provides an opportunity to improve one's own documentation.
- Make sure that the indicators on which records are to be assessed are clear. If uncertain, ask questions, and be prepared to suggest ways to make the indicators more clear and pertinent.
- It is easy to become defensive when receiving feedback, but keep in mind that the activity is designed to help, not harm. Accept the feedback graciously and without argument, consider ways in which it might be helpful, and plan on making improvements. If feedback is provided in a manner that is disrespectful, unfair, or not confidential, this concern should be raised with one's supervisor.

SUPERVISORY REVIEW

As its name suggests, supervisory review involves obtaining feedback from supervisors regarding documentation. Often supervisors must review and approve the records maintained by staff reporting to them (Reamer, 2001). A supervisor is responsible for knowing the status of open cases, but specific feedback regarding case file documentation requires more focus from the supervisor, so a social worker may need to directly ask supervisors for this sort of review.

Suggestions for getting the most benefit from supervisory review include the following:

- Present the entire case file to be reviewed to the supervisor (Ward & Mama, 2010). In the interest of time, flag those places in the file regarding which you have questions.
- Allow the supervisor time to conduct an in-depth record review.
- The same criteria used in the self-review may be used during the supervisory review, and a comparison can then be made between one's own assessment and supervisory comments.
- When receiving feedback, remain open-minded and objective (Sidell & Smiley, 2008). Use the information provided as a springboard to improve recording skills.
- One of the tasks of supervision is to assist the staff in developing the skills necessary for lifelong professional learning (Shulman, 2008). It may be helpful to frame supervisory review in this context.

Enabling the evaluation of the quality of social work services is a central function of the case record. Kagle (2002) stated that one meaningful reason to maintain records is to improve practice: "Recording causes practitioners to rethink their assessment of the client-situation, the feasibility and suitability of the service plan, and barriers to and movement towards goals" (p. 28). The very process of documentation requires critical thinking that can only improve the services provided. There are several ways in which records can be useful when evaluating services. One of those ways is process recording, an educational method of documentation.

PROCESS RECORDING

Process recording has been described as a specialized form of documentation in which an interview is reconstructed as accurately as possible (Kagle & Kopels, 2008; Wilson, 1980). It is rarely used in practice today, although Wilson noted that it was commonly used in early social work. Now it is applied only as a training and supervision tool, particularly in graduate social work programs, to help a new worker develop assessment and self-reflection skills and as a way to teach interviewing skills (Kagle & Kopels, 2008; Wilson, 1980).

"The focus is two-fold: understanding the client-need-situation and developing the student's knowledge and skills" (Kagle & Kopels, 2008, p. 96). For seasoned workers, process recording can also be a useful tool. "When they are really stuck, process recording is still the best way . . . to understand what is happening in their interaction with the client and what their gut feelings are about that interaction" (Ward & Mama, 2010, p. 86). In addition, process recording can help a worker identify transference and countertransference issues that may be present (Wilson, 1980). Although traditionally used in one-on-one settings, it has been useful in processing contacts with other treatment team members, in group interactions, or in contacts with community-based service providers.

In a process recording, a written script of the interview and social worker reactions to it is reviewed by both the worker and the supervisor. Everything that occurs during an interview is noted, beginning with introductions at the office door. For the sake of accuracy, the interview is typically audiotaped or videotaped, with the client's written consent. A transcript is then prepared, usually by the social worker, or (if one is fortunate) a clerical assistant.

Columns are a defining feature of a process recording. The first column typically contains the actual words that were stated. In a separate column, the social worker notes comments or feelings about the interview. Sometimes a third column is used for supervisor comments. There are variations to this model: Wilson (1980), for example, suggested that the middle column contain the interview's content, with the left-hand column reserved for supervisory comments and the right-hand column for the social worker's comments. Some versions use only two columns, with the supervisory comments discussed one-on-one with the worker. A sample process recording follows.

Process Recording Sample 1

Interview Content	Social Worker Comments	Supervisor Comments
Worker: Hello, please come in.		
Client: Thanks. [pause] Should I sit here?		
Worker: Wherever you're comfortable. Let me take your coat and hang it here.		
Client: Thanks.		
Worker: I'm [name] and I'm your assigned worker today. This is the first time you've been to the agency?	I'm nervous and it shows here. I already knew from the file that she hadn't been here before. I don't know why I asked this.	
Client: Yeah [long pause]. I've never been to anyone before to talk like this.		
Worker: Well, I hope this goes well.	I don't think I handled this very professionally, did I? I'm really nervous here.	
Client: [no response]		
Worker: It looks like you've signed all of our agency forms and have agreed to this interview being taped. Do you have any questions about this?	I wanted to get this out of the way before we started.	
Client: No. Except what happens to the tape when you're done with it?		
Worker: It will get destroyed and no one else will listen to it but me. So, let's begin. I have a lot of questions for you, but I want to start with what brings you here.	Let's get on with this!	Do you think the client was okay with this explanation about what happens to the tape?

Although it can provide an important perspective, process recording has several limitations. It is not practical or cost-effective for widespread use (Kagle & Kopels, 2008; Wilson, 1980). Efforts have been made to summarize process recordings as a way to retain their value while lessening the time and cost involved in preparing them. If meaningful feedback is not obtained from a supervisor, negative reactions about documentation in general can result.

It can be tempting for workers to alter process recordings to make themselves look better to a supervisor. "It has been demonstrated that if five different social workers observe the same interview, five different process recordings will be produced" (Wilson, 1980, p. 24). For the process recording to be most meaningful, the worker must resist the urge to muddy facts and the supervisor must offer constructive feedback in a positive manner. The supervisor must also create an atmosphere of open exchange that features a helpful learning context.

The development of any process recording is time-consuming, another negative feature. Interviewing before one-way mirrors and electronic recording, for example, have been suggested as more beneficial methods of teaching basic interviewing skills than process recording (Wilson, 1980).

Wilson (1980) offered an alternative to process recording that is not a verbatim transcript but a paraphrased summary of the worker–client interactions.

Process Recording Sample 2

Interview Content	Social Worker Comments	Supervisor Comments
I asked Mrs. D what she meant when she said that she was thinking of walking away from it all. She said she was just tired, that was all. I wondered what tired meant to her and she started crying. I gave her tissues and waited for her to calm down. It took her quite a while to compose herself. I reflected by noting that she must be feeling very upset right now.	I felt I needed to follow up on this statement. Was this a self-harm comment?

I was trying to get a sense of what she meant, but I upset her.

I felt terrible and helpless. I hate it when someone—anyone—cries. I found myself tearing up, too, and got mad at myself for this.

I was upset, too. . . . | This is important to follow up on.

Let's talk about your gut reactions here. You felt a need to not respond emotionally, but that's part of who you are. How can you use this to your advantage in an interview? |

Neither verbatim nor summary process recording prepares one to record in a manner used in most agencies today (Kagle & Kopels, 2008; Wilson, 1980). If it is used, the process recording does not belong in the client's official record. It is a training tool that should be destroyed once the exercise is completed.

SUMMARY AND EXERCISES

Quality of documentation can be assessed in a variety of ways. Three key formats are self-review, peer review, and supervisory review. Using a combination of these types of reviews can result in improved quality of social work recording skills.

The following exercises will provide experience with each of these processes. Whenever possible, complete them with a peer. Once each of you has done the exercises, compare and critique each other's work.

Exercise 10.1: Agency Documentation Review

Ask a local social work agency for a copy of its policy on documentation. If you are employed in a social work agency, ask for a copy of your own agency's policy. Read it with the following questions in mind:

1. What major issues does the policy cover?
2. Does it have any gaps? Explain.
3. Does it list the characteristics of high-quality records?
4. Does it require or encourage staff to review the documentation of peers? If so, how does that process work?
5. How are peer review findings shared with staff? Are there other ways in which peer review may be useful at the agency?
6. What is the agency policy regarding supervisory review of records? How often is this expected to take place? What typically occurs during the process?

Exercise 10.2: Rating, Rewriting, Improving

The following two notes describe the same case. Review them, and rate each on a scale of 1 to 10, with 1 being the worst and 10 being the best. Indicate why you selected the rating. Consider all aspects of each note when rating it, including format, content, and language used. Write a new version of the note that you consider better than the two presented here.

Note 1

April 1, 2015. A referral was made by the emergency room physician for a social work assessment. Upon arriving in the ER, I talked to the charge nurse who said that the patient was brought in via ambulance two hours ago, after being found under a tree with a bicycle and a bag of clothes. Identification indicated an out-of-state address. Could he have ridden his bike that far? He looked to be about 70 years old and pretty frail and thin, almost emaciated, the nurse said. He had suffered a stroke, according to the attending, and couldn't communicate very well. They have him on medication now so talking to him isn't going to work at all. My job is gonna be to play detective and try to locate some family member or next of kin somewhere. The only thing I had to go on was his wallet, which contained $18 and a note that had a name and phone number on it. Was that him or someone else? No answer at the number that was written down and no answering machine to leave a message. Not that leaving a message is a good idea. Next step: check information to see about the name that was written down on the piece of paper. Prolly the internet too. He's being moved to the ICU so hopefully will stabilize soon. Maybe tomorrow he'll be able to talk better too, although that's a long shot. [Name], LSW

Note 2

April 1, 2015. An unidentified older man was referred to this social worker. He has been admitted to the ICU and is unable to communicate. There is a need to find next of kin. [Name], LSW

Exercise 10.3: Self-Review

Each evening for the next five days, write a narrative-style note about that day's events on a separate sheet of paper. Write the note as if you were a social worker objectively documenting what was experienced each day by you, a client.

After five days, review your notes as if you were a supervisor and the notes were written by a supervisee. Use the self-review worksheet presented earlier (not all items will be applicable).

Exercise 10.4: What Makes a Case Note Good?

Each of the three examples below contains two notes. Compare the two and decide which is better and why. Be as specific in your reasoning as possible.

Example 1

September 15, 2015. The intake screener referred Ms. Hakim to this worker for further assessment. The client is interested in becoming a foster parent. She wrote "I need the money" when asked why she wished to foster parent. She presented as an intelligent 36-year-old woman who considers herself "brutally honest." [Name], LSW

September 15, 2015. Ms. Hakim was referred for assessment about her desire to become a foster mom. The intake screener was concerned because she told her that she needs the money that foster children would bring in. She appeared neat and clean when this social worker met with her. She interacted well but admitted to being "brutally honest" about her views of the world. [Name], LSW

Example 2

December 21, 2015. The client came in for her second appointment and apologized for being 10 minutes late. Her mother, for whom she is the primary caregiver, had a minor problem. The mother fell but was not hurt, thankfully. The client indicated that this is a good example of how "my life is not my own." She indicated she never knows if she can be on time for anything, between her mother and her daughter who just turned 15. "Separately, each is a handful, but together, they have me in a spin." This worker normalized her feelings of being sandwiched between the needs of the older and younger generations. [Name], LSW

December 21, 2015. The client, arriving 10 minutes late, apologized and seemed very flustered. This worker encouraged her to take a deep breath and calm down. Her mother fell this morning, but is okay and that's what caused her to be late. "My life is not my own." Between her mother and her daughter, she feels like her life is whirling out of control. This social worker recognized her feelings and discussed her problems with being caught in the middle between two generations and their unique needs. [Name], LSW

Example 3

May 3, 2015. Conducted a home visit to find out what the problems are that's causing client to miss so much school. Mom had no idea, thinks daughter has had perfect attendance since before spring break. Needs to get a handle on her kids and find out where client has been going instead of going to school. Mom is clearly overloaded, with three preschoolers at home in addition to daughter in school. Plan: consult with supervisor. [Name], LSW

May 3, 2015. This worker visited the client's home to determine why so many school days have been missed this term. The client's mother thought she had perfect attendance for the last six weeks. When informed that the daughter has not attended at all in the last week, mom expressed surprise. There are three preschool-age children in the home and mom appeared overwhelmed. The next step is to discuss situation with supervisor. [Name], LSW

Exercise 10.5: Expanding Oversimplified Notes

The following notes are examples of oversimplification. Rewrite each note to improve it. Add additional information if you feel it will improve the note.

Note 1

1/29/2015. Met with client—agitated when suggestion made to terminate next week—goals met—but wants to add new goals—explained agency policy—reminded that this has been discussed weekly—encouraged discussion of why he finds this so upsetting. [Name], LSW

Note 2

3/4/15. Couple seen for fourth time. No progress seen in working through marital issues. Lack of trust is barrier for both parties. Assigned homework. Next meeting in one week, same time.

Note 3

Family meeting to discuss progress was chaotic. This worker pointed out that no one was listening to the others, a recurring pattern for this family system. Technique of using talking stick seemed to help, as long as everyone remembered. Then, back to old pattern. They gave this worker a massive headache. [Name], LSW

Note 4

> S: Client sad.
> O: Dad canceled trip due to dad's job loss and economic insecurity.
> A: Client's self-centered attitude is making this divorce hard for her.
> P: Refer to support group of kids whose parents are divorced.
[Name], LSW

Exercise 10.6: Improving a Note's Quality

Read and evaluate the note below. Then write an improved version and explain why it is better.

> August 9, 2015. This first session did not start off on the right foot. In fact, it was probably the worst first session I've ever had. To start with, I was late due to babysitting problems. The client had been waiting for me to arrive about 15 minutes. She should of gotten a babysitter for her child too, because he wasn't well behaved. Interruptions, so many that it was hard to get anywhere. Plus, I had to get caught up because my next appointment was coming soon. Agency confidentiality was explained and consent forms were signed. Her next appointment is set for August 12 at 1:00 (afternoons will be better for both of us, I think). So the problem she wants help with is her boyfriend, who sounds abusive: controlling, impossible to please, mistrustful. He's the father of the 4-year-old that needs to learn better behavior. Safety plan: none. I explained the importance of having one, especially since he's turned violent in the last few weeks. No harm to the child—yet. Living situation: rented apartment, in his name. He works, she doesn't. No income except his. Not to be repetitive but this seems like a classic case of domestic violence here. Explored other supports for her. Her

mom is about it, and they aren't all that close. Her mom has problems of her own, and lives with a crack addict, according to the client. Educated her about shelter options, and safety. Made an appointment for her to meet with a shelter worker for this afternoon, although she wasn't sure she'd keep it. She has her hands full with her child, who is a handful based on what I saw. [Name], LSW

Exercise 10.7: Consistency

Review the following notes from a case file. Are the notes consistent? Why or why not? If not, what could be done to make them more consistent? Is any note better than the others? Why? Is there any note you would be unwilling to claim as your note? Why? What would make it better?

Note 1

February 22, 2015. The client arrived in the unit and was oriented to the rules of the residential treatment facility. She met her roommate and was rude to the staff. She was taken to the time-out room to calm down and process her reactions. [Name], LSW

Note 2

February 23, 2015. Quiet night last night, once the client settled down. Obviously scared and unsure of how to react to being here. Trying to put up a brave front for everyone. Today, went to the school program in the morning and returned to the unit for lunch. Met with her for one hour, as her primary counselor. See assessment plan. Immediate goal is to assist in adjusting to setting, then we'll work on the issues that brought her here.

Note 3

2/24/15. This worker met with the client for second session as primary counselor. The client is beginning to settle into the unit's routine and had begun a tentative friendship with another client, in the room next door. The client revealed today that she believes she is six weeks pregnant. A medical evaluation, completed at intake, did not indicate this. A referral has been made to the program nurse. The client began to open up about her history of stealing, breaking and entering, and drug use. She is not taking responsibility for her actions, however, which will be an objective of meetings with her. She blames her mother for being "a rotten mom" and her dad for being "not there, even when he is there." She appears to be bright and intelligent, and a strength appears to be her interest in others, evidenced when she expressed concern for a client who was hurt in an accident on her way back to the unit from court yesterday. These strengths will assist her, if they can be tapped into. This social worker will meet with the client 2/25 at 10:15 a.m. [Name], LSW

Exercise 10.8: Preparing for Supervisory Review

Imagine you are meeting with your supervisor after having asked him or her to complete a documentation review of a sample of your case files. You bring three files to be reviewed with you. In advance of the meeting, you have flagged areas in which you have questions. You enter the supervisor's office, close the door, and take a seat. You give the three files to the supervisor, who begins to review them. For each of the supervisor's comments below, note your initial reaction and write what you would say to the supervisor.

1. I'm having a hard time reading this note. Were you in a hurry when you wrote it?
2. Agency policy suggests that this assessment should have been updated two weeks ago. When do you plan on completing it?
3. This note is very complete, except you forgot to sign it.
4. The consent-to-treat form is filled out properly. Nice job!
5. I don't get a sense of what's currently happening here, as the last note was made 10 days ago.
6. Your SOAP notes are very complete, except you're weak on the A part of them. How can I help you in developing those skills further?
7. Would you be willing to provide training on documentation to the new group of interns starting next month? They could learn from you, I think.
8. Your termination summary looks incomplete on this case you just closed. How do you think it could be improved?

Exercise 10.9: Providing Supervisory Review

For this exercise, working with a peer who can help you role-play would be especially helpful.

Imagine you are a supervisor who has reviewed a case file completed by a social work intern assigned to you. You have completed the review sheet that appears below and now need to discuss your findings with the intern. Your goal is to help the intern improve her documentation skills. Prepare for that meeting by reviewing the notes in the Completed Self-Review Worksheet that follows.

Role-play giving this feedback to the intern. How would you handle this? What would you say? Ask for feedback after you have completed the role play. What did you learn?

Completed Self-Review Worksheet

	Yes	No	N/A	Comments
Format				
1. All entries dated and signed?		x		Three notes not signed; one note initialed only.
2. All entries legible?		x		Difficult to read handwriting.
3. Agency forms used?	x			
4. Agency note structure followed?	x			
5. Frequency of notes acceptable?	x			Notes are dated every other day, which is acceptable.
6. Assessment timely?		x		Assessment four days later than policy requires.
7. Closing summary done?	x			
Content				
1. Reason for referral stated?		x		No reason stated for seeking services.
2. Client feelings noted?	x			Very nice job with noting feelings.
3. Confidentiality, informed consent noted?		x		Confidentiality form not signed, no consent to treat in file.
4. Clear plans established?	x			
5. Goals measurable and noted?		x		Goals are vague; "client wants to feel better" not clearly stated.
6. Service provisions clearly indicated?	x			Good notes about what services have been offered and provided.
7. Comprehensive assessment noted?	x			Assessment weak in family background area.
8. Client strengths noted?	x			
9. Referrals noted?	x			
10. Closing summary clear?		x		Closing summary not clear.
11. Date of best note: 3/8/2015	Why was this best? Note contained information about situation, client's response, worker's assessment, services provided, plan for next time.			
12. Date of worst note: 3/11/2015	Why was this worst? Difficult to read, brief, vague statements used such as "services were provided." What services?			
13. How could this record be improved?	Assessment strengthened, notes more consistent and concretely worded.			

Exercise 10.10: Process Recording (I)

Go to your favorite search engine and enter the phrase "social work process recording samples." You will find a variety of guidelines for completing a process recording, many from graduate schools of social work that have posted manuals about the procedure. Review at least two sets of guidelines and answer the following questions about what you found.

1. Why have schools of social work posted these guidelines? Who is the intended audience?
2. What similarities did you find in the suggested structures for process recordings? What differences did you observe?
3. Do all of the guidelines you reviewed require taping and transcribing? Is the student asked to complete a verbatim process recording or a summary of what occurred? Which do you think would be most helpful from the perspective of the student?
4. If you were teaching a graduate-level class, would you require students to complete a process recording during their internships? Why or why not?
5. What have you learned from looking at these documents?

Go back to the Internet and locate one or more sample process recordings. You may find them in the guidelines you already looked at, or they may be separate documents. Select one and answer the following questions about it:

1. How are the columns labeled?
2. What are the strengths of this process recording? How might it be improved?
3. If you were the supervisor of the student who produced this process recording and it was given to you for review, how would you respond? What feedback would you give this student?

Exercise 10.11: Process Recording (II)

Review the following excerpt from a summary process recording of a group session. Imagine you are a supervisor who has been given this document by your new student intern. He or she is very upset about what happened and has asked you for feedback.

Review the document and write down the comments you would add as a supervisor. What are this student's strengths? Areas that need work?

What did you learn about yourself in this exercise?

Process Recording Sample 3

Interview Content	Social Worker Comments	Supervisor Comments
My cofacilitator called in sick today. I began by explaining that it was just me today and introduced the new member, T. D said she didn't want her here, and two others agreed. I asked why, and D said, "we don't need no one else in here. And besides, she looks like she's stupid." I reminded D of the group rules of respect for all members. D said, "She's not a group member, so I don't have to show her any respect." T started crying. M said, "Look at the crybaby." D laughed, and so did most of the others. I asked if we could get started, and T got up to leave. I stopped her and encouraged her to sit back down. D said, "Let her go." I said, "We're going to begin reviewing the rules of the group, after we introduce ourselves to T." D said, "I don't want to introduce myself to someone who doesn't belong here." She asked to take a vote on whether T should leave. T said forget it, why should she stay where she wasn't wanted. I said maybe we'd be better off trying again tomorrow.	I was very nervous, and the group probably picked up on this. D has always had control issues, but my cofacilitator has always dealt with her. I guess I was intimidated. I tried to focus on the facts of the group rules. It didn't work very well. I should have handled this differently. I felt good about getting T to stay. I thought it would be a mistake to let D "win." I decided to focus on the group tasks and move on past the emotion. That didn't work either. D is clearly in control here. T is demoralized. All I can think about is getting out of here. Maybe my cofacilitator will be back tomorrow. Maybe I'll be sick tomorrow.	

Exercise 10.12: Process Recording (III)

This exercise requires the help of two volunteers—one to role-play a client or interviewee and one to role-play your supervisor.

Audio- or videotape a three- to five-minute interview in which you assume the role of social work interviewer and the first volunteer plays him- or herself. During the interview, find out as much detail as possible about that person's plans for the weekend or for an upcoming trip or special event.

After the taping is finished, complete a verbatim process recording, using the same format as in the previous exercise. When you have completed the first two columns, give the work to the second volunteer for supervisory feedback.

What did you learn from completing this exercise?

Exercise 10.13: Problem Solving Ways to Obtain Feedback

Think about how you would react to the following scenarios and review your responses to the questions with a peer who also completed the exercise. What did you learn that you can apply to your future social work practice?

1. Your supervisor says she does not have time to review your documentation and give you feedback. What will you do?
2. You are the only social worker employed in a community action agency. You would like feedback on notes you have kept about your work with a coalition of community leaders. Your supervisor is the chair of the agency's board of directors and is not a social worker. What will you do?
3. You feel you are spending too much time documenting notes about the several groups you facilitate. Your supervisor says he spends too much time documenting too and offers you no helpful advice on how to proceed. What will you do?
4. You meet with your clinical supervisor electronically to discuss cases and concerns. The supervisor is employed at an agency other than yours. You are careful not to discuss names or other identifying information with her. You would like her feedback on your clinical notes but do not know how you can share them with her in a confidential, private manner. What will you do?
5. As a supervisor in a large agency, you keep notes of supervision sessions with supervisees. You would like feedback on the quality and frequency of your notes. The agency administrator looked at the notes briefly and said they were fine. No additional feedback was given, even though you tried to elicit more. What will you do?
6. You are a member of a hospital treatment team and would like feedback on your notes. The team leader is a very busy physician who does not want to review any records. What will you do?

CHAPTER 11

Supervision and Documentation

Supervision is an important component of one's growth and development as a professional. As such, documentation should be a topic of regular review in supervisory sessions. "It is recommended that documentation be a standing item for supervision. Overall, there needs to be a framework of cultural shift where report writing is valued in and for itself and is considered more than an administrative task" (Cumming et al., 2007, p. 255).

Supervisors of social workers have unique perspectives and issues related to documentation. Shulman (2008) noted two types of presentations frequently used by supervisors to understand staff members' direct practice activities: case presentations, which focus on assessment and treatment issues, and process presentations, which involve, at some level, a review of case files.

Kagle (1984a) rightly pointed out that a great deal of variance exists in the quality and quantity of supervisor use of case files. The way in which feedback is provided also varies tremendously.

> For many practitioners, however, the problem lies not in the record's use as the basis for discussion of issues concerning substantive service delivery but in its use as a basis for criticisms of the practitioner's work habits. When this occurs, recording can be a focal point for dissension. (Kagle, 1984a, p. 49)

Documentation can be a source of conflict between supervisor and supervisee, but precautions can prevent this from occurring. "Clear, explicit, and reasonable guidelines" (Kagle, 1984a, p. 49), developed with input from all parties, can assist. It is the supervisor's task to explain these guidelines to supervisees.

At a minimum, a supervisor should clearly state what is expected of a social worker regarding documentation, including the forms to be used, the style of documentation used at the agency, and expectations regarding frequency and content of notes. Providing examples of appropriate documentation is a helpful way to introduce and model acceptable recording behaviors. Allowing adequate time in which to document is also a critical factor. In Kagle's 1993 study, over three-quarters of participants indicated that they did not have enough time to complete documentation requirements during work hours. "Only a few agencies made sure that workers had enough time to record or that they used available time for record keeping" (Kagle, 1993, p. 195). It is clearly important for supervisors to work with staff to develop realistic and meaningful guidelines for documentation.

SUPERVISORY RECORDS

Documenting social work supervision sessions has received limited attention. Most of the literature on record keeping in supervision focuses on the supervision of social workers' record keeping (Gillanders, 2005). Somewhat more has been written about documenting clinical social work supervision. This has been cited as one way for a clinical supervisor to reduce malpractice risks (Houston-Vega & Nuehring, 1997) and as an element of good clinical supervisory practice (NASW, National Council on the Practice of Clinical Social Work, 1994). "Documentation is important in supervision and verifies that the service actually occurred" (NASW, 2003, p. 3).

Documentation is important regardless of the method in which supervision is delivered. For example, supervision may occur in person or through technology, such as Skype. "When using or providing supervision and consultation by technological means, social work supervisors and supervisees shall follow the standards that would be applied to a face-to-face supervisory relationship and shall be competent in the technologies used" (NASW & ASWB, 2005, p. 16).

It is helpful for both clinical supervisor and supervisee to document, for each supervision session, the date and duration of the meeting, issues covered, and follow-up plan. Any cancellations should also be documented, as should the dates and nature of telephone and electronic communications. A written contract can be helpful in clarifying and setting goals and objectives. It should set out the clinical supervisory relationship and describe the rights and responsibilities of both parties, the supervisor's authority, the limits of confidentiality, payment issues if appropriate, the time frame for supervision, and a process for ending the relationship.

The issue of recording social work supervision of a nonclinical nature has not been well addressed. Shulman (1993) decried the general lack of attention to recording supervisory sessions: "Supervisors who adopt some form of recording will probably find themselves going against the trend in the profession, . . . [because] attention to the details of the work is seldom encouraged" (p. 313).

This trend is changing as the profession recognizes the risks involved in not documenting supervisory contacts. Atherton (1986) cited compelling reasons for supervisors to document supervisory sessions, despite the time this requires. For example, doing so promotes reflection on what occurred and helps to ensure continuity between sessions. In addition, it assists in overseeing and evaluating the effectiveness of supervision.

If these reasons are not enough to convince the busy supervisor to document sessions, risk management provides another rationale. "Particularly given the recent national trend towards managed care, increased risk is assumed by agencies and human service providers who are treating more clients over shorter periods of time" (Falvey, Caldwell, & Cohen, 2002, p. 3). A need exists to monitor important aspects of client services and employee development, regardless of the setting in which one is employed. As Gillanders (2005) argued, "In the present climate of making social work practitioners accountable for their work, pressure will come on the supervision relationship and the records which result from it" (p. 2).

Any individual supervising a social worker or student intern who provides client services of any type should maintain records of supervisory sessions. At a minimum, a separate file should be maintained for each supervisee. What information is specifically documented will depend upon the practice setting, but the format of the note should be agreed upon by both parties. Both should maintain copies of the notes (Zuckerman, 2008). Just as a client has access to his or her case file, a supervisee also has access to supervisory records. Atherton (1986) recommended that the supervisee maintain the supervisory record as a way to feel more secure and involved in the process. Given this, care should be taken to avoid subjective, derogatory, or inflammatory language.

The content of a supervision note should include, at a minimum, the name of the supervisee and date of supervision; whether the contact occurred in person or electronically; the clients and client interventions discussed; concerns or issues raised by the supervisee; the supervisor's concerns, suggestions, or observations for the supervisee; recommendations or suggestions for future work; any risk-management issues discussed; and signatures of both supervisor and supervisee (Falvey et al., 2002; Zuckerman, 2008).

Supervision notes can use a narrative format or a form that is tailored to the needs of the setting. Examples of forms are provided in Zuckerman (2008) and Falvey et al. (2002).

As a guide for supervisors in structuring their notes, the acronym SUPERS may be helpful:

- S—supervisee-initiated items
- U—useful feedback or suggestions from the supervisor
- PE—performance expectations that have been discussed
- R—recommendations for future goals
- S—strengths of the supervisee.

A positive feature of this format is that it notes strengths of the supervisee and is written with an eye toward continual improvement. An example follows.

6/3/2015 Supervision Note

S: [Name] brought up problems locating resources for the Frauhiger family. She also raised questions about how best to proceed with the Yang case.

U: Several resources were suggested for the Frauhigers, including the Family Resource Center and the local food bank. Consent forms will need to be completed. Processing of work with the Yang case was discussed and a plan established to use solution-focused techniques.

PE: A review of the files for the Frauhiger and Yang cases revealed good efforts at documentation. A suggestion was made to further explore family-of-origin issues with Ms. Yang.

R: Readings related to solution-focused techniques were suggested to increase [Name]'s comfort level. In addition, agency guidelines related to consent forms should be reviewed.

S: [Name] is motivated to provide high-quality services and receives feedback well. She possesses solid documentation skills.

Supervisor's signature: [Name]

Social worker's signature: [Name]

Group supervision should also be documented. A separate file should be maintained by the supervisor that indicates date, participants, topics explored, outcomes (if any), and additional follow-up. A sample format for documenting group supervision follows.

Group Supervision Record

Date:	Time Started	Time Ended
Participants:		
Topics explored:		
Follow-up:		
Next meeting:		
Supervisor signature:		

SUPERVISORY ISSUES

Several documentation issues specific to supervisors are addressed in this section.

Positive Feedback

A parallel process has been found with interactions between supervisors, staff, and clients: How supervisors engage and interact with their staff tends to affect the way workers engage and interact with their clients (Shulman, 2008). This important role-modeling function can be applied to the ways that feedback is given to staff on documentation practices. Kagle (1993) found that "an angry impasse" over record keeping existed between some managers and staff: "Managers blamed workers for not recognizing the importance of records, for neglecting their obligations, or for being actively resistant to the task" (pp. 192–193), whereas workers blamed managers for making unrealistic demands or for confusing client priorities.

Providing feedback to staff and engaging them in meaningful discussions about recording practices is essential if one wishes to avoid such confrontation. Noting strengths is one important way for a supervisor to communicate with a supervisee about documentation, just as it is when social workers communicate with clients. Supervisory discussions with a social worker about documentation should involve more than criticisms. A review of a case file should readily lend itself to a mutual discussion about important practice issues (Kagle & Kopels, 2008). In addition, supervisee strengths should be noted. Kahn and Holody (2012) further recommended that if a supervisee is experiencing extensive writing problems, a supervisor could identify a maximum of three persistent errors and ask that attention be focused there. The supervisee will not be overwhelmed with negative feedback and will have a specific plan to improve writing skills.

Documentation Policy

Documentation should be perceived as important to practice and helpful in making treatment decisions and enhancing client services. If social workers see the record as an administrative activity only, they will not value it as a legitimate social work function (Kagle & Kopels, 2008). Supervisors can help foster a commitment to good documentation by emphasizing the usefulness of the record. A well-developed policy can begin this process.

A supervisor may find that agency policy scarcely addresses documentation. Creating or enhancing existing agency documentation protocols is a valuable means of establishing better practices. "It is wasteful for practitioners to spend too much time recording too much, too little, or too late" (Kagle & Kopels, 2008, p. 180). Policies can simplify the documentation process by clarifying what is important to note and what is not.

Staff input is critical to policy development and review. A supervisor may wish to establish a work group to help explore reasonable guidelines but should ensure that the process is transparent and inclusive of all staff involved in case file documentation.

A supervisor can consider several issues when formulating policy regarding documentation. Adapted from Kagle and Kopels (2008), the following questions can assist in assessing documentation practices and efficiencies:

- Is there redundancy in documentation practices? If so, can it be reduced or eliminated?
- Is overdocumentation occurring? If so, how can it be reduced?
- Can open-ended narratives be replaced without harming the quality of the record? For example, can a checklist be used for routine 30-day case reviews?
- Are formats or examples available that model best practices and help staff to understand expectations? If not, can they be developed?

- Can routine cases be identified as eligible for shortened documentation standards?
- How are clerical and support staff used in the documentation process? Are social workers spending large amounts of time completing work that could be accomplished by less highly trained staff?

A documentation policy should contain both standard elements and elements that are unique to the agency's setting. Kagle and Kopels (2008) suggested that, at a minimum, policy guidelines should indicate the types, purpose, and use of records; information to be recorded in all instances and information that can be noted only in special circumstances; the acceptable forms and formats and how they are used; and the frequency with which various records must be created and updated. A sample record can be developed to serve as a reference and training tool for incoming staff and student interns.

Storage of Records

The NASW (2008) *Code of Ethics* states, "Social workers should store records following termination of services to ensure reasonable future access" (section 3.04[d], p. 20). The CASW (2005) ethical guidelines address the issue similarly in section 1.7.8: "Social workers protect clients' records, store them securely and retain them for any required statutory period" (p. 10).

Storage of records can create problems for agencies, supervisors, and social workers. Storage space can be expensive to maintain and complicated to keep organized. Ask any hospital medical records department worker about the issues involved in storing massive amounts of data! Records must be stored in a secure manner that protects them from breaches of confidentiality, theft, or accidental discarding. They must be preserved against damage from fire, water, and vermin (Zuckerman, 2008) as well as from computer failures (Houston-Vega & Nuehring, 1997).

If a private practitioner becomes ill or dies unexpectedly, someone must be responsible for the physical storage of records. Ethically, a responsibility to preserve and protect the written record continues to exist even after the person who created the records is no longer actively working. Social workers "should make special provisions for proper storage and maintenance of records in the event of their disability, incapacitation, termination of practice (because of retirement or disciplinary proceedings, for example), or death" (Reamer, 2001, p. 27).

Several options exist for records management. An electronic record will still need to be stored on a computer or server somewhere, and careful consideration should be given to how this will be best accomplished. It may make sense to preserve paper records electronically (for example, scanning and saving the records as PDF files). Older electronic records may not be readable in updated versions of programs, so saving files in plain text format may be the best option (Zuckerman, 2008). Microfilming records may be another option. Regardless of the storage option selected, it is typical for a single person to be responsible for overseeing agency records. The custodian could be an office manager, a system administrator, or an outside contractor (Zuckerman, 2008).

It is important that records be stored in a way that makes them easily accessible to those who need them yet protects them from damage or loss. Horror stories exist of records that could not be found or paper files that blew across a busy highway because a worker forgot them on top of a car. Agency policies should account for how records are to be stored with an eye toward limiting damage and liability.

Records Retention

The length of time that records should be maintained after case closure is also an important consideration, particularly for supervisors and independent practitioners. The NASW (2008) *Code of Ethics* states that "records should be maintained for the number of years required by state statutes or relevant contracts" (section 3.04[d], p. 20). The CASW (2005) ethical guidelines advise that

> social workers transfer or dispose of clients' records in a manner that protects clients' confidentiality and is consistent with provincial/territorial statutes governing records and social work regulation. Social workers also ensure that mechanical or electronic records are properly transferred or disposed of. (section 1.79)

There is some disagreement in the professional literature regarding time frames for record retention. Rules on this are "complex, overlapping, and dependent on a host of variables—such as type of services, location, professional discipline, contractual obligations, and contents of the record" (Zuckerman, 2008, p. 34). Zuckerman (2008) said if storage space is secure, for the best protection, one should "keep the whole record forever" (p. 34). Others have also recommended keeping records in perpetuity ("Don't Throw away Your Records Yet," 1993; Houston-Vega & Nuehring, 1997).

If permanent storage is not a reasonable option, Zuckerman (2008) suggested retaining a minor's records for five years after he or she reaches the age of adulthood, keeping adult records for at least 12 years, and saving at least a summary of services forever. After the storage period, records could either be destroyed or be given to another professional who is actively providing services to the client (Zuckerman, 2008). No matter what time frame is chosen, he stressed that consistency is key, "because any exceptions would suggest to a malpractice attorney that you have something to hide" (Zuckerman, 2008, p. 35).

Rules can vary from state to state and can depend on the type of case. Kagle and Kopels (2008) pointed out that some states require record retention for long periods when the situation involves serious physical injury. For example, in Illinois, records of a case in which a child has died must be kept for 50 years.

Before policy is set, a close review of relevant law is necessary. Whatever the minimum time period mandated, "practitioners may want to increase that minimum or elect to keep closed files indefinitely" (Houston-Vega & Nuehring, 1997, p. 45).

When client paper records are discarded, they should be shredded (Houston-Vega & Nuehring, 1997; Zuckerman, 2008) or disposed of by a professional disposal firm that can provide a certificate of destruction to verify that the records were handled in a confidential manner (Zuckerman, 2008). Merely tossing a case file's contents into a recycling bin is neither acceptable nor ethical.

SUMMARY AND EXERCISES

Supervision plays an important role in the recording process. This chapter has described its importance and reviewed ways in which recording can be a helpful supervisory tool. Policies should be in place in every practice setting to clarify for both supervisor and supervisee three documentation issues: what content should be found in case records, how they should be stored, and how long they should be retained.

The following exercises are best carried out with a peer who can give feedback and share responses.

Exercise 11.1: Writing a SUPERS Note

Imagine you are a supervisor who has just completed a supervisory session with a new social worker and need to document it. Using the SUPERS format, write a supervisory note based on these facts:

1. The new worker began last week and has completed his orientation session. This is his first supervision meeting.
2. He has no prior work experience but is motivated and has a great deal of energy. He seemed very nervous during the session and admitted this.
3. He was not prepared for this meeting and did not appear to know what to expect. He had no agenda established. You had to educate him about expectations for future meetings.
4. He did bring the case files for the four cases that he has been assigned to the meeting.
5. The next supervision meeting is set to occur within two days.
6. He appeared to understand the agency time frame for assessment completion but had not written any progress notes yet. He should have written at least one progress note for each case. He doesn't appear to understand progress note guidelines.
7. His writing skills need work. He uses "I" and "my" in his assessments. He may also be dyslexic, as several words were missing, misspelled, or in the wrong order.
8. He is signed up for training on crisis intervention in three weeks; agency reimbursement for training costs was explained.
9. He has a nice sense of humor and seems very personable.
10. He seems to be clear about the goals that have been established with the clients on his caseload. All issues with the cases seem fairly routine at this point.

Exercise 11.2: Writing a Supervisory Narrative Note

Using the information presented in exercise 11.1, write a note about the supervisory meeting in a narrative format.

When you have completed the note, compare what you wrote for this and the previous exercise. Which style of supervisory note did you prefer? Why?

As the supervisor, plan a written agenda for the second meeting with the supervisee you just wrote about. Include those items that require follow-up attention from the first session.

Imagine you are now the supervisee. What written agenda will you bring to the next supervisory meeting?

Exercise 11.3: Responding to Staff Behavioral Statements about Documentation

Read the following statements, each made to you by a different supervisee reporting directly to you. How would you respond? What information would you need?

Lost File

I hate telling you this, but I want to be honest. I can't find the case file for Mrs. Esteban. I had it yesterday on my desk, and now I can't find it anywhere. I'm starting to panic.

Possible Security Breach

I think there's a problem with the maintenance worker. He was asking me about a client of mine and how much progress she's making with her addiction. I don't want to make any false accusations, but I think he may have been reading the file when I was out for lunch the other day. I'm not sure what I should do.

Car Accident

I was in an accident on the way to work this morning. Someone rear-ended my car. I can't get the trunk lid open; it's all mashed in. I'm fine, but my car isn't. It was towed, and I'm afraid it's been totaled. The problem is that the case files from yesterday's home visits were in the trunk. What should I do?

Red Ink

I had to use red-colored ink when I documented yesterday because my black pens all ran out and that was the only pen I had available. If I hadn't used red, I wouldn't have been able to document at all.

Case Notes Destroyed

My dog ate my notes on Mrs. Junius's case last night. I know I shouldn't have taken the notes home with me, but I wanted to get caught up. I knew I was going to have a crazy day today. I'm really sorry.

Computer Problems

Somehow, I erased all of my notes from the electronic file of Mr. Wisniewski. I've tried everything I can think of and they are just gone. I hate this computer program.

Exercise 11.4: Responding to Concerns about Documentation Practices

Imagine that you are a new supervisor responsible for several staff members. Each of the following statements is made to you in your first week by a different supervisee. What problem has the staff member identified? What additional information do you need? What is your immediate response? What is your long-term plan?

1. I am two months behind in my case note documentation.
2. I believe that my first priority here is my clients. Documenting is way down on my list of important tasks.
3. I didn't go to school for all of these years to just sit around and spit out case notes that no one uses. I don't see how it's important to me or to my clients.
4. I don't like to use this computer program to document, so I haven't been using it. My last supervisor said it was okay to just keep personal notes on scraps of paper.
5. I'm sorry that my notes are so long, but I like to document everything I possibly can about a case. I know it takes time but I don't want to miss anything. Do you think a five-page progress note on an hour-long session is long enough? I can write more if you think I should.
6. I'm a community organizer. I don't have any records for you to review because I don't have to document what I'm doing. It would be too involved. I'll answer whatever questions you have, though.
7. My group interventions are too involved to document about and it would be too time-consuming anyway. When I was in school, my field supervisor said she never wrote notes on her groups, so I haven't either.
8. My writing skills are excellent and I don't think there are any ways to improve them. What I really need help with is this overwhelming caseload of clients.

Exercise 11.5: More Practice with SUPERS

Imagine that you conducted supervisory sessions with three of the supervisees from Exercise 11.4. Write a SUPERS note to document each meeting. Add additional information as you see necessary.

CHAPTER 12

The Future of Documentation

In 1925, Mary Richmond stated, "As you know, we still have much to learn about records" (p. 216). Richmond's words could have been written today rather than in 1925, as there remains much to learn about records and documentation practices. Examining the current status of documentation leads to questions about what future issues social workers will face in case recording. This chapter explores some challenges that are already emerging and are likely to become more important in the future.

Kagle (2008) identified three factors changing social work documentation today. The first is technological advances and increasing reliance on computers to manage client information. Kagle predicted that many agencies will completely automate records and that social workers will use computers and other advanced technologies for all documentation tasks. Second, the accessibility of client information has changed how records are managed. Personal information about a client is available to agency staff and oversight agencies involved in authorizing services. Despite best efforts to protect client privacy, breaches persist and will likely continue to do so. Third, the increasing complexity of reporting requirements makes managing records difficult. Contradictory jurisdictional requirements overlaid with HIPAA requirements and managed care demands will continue to challenge social workers. Not even 10 years have passed since Kagle identified these issues, and they are on target.

Much to the dismay of social workers who labor under increasing documentation demands, record keeping is here to stay—the many reasons for documenting the social work helping process are too compelling. Recording will continue, although its format is likely to change as the society in which social workers practice continues to evolve.

TECHNOLOGY

Much as the typewriter revolutionized social work documentation, so too has the computer. While Gingerich (2002a) noted that existing computer technology has been slow to move past financial management and word processing into social work activities, today's technology has become pervasive throughout the profession. Technologies that are currently unheard of will undoubtedly become routine parts of future social work practice, and tomorrow's social workers will grapple with issues that today's social workers cannot imagine. For some, the future is already here. For example, those providing online social work services are faced with questions of how best to document this emerging mode of practice (Gingerich, 2002b). Another example is the use of wireless technologies by social workers in the field (NASW & ASWB, 2005). Complex practical and ethical issues will emerge as new technologies become even more commonplace.

It is instructive to turn to the past to learn how older technologies were successfully incorporated into practice. Sheffield (1920) likely envisioned eliminating pen and paper in favor of the more efficient typewriter, but the reality is that pen and paper still serve social workers today—it is the typewriter that has been replaced. It has become important to conduct meaningful research on emerging technologies and their usefulness to social workers' documentation practices.

It can be argued that today's technology has resulted in damage to basic skills in reading and writing. For example, it is not uncommon for social work instructors to receive formal papers from undergraduate students that include abbreviations such as "u" for *you* and "r" for *are*. This seems to be a result of confusing common electronic texting abbreviations with acceptable formal writing. Similarly, instances of sentences beginning with lowercase letters, incomplete sentences, and grammatical errors also seem to be on the rise. This will be reflected in future social work documentation if efforts are not made, beginning in academia and extending into agencies, to correct the situation.

Technology in some form is here to stay and has become part of the fabric of today's society. It is the social worker's responsibility to "acquire adequate skills that use technology appropriately, and adopt traditional practice protocols to ensure competent and ethical practice" (NASW & ASWB, 2005, p. 3). Ongoing training is necessary to become proficient in technology and remain current in its use.

EMPHASIS ON OUTCOMES

Funding sources and accrediting bodies have become increasingly concerned with the documentation of service outcomes, at both the case and the program levels (Swenson, 2002). Social workers are expected to document service provision in concrete, measurable terms and not only in managed care settings. This emphasis can be reasonably expected to continue into the future, and social workers will need to develop dual voices: talking the outcomes-oriented talk with funding sources and the service talk with clients (Kane et al., 2002). In addition to talking, social workers will need to be writing.

CLIENT RECORD KEEPING

Client access will continue into the future, but is there a way to make record keeping more meaningful to clients? Some attempts have been made to involve clients in the documentation process (Albeck & Goldman, 1991; Kagle, 1984a; Wilczynski, 1981). Seeing it as a way to make recording more dynamic, to demystify the recording process for clients, and to obtain immediate feedback, proponents of this practice have noted that it is an adjunct, not a replacement, for documentation by the social worker. "Client recording should facilitate and enhance—but should not be used as a substitute for—the social worker's disciplined, professional thinking" (Wilczynski, 1981, p. 317). Little research on the efficacy of this practice appears in the literature. This may be an area in which future growth will occur.

STREAMLINING

In 1993, Kagle wrote that agencies in the 1990s would have to make "critical choices about how to use diminishing resources" (p. 196). This remains true today and will likely continue to be so in the future. Agencies and social workers will continue to make difficult decisions about managing their workload in the face of budgetary constraints. Can documentation be streamlined?

Kagle (1984a) suggested that the record could be simplified through the use of logs or abbreviated recording. She suggested that narrative notes could be less burdensome to write if social workers excluded redundant information, used diagrams rather than words to more efficiently depict some situations, and eliminated information unrelated to service provision. These suggestions are important, but do they go far enough? In what other ways could a social worker simplify a record while retaining necessary information? Research is needed to help answer these questions.

SKILL BUILDING FOR NEW PRACTITIONERS

The more skilled at documentation social workers are, the more efficiently they can record service delivery. Inexperienced workers often chart more detail than is necessary. As one practices the art of documentation and gains a better understanding of what is important and what is not, one's records will become simpler and better organized.

Training in documentation is necessary across practice settings, and research has identified some successful models for specialized settings such as hospitals (Leon & Pepe, 2013). However, training must begin in educational programs. "Although in-service workshops can help practitioners establish and improve their skills, clinical recording will not be significantly improved until education for it returns to the classroom" (Kagle, 1984a, p. 50). Kagle (1984a) suggested that documentation skills be included throughout the social work curriculum, with increased exposure to narrative summary style. Savaya (2010) provided an example of the importance of raising awareness through student intern reviews of two completed case files at the internship site. All social work programs should aim to instill an awareness in students of the vital importance of documentation. In addition, the benefits of process recording, a mainstay of many educators, can be obtained in alternate ways, for example, by taping student sessions. Educational culture must change to give greater importance to practical documentation skills.

HOW CAN DOCUMENTATION IMPROVE?

Understanding expectations is critical to good documentation. "Writing in social work takes on many dimensions. Find out what is expected and get help if you need it. It can be complicated, confusing, and overwhelming, but stay on top of your documentation and you will be fine" (Ward & Mama, 2010, p. 87).

How can social workers' documentation skills improve, particularly when faced with a lack of time, preparation, experience, or agency guidance? In addition to enhancing practitioner skills, three steps can help: clarifying agency guidelines, offering more resources to help with documentation, and placing increased value on the case record in an agency's culture (Kagle & Kopels, 2008).

Agencies must develop or revise their policies on documentation. Simple guidelines, developed jointly by administrators and practitioners, can help staff to create timely, high-quality records of services provided. Kagle and Kopels (2008) recommended that minimum guidelines should explicitly address the types, purpose, and intended use of records; under what circumstances different types of information should be recorded; the forms and formats to be used; and how often files should be updated.

Agencies should allow sufficient resources for preparing, storing, and retrieving client files. The assumption is often made that social workers will find time to document during the course of their work day. A survey conducted in the late 1980s revealed that 65 percent of social work managers felt that there was not enough time available for documenting (Kagle, 1993). One can only speculate whether this situation remains true today, as research on documentation practices has not been forthcoming. Lack of research on deficient time is not acceptable and needs to be corrected.

Agency culture must be changed to reflect the importance of the record-keeping process. Kagle (1984a) suggested that if agencies do not view recording as central to the helping process, neither will employees. Agencies must commit to valuing documentation as essential to high-quality service provision.

Professional organizations have a role to play in elevating the importance of the documentation process. For example, several states' licensing laws now require licensees to complete a minimum number of continuing education hours in ethics content. In addition, at least one state requires continuing education hours related to cultural issues. It is reasonable to expect that laws could be revised to require a minimum number of continuing education hours focused on documentation issues as well. State social work associations could make this a clear priority. NASW's (2011) publication *Strengthening Your Writing Skills: An Essential Task for Every Social Worker* captures key elements of professional writing. This tool, offering a convenient reference guide and resources to access, should be readily available in agencies and social work education programs. Similarly, the importance of documentation could be further elevated by CSWE and other professional organizations invested in the future of the profession.

Tips from NASW (2011) include the following actions that should be taken by every social worker, regardless of his or her practice setting, to continually improve his or her documentation skills:

- Use reference books such as a thesaurus, style manuals, or specialty dictionaries.
- Take a workshop or class in writing and editing.
- Proofread and ask others for feedback.
- Keep track of writing tips learned and apply them consistently.
- Save writing samples, taking care to protect any confidential information.
- Seek out opportunities to write.
- Remember that everything written reflects on the writer professionally.
- Read well-written documents and books of all kinds to absorb good writing by example.

Each individual social worker has a responsibility to improve his or her documentation skills, whether documentation occurs electronically or in print. Complete, succinct documentation is often used as a measure of an efficient, competent social worker (Young, 2014). Taking every opportunity to improve these skills will enhance the professionalism of the social worker and the services that are provided to clients.

SUMMARY AND EXERCISES

Documentation is a critical skill, and developing it is a continuing professional journey. Social workers depend on recording for many purposes, but future social workers would do well to reflect on what Mary Richmond wrote early in the 20th century. She said that the profession "would have to depend upon recording for advancing standards and new discoveries within the profession" (Richmond, 1917, p. 26). The profession will not grow, flourish, and continue to meet the needs of the clients it serves without effective documentation.

Confidently predicting the future of social work recording is impossible, but the goals of social work recording are clear. Richmond put it simply when she said, "I plead for honest, intelligent, and full, day-by-day recording of what is happening" (Richmond, 1925, p. 216).

The following exercises will be most beneficial if you work through them with a peer.

Exercise 12.1: Documentation Self-Assessment

Honestly rate yourself on each statement below, with 1 = strongly disagree, 2 = disagree, 3 = agree, and 4 = strongly agree.

1. I can usually select the best words to express myself.
2. I can usually write in a focused way.
3. My writing is usually well organized and logical in sequence.
4. I am highly skilled at expressing myself in writing.
5. I am highly skilled at comprehending what I have read.
6. I have confidence that I know how to write about a client.
7. I have a good memory for details.
8. I know the difference between objective and subjective information.
9. I know the difference between a summary and a SOAP note.
10. I can tell what is important about a client session and what is not.
11. I am highly skilled at homing in on what is important in a conversation.
12. I know the difference between a complete sentence and an incomplete sentence.
13. I know the difference between "your" and "you're."
14. I know the difference between "its" and "it's."
15. I know when to use commas, periods, semicolons, and colons.
16. I understand what is meant by subject and verb agreement.
17. I know the difference between writing in the first, second, and third person.

Total your score and see where you fall in the scale below:

0–17:   Your skills are poor but can be improved with hard work and diligence.
18–35: Your skills are fair, with plenty of room for more improvement.
36–53: Your skills are good, with room for improvement.
54–68: Your skills are excellent.

Complete each sentence with a short phrase.

1. Areas in which I am most confident about documenting are . . .
2. I think my documentation strengths are . . .
3. I am least confident about documenting . . .
4. Areas in which I think I need the most help are . . .

When finished, compare your responses with those from exercise 3.1. Were there differences?

Exercise 12.2: A Note about Today

Write a detailed note about your day, as if you were an outsider observing it rather than experiencing it. Refer to yourself as "he" or "she." Use the following example to get you started:

Today she got up after sleeping in. Her alarm went off, but she didn't feel like getting up right away. She dozed off and on for over 15 minutes. When she finally decided that she had better get moving, she showered and had a quick breakfast that consisted of an eight-ounce glass of orange juice and a large cinnamon roll. She checked her e-mail messages and found that she had several to return. She took a few minutes to do that but couldn't get to all of them because she was running out of time. She packed up and headed out the door.

Include as much detail as you can.

Next, critically analyze what you just wrote. Name three things you like about your note. Name three things you do not like.

Compare this note with the one you wrote in exercise 3.2. How do they differ? How are they similar?

What have you learned from this exercise?

Exercise 12.3: Improvement Plan

Be sure to complete the exercises above before you start this one. Answer the following questions about your current level of documentation skills.

1. What improvements are evident in your documentation when you compare the results of exercise 3.1 with those of exercise 12.1?
2. What improvements are evident when comparing exercise 3.2 with exercise 12.2?
3. In what documentation areas do you feel you need further development?
4. On the basis of your answer to the previous question, develop a specific goal and a plan to address it. Develop at least three objectives that address this goal.

References

Addressing an envelope. (n.d.). Retrieved from http://www.letterwritingguide .com/addressingenvelope.htm

Albeck, J. H., & Goldman, C. (1991). Patient–therapist co-documentation: Implication of jointly authored progress notes for psychotherapy practice, research, training, supervision, and risk management. *American Journal of Psychotherapy, 3*, 317–334.

American Psychiatric Association. (2013). *Diagnostic and statistical manual of mental disorders* (5th ed.). Arlington, VA: Author.

Ames, N. (1999). Social work recording: A new look at an old issue. *Journal of Social Work Education, 35*, 227–238.

Ames, N. (2002). What are we teaching our students about social work recording? An exploratory study. *Areté, 26*(2), 100–106.

Ames, N. (2008). Teaching recording and documentation to BSW students: An exploratory study of field instructors' views. *Journal of Baccalaureate Social Work, 13*(2), 69–82.

Anderson, D. (2003). Improving writing skills among undergraduate social work students. *Areté, 27*(2), 79–83.

Atherton, J. S. (1986). *Professional supervision in group care: A contract-based approach.* London: Tavistock.

Barker, R. L. (2014). *The social work dictionary* (6th ed.). Washington, DC: NASW Press.

Bartlett, T. (2003, January 3). Why Johnny can't write, even though he went to Princeton. *Chronicle of Higher Education*, pp. 39–40.

Beer, P., & Leonard, T. (2001). *Community how to guide on needs assessment and strategic planning* [Booklet]. Retrieved from http://www.nhtsa.gov/people/injury/ alcohol/community%20guides%20html/Book2_NeedsAssess.html

Behavioral Health Innovation. (2014). *Telemental health therapy comparisons.* Retrieved February 20, 2015, from http://www.telementalhealthcomparisons.com

Belluomini, E. (2013, Spring). Technology changing the face of social work. *New Social Worker, 20*(2). Retrieved from http://www.socialworker.com/

Berner, M. (1998). Write smarter, not longer. In L. Lifson & R. Simon (Eds.), *The mental health practitioner and the law: A comprehensive handbook* (pp. 329–343). Cambridge, MA: Harvard University Press.

Borcherding, S. (2000). *Documentation manual for writing SOAP notes in occupational therapy.* Thorofare, NJ: Slack.

Braaten, E. (2007). *The child clinician's report-writing handbook.* New York: Guilford Press.

Bristol, M. C. (1936). *Handbook on social case recording.* Chicago: University of Chicago Press.

Brown, J. C. (1922). A city case worker in the country. *Family, 8*(3), 187–193.

Brown, J. C. (1932). Research relating to rural social work. In J. D. Black (Ed.), *Research in rural social work: Scope and method* (pp. 3–18). New York: Social Science Research Council.

Brown, J. C. (1940). *Public relief 1929–1939.* New York: Octagon Books.

Burack-Weiss, A. (2012). Writing in the field of aging. In W. Green & B. L. Simon (Eds.), *The Columbia guide to social work writing* (pp. 276–293). New York: Columbia University Press.

Business and workplace email etiquette. (n.d.). Retrieved from http://www.letter writingguide.com/emailetiquette.htm

Business email writing. (n.d.). Retrieved from http://www.letterwritingguide.com/businessemail.htm

Canadian Association of Social Workers. (2005). *Guidelines for ethical practice.* Ottawa: Author.

Chase, Y. (2008). Professional liability and malpractice. In T. Mizrahi & L. E. Davis (Eds.), *Encyclopedia of social work* (20th ed., Vol. 3, pp. 425–429). Washington, DC, and New York: NASW Press and Oxford University Press.

Colcord, J. C., & Mann, R. Z. S. (Eds.). (1930). *The long view: Papers and addresses of Mary E. Richmond.* New York: Russell Sage Foundation.

Conference of Boards of Public Charities. (1874). *Proceedings of the first national conference on charities and corrections.* Retrieved from http://quod.lib.umich.edu/n/ncosw

Coulton, C. J. (1982). Quality assurance for social service programs: Lessons from health care. *Social Work, 27,* 397–402.

Council on Social Work Education. (2008). *Educational policy and accreditation standards.* Alexandria, VA: Author.

Council on Social Work Education. (2012). *Advanced social work practice in trauma* [Brochure]. Retrieved from http://www.cswe.org/File.aspx?id=63842

Cournoyer, B. R. (2011). *The social work skills workbook* (6th ed.). Belmont, CA: Brooks/Cole.

Cumming, S., Fitzpatrick, E., McAuliffe, D., McKain, S., Martin, C., & Tonge, A. (2007). Raising the Titanic: Rescuing social work documentation from the sea of ethical risk. *Australian Social Work, 60,* 239–257.

DeAngelis, T. (2012, March). Practicing distance therapy, legally and ethically. *Monitor on Psychology, 43*(3), 52–53.

Documentation. (2013). In *Oxford English dictionary online.* Retrieved December 1, 2013, from http://www.oed.com/

Doel, M. (2006). *Using groupwork.* London: Routledge.

Don't throw away your records yet. (1993, July). *Mental Health Legal Review,* p. 1.

Dorn, E. (2007). *Goodbye, good luck and thanks.* Retrieved from http://www.utexas.edu/lbj/archive/news/fall2007/dorn_oped.php

Drozdowski, M. J. (2003, September 23). The write stuff. *Chronicle of Higher Education.* Retrieved from http://chronicle.com/article/The-Write-Stuff/45310

Drude, K., & Lichstein, M. (2005, August). Psychologists' use of e-mail with clients: Some ethical considerations. *Ohio Psychologist*, pp. 13–17.

Ephross, P. H., & Greif, G. L. (2009). Group process and group work techniques. In A. R. Roberts (Ed.), *Social workers' desk reference* (2nd ed., pp. 679–685). New York: Oxford University Press.

Falk, D., & Ross, P. (2001). Teaching social work writing. *Journal of Baccalaureate Social Work, 6*(2), 125–141.

Falvey, J. E., Caldwell, C. F., & Cohen, C. R. (2002). *Documentation in supervision: The focused risk management supervision system.* Pacific Grove, CA: Brooks/Cole.

Fax cover sheet. (n.d.). Retrieved from http://business.lovetoknow.com/wiki/Fax_Cover_Sheet

Fax cover sheet info. (n.d.). Retrieved from http://www.faxcoversheets.net/info.htm

Finnegan, D. J., & Ivanoff, A. (1991). Effects of brief computer training on attitudes toward computer use in practice: An educational experiment. *Journal of Social Work Education, 27,* 73–82.

Fogarty, M. (2007, March 9). Who versus whom [Blog post]. *Quick and Dirty Tips.* Retrieved from http://www.quickanddirtytips.com/education/grammar/who-versus-whom

Fogarty, M. (2010, July 22). Active voice versus passive voice [Blog post]. *Quick and Dirty Tips.* Retrieved from http://www.quickanddirtytips.com/education/grammar/active-voice-versus-passive-voice

Freedheim, D. K., & Shapiro, J. P. (1999). *The clinical child documentation sourcebook.* New York: Wiley.

Garvin, C. (2002). Developing goals. In A. R. Roberts & G. J. Green (Eds.), *Social workers' desk reference* (pp. 309–313). New York: Oxford University Press.

Gellman, R. (2009). *Privacy in the clouds: Risks to privacy and confidentiality from cloud computing* [World Privacy Forum report]. Retrieved from http://netop.com/fileadmin/netop/resources/products/administration/remote_control/whitepapers/WPF_Cloud_Privacy_Report.pdf

Gillanders, M. (2005). The hidden power of the written word: Record-keeping in supervision. *Social Work Review, 17*(3), 2–9.

Gillett, A. (2010). *Common spelling problems* [Quiz]. Retrieved from http://www.uefap.com/writing/exercise/spell/spell.htm

Gingerich, W. J. (2002a). Computer applications for social work practice. In A. R. Roberts & G. J. Green (Eds.), *Social workers' desk reference* (pp. 23–28). New York: Oxford University Press.

Gingerich, W. J. (2002b). Online social work: Ethical and practical considerations. In A. R. Roberts & G. J. Green (Eds.), *Social workers' desk reference* (pp. 81–85). New York: Oxford University Press.

Glicken, M. D. (2008). *A guide to writing for human service professionals.* Lanham, MD: Rowman & Littlefield.

Gold, E., & Simon, E. (2002). *Successful community organizing for school reform.* Retrieved from http://comm-org.wisc.edu/papers2003/goldsimon/goldsimon.htm

Griffith, E. (2013, March 13). What is cloud computing? *PC Magazine.* Retrieved from http://www.pcmag.com

Grise-Owens, E., & Crum, K. (2012). Teaching writing as a professional practice skill: A curricular case example. *Journal of Social Work Education, 48,* 517–534.

Hacker, D. (1996). *Rules for writers* (3rd ed.). Boston: Bedford Books.

Hamilton, G. (1936). *Social case recording.* New York: Columbia University Press.

Hammerstrom, G. (2014). *Say cheese: Patient photos being added to medical record* [News brief]. Retrieved from http://med.stanford.edu/news/all-news/2014/03/say-cheese-patient-photos-being-added-to-medical-record.html

Hartman, B. L., & Wickey, J. M. (1978). The person-oriented record in treatment. *Social Work, 23,* 296–299.

Health Information Technology. (n.d.). *Learn EHR basics.* Retrieved from http://www.healthit.gov/providers-professionals/learn-ehr-basics

Hepworth, D. H., Rooney, R. H., Rooney, G. D., & Strom-Gottfried, K. (2012). *Direct social work practice: Theory and skills* (9th ed.). Belmont, CA: Brooks/Cole.

Homophones. (2010). Retrieved from http://individual.utoronto.ca/h_forsythe/homophones.html

Houghkirk, E. (1977). Everything you've always wanted your clients to know but have been afraid to tell them. *Journal of Marital and Family Therapy, 3*(2), 27–33.

Houston-Vega, M. K., & Nuehring, E. M. (1997). *Prudent practice: A guide for managing malpractice risk.* Washington, DC: NASW Press.

How to write a business letter. (n.d.). Retrieved from http://www.letterwritingguide.com/businessletter.htm

How to write a complaint letter. (n.d.). Retrieved from http://www.letterwritingguide.com/complaint.htm

Illinois Department of Human Services. (2013). *Module 5 DSP notebook: Individual service plan development and implementation.* Retrieved from http://www.dhs.state.il.us/OneNetLibrary/27896/documents/By_Division/Division%20of%20DD/DirectSupportPerson/Module5NotebookIndividualServicePlan.pdf

Jongsma, A. E., & Peterson, L. M. (2003). *The complete adult psychotherapy treatment planner.* Hoboken, NJ: Wiley.

Kagle, J. D. (1984a). Restoring the clinical record. *Social Work, 29,* 46–50.

Kagle, J. D. (1984b). *Social work records.* Homewood, IL: Dorsey Press.

Kagle, J. D. (1993). Record keeping: Directions for the 1990s. *Social Work, 38,* 190–196.

Kagle, J. D. (2002). Record-keeping. In A. R. Roberts & G. J. Green (Eds.), *Social workers' desk reference* (pp. 28–33). New York: Oxford University Press.

Kagle, J. D. (2008). Recording. In T. Mizrahi & L. E. Davis (Eds.), *Encyclopedia of social work* (20th ed., Vol. 3, pp. 497–498). Washington, DC, and New York: NASW Press and Oxford University Press.

Kagle, J. D., & Kopels, S. (2008). *Social work records* (3rd ed.). Prospect Heights, IL: Waveland Press.

Kahn, J. M., & Holody, R. (2012). Supporting field instructors' efforts to help students improve writing. *Journal of Social Work Education, 48,* 65–73.

Kane, M. N. (2002). Are social work students prepared for documentation and liability in managed care environments? *Clinical Supervisor, 20*(2), 55–65.

Kane, M. N., Houston-Vega, M. K., & Nuehring, E. M. (2002). Documentation in managed care: Challenges for social work education. *Journal of Teaching in Social Work, 22*(1/2), 199–212.

Kincaid, S. (Ed.). (2004). *Technology in human services: Using technology to improve quality of life* [Council for Standards in Human Service Education monograph]. Retrieved from http://www.cshse.org/documents/Technology_in_HS.pdf

Kirst-Ashman, K. K., & Hull, G. H. (2011). *Understanding generalist practice* (6th ed.). Belmont, CA: Thomson.

Kirst-Ashman, K. K., & Hull, G. H. (2015). *Generalist practice with organizations and communities* (6th ed.). Stamford, CT: Cengage Learning.

Kurzweil, R. (2001). *The law of accelerating returns.* Retrieved from http://www.kurzweilai.net/the-law-of-accelerating-returns

Latner, A. W. (2012, July 28). Including pictures in electronic medical records reduces errors. *Renal & Urology News.* Retrieved from http://www.renaland urologynews.com

Leiner, B. M., Cerf, V. G., Clark, D. D., Kahn, R. E., Kleinrock, L., Lynch, D. C., et al. (2000). *A brief history of the Internet.* Retrieved from http://www.internet society.org/internet/what-internet/history-internet/brief-history-internet

Leon, A. M., & Pepe, J. (2010). Utilizing a required documentation course to improve the recording skills of undergraduate social work students. *Journal of Social Service Research, 36,* 362–376.

Leon, A. M., & Pepe, J. (2013). Utilizing a continuing education workshop to increase knowledge of documentation among hospital psychosocial staff. *Journal of Social Service Research, 39,* 115–128.

Letter writing tips. (n.d.). Retrieved from http://www.letterwritingguide.com/ tips.htm

Lukas, S. (1993). *Where to start and what to ask: An assessment handbook.* New York: Norton.

Mathews, H. J. (1980). Special problems of rural social work. In E. E. Martinez-Brawley (Ed.), *Pioneer efforts in rural social work: Firsthand views since 1908* (pp. 163–172). University Park: Pennsylvania State University Press. (Original work published 1927)

Mattison, M. (2012). Social work practice in the digital age: Therapeutic email as a direct practice methodology. *Social Work, 57,* 249–258.

Moellinger, T. (2010). Santa or the Grinch: Paradoxes presented by the use of today's popular media. *Human Studies, 33,* 205–220.

Moline, M. E., Williams, G. T., & Austin, K. E. (1998). *Documenting psychotherapy: Essentials for mental health practitioners.* Thousand Oaks, CA: Sage Publications.

Moreland, M. E., & Racke, R. D. (1991). Peer review of social work documentation. *Quality Review Bulletin, 17*(7), 236–239.

Morgan, S. (2013, May). Social workers and the 2013 Omnibus HIPAA rule. *National Association of Social Workers Washington Chapter Newsletter.* Retrieved from http://nasw-wa.org/social-workers-and-the-2013-omnibus-hipaa-rule/

National Association of Social Workers. (1996). *Code of ethics.* Washington, DC: Author.

National Association of Social Workers. (2003). Supervision and the clinical social worker. *Clinical Social Work Practice Update, 3*(2), 1–4.

National Association of Social Workers. (2008). *Code of ethics of the National Association of Social Workers.* Washington, DC: Author.

National Association of Social Workers. (2011). *Strengthening your writing skills: An essential task for every social worker.* Retrieved from http://careers.socialworkers .org/documents/WritingSkillsLL.pdf

National Association of Social Workers. (2012). *Social workers and Skype: Part 1.* Retrieved from https://www.socialworkers.org/ldf/legal_issue/2011/112011 .asp?back=yes

National Association of Social Workers. (2013, Winter). Progress notes versus psychotherapy notes: What is the difference? *Pennsylvania Social Worker*, pp. 21–22.

National Association of Social Workers & Association of Social Work Boards. (2005). *NASW & ASWB standards for technology and social work practice.* Retrieved from http://www.socialworkers.org/practice/standards/naswtechnologystandards .pdf

National Association of Social Workers, National Council on the Practice of Clinical Social Work. (1994). *Guidelines for clinical social work supervision.* Washington, DC: Author.

National Child Traumatic Stress Network. (n.d.). *Empirically supported treatments and promising practices.* Retrieved from http://www.nctsn.org/resources/ topics/treatments-that-work/promising-practices

Netting, F. E., Kettner, P. M., McMurtry, S. L., & Thomas, M. L. (2012). *Social work macro practice* (5th ed.). Upper Saddle River, NJ: Pearson.

O'Hare, T. (2009). *Essential skills of social work practice: Assessment, intervention, evaluation.* Chicago: Lyceum Books.

Oxford Dictionaries. (2014). *Common misspellings.* Retrieved from http://www .oxforddictionaries.com/us/words/common-misspellings

Paré, A., & Allen, H. S. (1995). Social work writing: Learning by doing. In G. Rogers (Ed.), *Social work field education: Views and visions* (pp. 164–173). Dubuque, IA: Kendall/Hunt.

Pennsylvania Department of Public Welfare. (1934). *Poor relief administration in Pennsylvania* (Bulletin No. 61). Harrisburg, PA: Author.

Putre, L. (2011, Spring/Summer). Are we finally ready to cut the paper out of doctors' paperwork? *Magazine of Case Western Reserve University*, pp. 29–33.

Reamer, F. G. (1998). *Ethical standards in social work: A critical review of the NASW code of ethics.* Washington, DC: NASW Press.

Reamer, F. G. (2001). *The social work ethics audit: A risk management tool.* Washington, DC: NASW Press.

Reamer, F. G. (2005). Documentation in social work: Evolving ethical and risk-management standards. *Social Work, 50,* 325–334.

Reamer, F. G. (2009). *The social work ethics casebook: Cases and commentary.* Washington, DC: NASW Press.

Reamer, F. G. (2011). Developing a social media ethics policy. *Social Work Today.* Retrieved from http://www.socialworktoday.com

Reardon, C. (2011, May/June). Building a practice in a digital world. *Social Work Today, 11*(3), 10–13.

Richardson, M. (2008, November 7). Writing is not just a basic skill. *Chronicle of Higher Education*, pp. 47–49.

Richmond, M. E. (1917). *Social diagnosis.* New York: Russell Sage Foundation.

Richmond, M. E. (1922). *What is social case work?* New York: Russell Sage Foundation.

Richmond, M. E. (1925). Why case records? *Family, 6*, 214–216.

Robertson, H. W., & Jackson, V. H. (1991). *NASW guidelines on the private practice of clinical social work.* Washington, DC: NASW Press.

Rothman, J. C. (2002). Developing therapeutic contracts with clients. In A. R. Roberts & G. J. Green (Eds.), *Social workers' desk reference* (pp. 304–309). New York: Oxford University Press.

Savaya, R. (2010). Enhancing social work awareness of the importance of full and accurate documentation in social work practice. *Social Work Education, 29*, 660–669.

Schmelter, B. (2012). *Implementing collaborative documentation: Making it happen!* Retrieved from SAMHSA-HRSA Center for Integrated Health Solutions Web site: http://www.integration.samhsa.gov/pbhci-learning-community/jun_2012_-_collaborative_documentation.pdf

Schoech, D. (1982). *Computer use in human services: A guide to information management.* New York: Human Sciences Press.

Sears, K. P. (2012). Improving cultural competence education: The utility of an intersectional framework. *Medical Education, 45*, 545–551.

Shea, J., Santos, J. J., & Byrnes, P. (2012). *Community needs assessment and data-supported decision making: Keys to building responsive and effective health centers.* Bethesda, MD: National Association of Community Health Centers.

Sheafor, B. W., & Horejsi, C. R. (2008). *Techniques and guidelines for social work practice* (8th ed.). Boston, MA: Allyn & Bacon.

Sheafor, B. W., & Horejsi, C. R. (2012). *Techniques and guidelines for social work practice* (9th ed.). Boston, MA: Allyn & Bacon.

Sheffield, A. E. (1920). *The social case history: Its construction and content.* New York: Russell Sage Foundation.

Shulman, L. (1993). *Interactional supervision.* Washington, DC: NASW Press.

Shulman, L. (2008). Supervision. In T. Mizrahi & L. E. Davis (Eds.), *Encyclopedia of social work* (20th ed., Vol. 4, pp. 186–190). Washington, DC, and New York: NASW Press and Oxford University Press.

Sidell, N. L., & Smiley, D. (2008). *Professional communication skills in social work.* Boston: Pearson.

Simon, B. L., & Soven, M. (1990). The teaching of writing in social work education: A pressing priority for the 1990s. *Journal of Teaching in Social Work, 3*(2), 47–63.

Smith, C. M. (2001). Documentation requirements for the acute care inpatient record (AHIMA practice brief). *Journal of American Health Information Management Association, 72*(3), 56A–56G.

Snow, K. (2009). *Disability is natural.* Woodland Park, CO: BraveHeart Press.

Social media. (2014). In *Wikipedia.* Retrieved January 16, 2015, from http://en.wikipedia.org/wiki/Social_media

Sormanti, M. (2012). Writing for and about clinical practice. In W. Green & B. L. Simon (Eds.), *The Columbia guide to social work writing* (pp. 114–132). New York: Columbia University Press.

Stanford School of Medicine. (2014). *Evidence.* Retrieved from http://domesticabuse.stanford.edu/reporting/evidence.html

Staniforth, B., & Larkin, R. (2006). Documentation in social work: Remembering our ABCs. *Social Work Review, 18,* 13–20.

Straus, J. (2008). *Blue book of grammar and punctuation* (10th ed.). San Francisco: Jossey-Bass.

Strode, J. (1940). *Introduction to social case work.* New York: Harper.

Strunk, W. (2006). *The elements of style.* Mineola, NY: Dover.

Substance Abuse and Mental Health Services Administration. (2009). *Suicide assessment five-step evaluation and triage (SAFE-T) pocket card for clinicians.* Retrieved from http://store.samhsa.gov/shin/content//SMA09-4432/SMA09-4432.pdf

Swaminathan, K. S. (2012). *4 technology trends to watch in human services.* Retrieved from http://www.govtech.com/e-government/4-Technology-Trends-to-Watch-in-Human-Services.html

Swenson, C. R. (2002). Clinical social work practice: Political and social realities. In A. R. Roberts & G. J. Green (Eds.), *Social workers' desk reference* (pp. 632–639). New York: Oxford University Press.

Swift, L. B. (1928). Can the sociologist and social worker agree on the content of case records? *Social Forces, 6,* 535–538.

Szuchman, L. T., & Thomlison, B. (2008). *Writing with style: APA style for social work* (3rd ed.). Belmont, CA: Brooks/Cole.

Tebb, S. (1991). Client-focused recording: Linking theory and practice. *Families in Society, 72,* 425–432.

Texas Council for Developmental Disabilities. (2007). *Describing people with disabilities* [Fact sheet]. Retrieved from http://www.ouhsc.edu/thecenter/products/documents/PeopleFirstLanguage.pdf

Timms, N. (1972). *Recording in social work.* London: Routledge and Kegan Paul.

True, M. S., & MacDougall, L. (n.d.). *Why do we use an Individualized Service Plan?* Retrieved from http://www.ilresources.com/articles/ISP.htm

University of Idaho Park Studies Unit. (2009). *How-to: Focus group study management: Step 9. Write the focus group report.* Retrieved from http://psu.uidaho.edu/focusgroup/evaluation/09.html

U.S. Department of Education, Office of Special Education and Rehabilitative Services. (2000). *A guide to the Individualized Education Program.* Retrieved from http://www2.ed.gov/parents/needs/speced/iepguide/iepguide.pdf

U.S. Department of Health and Human Services. (2014). *HIPAA privacy rules and sharing information related to mental health.* Washington, DC: Author. Retrieved from http://www.hhs.gov/ocr/privacy/hipaa/understanding/special/mhguidance.html

Vandiver, V. L., & Corcoran, K. (2009). Guidelines for establishing effective treatment goals and treatment plans with Axis I disorder. In A. R. Roberts (Ed.), *Social workers' desk reference* (2nd ed., pp. 497–505). New York: Oxford University Press.

Waller, M. (2000). Addressing students' writing problems: Applying composition theory to social work education. *Journal of Baccalaureate Social Work, 5*(2), 161–166.

Warchol, K. (2010, October 29). A discussion of cognitive screening instruments and executive functions [Blog post]. Retrieved from http://www.crisisprevention

.com/Resources/Article-Library/Dementia-Care-Specialists-Articles/Assessment/A-Discussion-of-Cognitive-Screening-Instruments-an

Ward, K., & Mama, R. S. (2010). *Breaking out of the box: Adventure-based field instruction* (2nd ed.). Chicago: Lyceum Books.

Weed, L. (1968). Medical records that teach and guide. *New England Journal of Medicine, 278,* 593–600.

Weisman, D., & Zornado, J. L. (2013). *Professional writing for social work practice.* New York: Springer.

Wilczynski, B. L. (1981). New life for recording: Involving the client. *Social Work, 26,* 313–317.

Wilson, S. J. (1980). *Recording guidelines for social workers.* New York: Free Press.

World Health Organization. (2010). *Telemedicine: Opportunities and developments in member states* (Global Observatory for eHealth Series Vol. 2). Retrieved from http://www.who.int/goe/publications/goe_telemedicine_2010.pdf

Young, D. J. (2014). *The writer's handbook: A guide for social workers.* Ogden Dunes, IN: Writer's Toolkit.

Zar, J. H. (1994). Candidate for a pullet surprise. *Journal of Irreproducible Results, 39*(1), 13.

Zuckerman, E. L. (2006). *HIPAA help: A compliance toolkit for psychotherapists.* Armbrust, PA: Three Wishes Press.

Zuckerman, E. L. (2008). *The paper office* (4th ed.). New York: Guilford Press.

Zur, O. (2012). *Utilizing interactive tele-video technologies (IATV) to provide telemental health, e-counseling, or e-therapy.* Retrieved from http://www.zurinstitute.com/telehealth_IATV.html

Index

In this index, *t* denotes table.

A

abbreviations, 47–48

access to records. *See* records accessibility

accountability. *See* agency policies; HIPAA (Health Insurance Portability and Accountability Act of 1996); social work practice; supervisory records

active versus passive voice, 41, 65

advocacy letter writing, 161–162

agency policies

  cloud server usage, 158

  confidentiality, 80

  documentation requirements, 26, 122, 193–194, 202

  documentation review, 173, 178

  envelope addressing, 152

  letter purpose and structure, 151

  signatures, 48

  social media usage, 157

  technology usage, 157, 165

agency records, 27, 81–82, 87–88, 129–130, 142

  See also specific forms, handouts, or sheets

Albeck, J., 159

Ames, N., 10, 11

apostrophes, 43–44, 60–61

assessments

  collaborative documentation in, 160

  cultural issues in, 97–98, 117–118

  definitions of, 89

  exercises about, 103–110

  organizational qualities of, 89–92

  pretests and posttests, 159

  types of, 92–97, 114, 116

  See also documentation self-assessments

asset mapping, 97, 119

Atherton, J., 190, 191

Austin, K., 29

B

background information, 81–82, 86–87

Barker, R., 94, 102

blank space cancellations, 123

blanket release forms, 82, 84

The Book of My [or Our] Therapy, 160

Borcherding, S., 23

boundary setting, 155

Braaten, E., 82, 84, 100

Brown, J., 4

Burack-Weiss, A., 24

C

capital letters and numbers, 44

care plans. *See* treatment plans

case notes and case records, 30–31, 33–34, 73

  See also client records

case numbers, 76

case presentations, 189

CASW *Guidelines for Ethical Practice*, 14, 80, 195

CFI. *See* Cultural Formulation Interview (CFI)

The Child Clinician's Report-Writing Handbook (Braaten), 84

Children's Hospital Colorado, 153

chronological organization, 91

  See also dates

client information diagraming, 92

client records

  accessibility of, 14, 16, 25

  documentation produced by clients in, 159–160, 200–201

  electronic sharing of, 17–18

  ethics and, 13–14

  maintenance and handling of, 14–15

  ownership of, 79

  potential readership considerations of, 23–24

  psychotherapy notes and, 27–28